Carpenters and Builders Library Volume Two

Builders Math — Plans — Specifications

By John E. Ball

Revised and Edited by Tom Philbin

Macmillan Publishing Company
New York

Collier Macmillan Publishers
London

FIFTH EDITION

Macmillan Publishing Company
866 Third Avenue, New York, N.Y. 10022
Collier Macmillan Canada, Inc.

Library of Congress Cataloging-in-Publication Data
Ball, John E.
    Builders math, plans, specifications.

    (Carpenters and builders library/by John E. Ball; v. 2)
    Includes index.
    1. Building—Mathematics. 2. Building—Contracts and specifications. I. Philbin,
Tom, 1934–   . II. Title. III. Series: Ball, John E. Carpenters and builders library; v. 2
TH437.B28   1982   692   82-1341
ISBN 0-672-23366-5   AACR2

10 9 8 7 6 5 4 3 2 1

Printed in the United States of America

Foreword

This book, the second in a four-volume series designed to give carpenters, builders, do-it-yourselfers, and students a solid knowledge of carpentry, not only concentrates on a number of basic areas but also considers some advanced building projects. A good portion of the book is devoted to mathematics needed by the carpenter, both the theoretical and the everyday math necessary for business computations.

A section on surveying is as basic as we could make it, yet it includes the techniques a surveyor must have and a consideration of the latest equipment. There is also information on reading plans and on how specifications are prepared when a structure is being built.

For the architect, carpenter, and builder there is a study of the effects of stresses on various wood and steel members. It is one thing to build a building—it is another to ensure that it stays standing!

An important area for the carpenter is drawing. While many technical aspects of the chapters on practical and architectural drawing will mainly interest technicians in those areas, there is much that should be of interest to the carpenter and the do-it-yourselfer. A solid foundation in drawing can make any carpenter's job easier, simply because such knowledge will allow him (or her) to be better prepared to conceptualize and plan jobs.

Finally, we consider what is involved in two specialized kinds of building: barns and motels.

All in all, the volume should be useful both to the specialist and to those seeking basic information.

Contents

CHAPTER 11

CHAPTER 1

Mathematics for Carpenters and Builders

Two thousand years ago, Hindu scholars invented and gave to the world the ten symbols that are now used by mathematicians all over the world—0, 1, 2, 3, 4, 5, 6, 7, 8, 9—and with only these ten symbols and the place system, we can express any number no matter how great or small. Later, in the tenth century, Arabian philosophers who had learned to use these symbols brought them to Europe in substantially the same form we know them, and we still call them the Arabic notation. Since in those days all writing was done by hand, the actual forms varied somewhat, and not until the invention of the printing press in the fifteenth century were the forms of the numerals fixed in the type styles we are familiar with and which are today used all over the civilized world.

Mathematics is, of course, crucial for building things, whether it be a shed for tools or a skyscraper. What follows is a consideration of fundamental mathematical principles and a variety of examples in which math comes into use.

ARITHMETIC

Definitions

1. *Arithmetic* is the art of calculating by using numbers. All of the sciences are based on arithmetic and the ability to use it. In fact, it has been said that we do not have a true science until we can number. It also can be said that the

true carpenter will understand numbers thoroughly and knows how to use them.

2. A *number* is a total, amount, or aggregate of units. By counting the units, we arrive at a certain number, such as *two* horses or *five* dozen.

3. A *unit* may mean a single article, but often it means a definite group adopted as a standard of measurement, such as *dozen, ton, foot, bushel,* or *mile.* Most commonly used units are standardized, and are defined and fixed by law.

4. A *concrete* number is a number applied to some particular unit, such as *ten* nails, *two* dozen eggs, *six* miles.

5. An *abstract number* is one that is *not* applied to any object or group, such as simply *two, four, ten.*

6. *Notation* is the art of expressing numbers by figures or letters. Our system of notation is the Arabic notation. The Roman notation uses letters, such as V = 5, X = 10.

7. *Cardinal numbers* are numbers used in simple counting or in reply to the question "How many?" Any number may be a cardinal number.

8. *Ordinal numbers* indicate succession or order of arrangement, such as *first, second, tenth.*

9. An *integer,* or *integral number,* is a whole number, not a fraction or part.

10. An *even number* is any number that can be exactly divided by 2, such as 4, 16, 96, 102.

11. An *odd number* is any number that is *not* exactly divisible by 2, such as 3, 15, 49, 103.

12. A *factor* of a number is a whole number that may be exactly divided into the number. For example, 3 is a factor of 27, 13 is a factor of 91.

13. A *prime number* is a number that has no factors other than itself and 1. Thus, 3, 5, 7, and 23 are prime numbers.

14. A *composite number* is a number that has factors other than itself and 1, such as 8, 49, and 100.

15. A *multiple* of a number is a number that is exactly divisible by a given number. For example, 91 is a multiple of 7, 12 is a multiple of 3.

16. A *digit* is any number from 1 to 9, and usually 0.

Signs of Operation

1. The *sign of addition* is +, and it is read "plus" or "add." Thus, 7 + 3 is read "seven plus three." The numbers may be taken in *any order* when adding; 7 + 3 is the same as 3 + 7.
2. The *sign of subtraction* is −, and it is read "minus." A series of subtractions *must* be taken in the order written—11 − 7 is *not* the same as 7 − 11.
3. The *sign of multiplication* is ×, and it is read "times" or "multiplied by." The numbers may be taken in *any order* when multiplying; 4 × 7 is the same as 7 × 4.
4. The sign of division is ÷, and it is read "divided by." A series of divisions *must* be taken in the order written— (100 ÷ 2) ÷ 10 = 5.
5. The *sign of equality* is =, and it is read "equals" or "is equal to." The expressions on each side of an equality sign must be numerically the same. The complete expression is called an *equation*.

Rules for Finding Divisors of Numbers

Sometimes useless labor can be avoided by making a check of divisibility using one of the following rules:

1. A number is divisible by 2 if its right-hand digit is 0 or is divisible by 2. Thus, 62, 114, 1078 are all divisible by 2.
2. A number is divisible by 3 if the sum of its digits is divisible by 3. Therefore, 27, 72, 201 are all divisible by 3.
3. A number is divisible by 4 if the number represented by the last two digits on its right are divisible by 4. For example, 2772 is divisible by 4 since 72 is divisible by 4.
4. A number is divisible by 5 if the last digit on its right is 0 or 5. Thus, 105, 255, and 1005 are all divisible by 5.
5. An even number the sum of whose digits is divisible by 3 is divisible by 6. For example, 2028 is divisible by 6, but the number 327,273 is not.
6. There is no quick check for divisibility by 7; it is necessary to try it out.
7. A number is divisible by 8 if the last 3 digits on the right of that number are divisible by 8. Therefore, the number 967,568 is divisible by 8 because 568 is divisible by 8.

11

8. A number is divisible by 9 if the sum of its digits is divisible by 9. Thus, the number 7,642,764 is divisible by 9 since the sum of its digits, 36, is divisible by 9.

How the Signs of Operation Are Used

Example—*The use of the sign of addition.* A builder when building a house buys 1762 board feet of lumber from one yard, 2176 board feet from another, and 276 board feet from another. How many board feet did he buy?

The problem: 1762 + 2176 + 276 = ?

The solution: 1762
         2176
        + 276
        ‾‾‾‾‾
         4214 board feet

Note how the numbers are aligned to permit addition. The units are all aligned on the right, then the tens, then the hundreds, then the thousands, each in the proper column.

Example—*The use of the sign of subtraction.* A carpenter bought 300 pounds of nails for a job, and he had 28 pounds left when he finished. How many pounds of nails did he use to complete the job?

The problem: 300 − 28 = ?

The solution: 300
        − 28
        ‾‾‾‾
         272 pounds

Note that the numbers must be aligned as they were for addition.

Example—*The use of the sign of division.* A man's car gets an average of 17 miles per gallon of gasoline. How many gallons of gasoline would be required for him to travel 2040 miles in his car?

The problem: 2040 ÷ 17 = ?

The solution:

$$\begin{array}{r} 120 \\ 17\overline{)2040} \\ \underline{17} \\ 34 \\ \underline{34} \\ 00 \end{array}$$

Example—*The use of the sign of equality.* A road contractor finds that he can lay the same amount of paving in 12 days using a 6-man crew that he can lay in 8 days using a 9-man crew. Express this statement as an equation.

$$12 \times 6 = 9 \times 8, \text{ or } 72 = 72$$

Roman Numerals

The Roman notation (Table 1) is still occasionally used for highly formalized inscriptions, such as the dates on cornerstones of buildings, on college diplomas, years of copyright in books, or numbers of chapters and sections in books.

Fractions

A fraction indicates that a number or a unit has been divided into a certain number of equal parts, and shows how many of these parts are to be considered. Two forms of fractions are in common usage—the decimal, which is expressed in the tenths system, and the common fraction. The common fraction is written by using two numbers, one written over or alongside the other with a line between them. The lower (or second) number, called the *denominator*, indicates the number of parts into which the unit has been divided, and the upper (or first) number, called the *numerator*, indicates the number of parts to be considered. In the fraction ⅔, the denominator shows that the unit is divided into 3 parts; the numerator indicates that 2 parts are being considered.

If the quantity indicated by the fraction is less than 1, such as ½, ¾, or ⁵/₆, it is called a *proper fraction*. If the quantity indi-

13

Table 1. Arabic and Roman Notations

0 = O		29 = XXIX	
1 = I		30 = XXX	
2 = II		31 = XXXI	
3 = III		32 = XXXII	
4 = IV		40 = XL	
5 = V		50 = L	
6 = VI		60 = LX	
7 = VII		70 = LXX	
8 = VIII		80 = LXXX	
9 = IX		90 = XC	
10 = X		100 = C	
11 = XI		101 = CI	
12 = XII		102 = CII	
13 = XIII		103 = CIII	
14 = XIV		104 = CIV	
15 = XV		150 = CL	
16 = XVI		200 = CC	
17 = XVII		300 = CCC	
18 = XVIII		400 = CD	
19 = XIX		500 = D	
20 = XX		600 = DC	
21 = XXI		700 = DCC	
22 = XXII		800 = DCCC	
23 = XXIII		900 = CM	
24 = XXIV		1000 = M	
25 = XXV		2000 = MM	
26 = XXVI		10,000 = $\overline{\text{X}}$	
27 = XXVII		100,000 = $\overline{\text{C}}$	
28 = XXVIII		1,000,000 = $\overline{\text{M}}$	

cated by the fraction is equal to or greater than 1, such as $^3/_3$, $^5/_4$, or $^7/_6$, it is called an *improper fraction*. When a whole number and a proper fraction are combined, such as 2¼, 6½, it is called a *mixed number*.

Addition of Fractions—Fractions cannot be added without first reducing them to a common denominator.

Example—Add $\frac{3}{4} + \frac{2}{9} + \frac{2}{3} + \frac{7}{12}$

To find the common denominator, place the denominators in a row, separated by dashes. Divide them by a prime number that will divide into at least two of them without leaving a remainder, and bring down the denominators with the dividends that did not contain the divisor without a remainder. Repeat this process as often as possible until there are no two numbers remaining that can be divided by the same number. Then, multiply the divisors and the remainders together, and the result will be the smallest common denominator.

The solution:

$$
\begin{array}{r}
2 \enspace) \enspace \underline{4-9-3-12} \\
3 \enspace) \enspace \underline{2-9-3-6} \\
2 \enspace) \enspace \underline{2-3-1-2} \\
1-3-1-1
\end{array}
$$

The common denominator will then be $2 \times 3 \times 2 \times 3 = 36$. The fractions are then reduced to the common denominator of 36 by multiplying the numerator and the denominator by the same number that will produce 36 in the denominator, as:

$$\frac{3}{4} = \frac{3}{4} \times \frac{9}{9} = \frac{27}{36}$$
$$\frac{2}{9} = \frac{2}{9} \times \frac{4}{4} = \frac{8}{36}$$
$$\frac{2}{3} = \frac{2}{3} \times \frac{12}{12} = \frac{24}{36}$$
$$\frac{7}{12} = \frac{7}{12} \times \frac{3}{3} = \frac{21}{36}$$

The sum of the fractions $= \dfrac{27 + 8 + 24 + 21}{36} = \frac{80}{36}$ or $\frac{20}{9}$

Multiplication of Common Fractions—A fraction may be multiplied by a whole number by multiplying the numerator of the fraction by that number.

Example—If $\frac{3}{4}$ of a keg of nails is used for siding a garage, how many kegs of nails will be used when siding 8 similar garages?

The solution: $8 \times \frac{3}{4} = \frac{24}{4}$

A fraction may be simplified by dividing both the numerator and the denominator by the same number, and its value will not be affected.

Example—Divide both the numerator and the denominator of the improper fraction $^{24}/_4$ by 4.

The result will be $^6/_1$, or 6. Therefore, 6 kegs of nails will be required to put the siding on the 8 garages.

Fractions may be multiplied by fractions by multiplying their numerators together and their denominators together.

Example—Multiply

$$^2/_5 \times ^1/_4 \times ^5/_{12} = \frac{2 \times 1 \times 5}{5 \times 4 \times 12} = \frac{10}{240} = \frac{1}{24}$$

Multiplication of Fractions by Cancellation—This may readily be done because any factor below the line may be divided by any factor above the line, and any factor above the line may be divided by any factor below the line, without altering the overall value of the expression. Take the example $^{12}/_{30} \times ^{14}/_{56} \times ^{10}/_{24}$ and write it in this form:

$$\frac{1 \times 1 \times 1}{\cancel{12} \times \cancel{14} \times \cancel{10}}$$
$$\cancel{30} \times \cancel{56} \times \cancel{24}$$
$$3 \times 4 \times 2$$

The 30 below the line may be divided by the 10 above the line—result, 3. The 56 below the line may be divided by the 14 above the line—result, 4. The 24 below the line may be divided by the 12 above the line—result, 2. The result of the cancellation, then, is

$$\frac{1}{3 \times 4 \times 2} = \frac{1}{24}$$

Division of Fractions—Fractions may be divided by whole numbers by dividing the numerator by that number or by multiplying the denominator by that number.

Example

$$\frac{7}{8} \div 7 = \frac{1}{8}$$

$$\frac{7}{8} \div 7 = \frac{7}{56} = \frac{1}{8}$$

Fractions may be divided by fractions by inverting the divisor and multiplying.

Example

$$\frac{7}{8} \div \frac{2}{7} = \frac{7}{8} \times \frac{7}{2} = \frac{49}{16}$$

which is the mixed number $3^1/_{16}$.

Subtraction of Fractions—Fractions cannot be subtracted from fractions without first reducing them to a common denominator, as is done for the addition of fractions.

Example—Subtract $\frac{13}{16}$ from $\frac{5}{6}$

Finding the least common denominator,

$$2 \underline{)\, 16 - 6 \atop 8 - 3} \qquad 2 \times 8 \times 3 = 48$$

$$\frac{13}{16} = \frac{13}{16} \times \frac{3}{3} = \frac{39}{48}$$

$$\frac{5}{6} = \frac{5}{6} \times \frac{8}{8} = \frac{40}{48}$$

$$\frac{40 - 39}{48} = \frac{1}{48}$$

To subtract a mixed number from another mixed number, it is usually most convenient to reduce both numbers to improper fractions and then proceed as shown in the last example.

To subtract a mixed number from a whole number, borrow 1 from the minuend, or upper number; reduce the 1 to an improper denominator of the fraction in the subtrahend, or lower number, thereby reducing the whole number by 1. Then make the subtraction in the normal manner.

Example—Subtract 6⅞ from 14.

The solution: $14 - 6\frac{7}{8} = 13\frac{8}{8} - 6\frac{7}{8} = 7\frac{1}{8}$

Applications of Cancellation—There are numberless applications where this method will save appreciable time and work, but care and thought must be given to the proper arrangement of the fractional expression if there are many factors. Also, it must be remembered that if addition or subtraction signs appear, cancellation *may not* be used.

Example—A circular saw has 75 teeth with a 1-inch spacing between each tooth. In order to do satisfactory work, the rim of the saw should travel at approximately 9000 feet per minute. How many revolutions should this saw make per minute? (Hint: 75 inches = $^{75}/_{12}$ feet.)

The solution:

$$\frac{\overset{120}{\cancel{9000}} \times 12}{\cancel{75}} = 120 \times 12 = 1440 \text{ rev. per min.}$$

Example—If you go to a bank and borrow $1000 to purchase a car, how much will the interest be, at 6% per annum (a theoretical example only), on the money you borrow for 1 year and 3 months? (Hint: 1 year 3 months = 15 months.)

The solution:

$$\frac{\cancel{6} \times \overset{\overset{5}{\cancel{10}}}{\cancel{1000}} \times 15}{\underset{\underset{2}{\cancel{100}} \times \cancel{12}}{}} = 5 \times 15 = \$75$$

Example—If 8 men in fifteen 8-hour days can throw 1000 cubic yards of gravel into wheelbarrows, how many men will be required to throw 2000 cubic yards of gravel into wheelbarrows in twenty days of 6 hours each?

The solution:

$$\frac{\overset{3}{\cancel{15}} \times \overset{2}{\cancel{8}} \times \overset{4}{\cancel{8}} \times \overset{2}{\cancel{2000}}}{\underset{4}{\cancel{20}} \times \cancel{6} \times \underset{2}{\cancel{1000}}} = 2 \times 4 \times 2 = 16 \text{ men}$$

Example—A building that is 30 feet × 30 feet with a 10-foot ceiling contains approximately 700 pounds of air. What will be the weight of the air in a room 120 feet long, 90 feet wide, and 16 feet high?

The solution:

$$\frac{\overset{4}{\cancel{120}} \times \overset{3}{\cancel{90}} \times 16 \times \overset{70}{\cancel{700}}}{\cancel{30} \times \cancel{30} \times \cancel{10}} = 4 \times 3 \times 16 \times 70 = 13,440 \text{ pounds}$$

Decimals

Decimal means numbering that proceeds by *tens*, and decimal fractions, usually simply called *decimals*, are formed when a unit is divided into 10 parts. When decimals are written, the point where the numbers start is called the *decimal point*. To the left of the decimal point, the numbers read in the regular manner—units, tens, hundreds, thousands, ten thousands, hundred thousands, millions, etc. To the right of the decimal point, the figures are fractional, reading, from the point, tenths, hundredths, thousandths, ten thousandths, hundred thousandths, millionths, etc.

The common fraction $^6/_{10}$ can be expressed decimally as .6, and the fraction $^{105}/_{1000}$ can be written as .105. The mixed number 106 $^6/_{100}$ may be expressed decimally as 106.06. The decimal .6 is read "six-tenths," the same as the common fraction

19

$^6/_{10}$, and the decimal 106.06 is read "one hundred six *and* six-hundredths," the same as the mixed number.

It is not necessary to place a zero before the decimal point, as 0.06, but it is sometimes convenient when it is necessary to align a column of decimals for addition. The decimal points must *always* be aligned for addition, as shown in the following example:

$$
\begin{array}{r}
.6 \\
6.29 \\
+10.72 \\
\hline
17.61
\end{array}
$$

The position of the decimal point in the sum is established directly under the column of decimal points above the line. *Note*: the number 327 is *not* read "three hundred *and* twenty-seven," but "three hundred twenty-seven"; however, the decimal 300.27 is read "three hundred *and* twenty-seven hundredths." The decimal .327 is read "three hundred twenty-seven thousandths," while the decimal 300.027 is read "three hundred *and* twenty-seven thousandths."

Reduction of Common Fractions to Decimals—Divide the numerator by the denominator, adding zeros and carrying the division to as many decimal places as are necessary or desirable. See Table 2 on pages 24 and 25.

Example—Reduce the common fraction $^{21}/_{32}$ to a decimal.

$$
\begin{array}{r}
.65625 \\
32\overline{)21.00000} \\
\underline{192} \\
180 \\
\underline{160} \\
160 \\
\underline{200} \\
192 \\
\underline{80} \\
64 \\
\underline{160} \\
160 \\
\underline{00}
\end{array}
$$

Count off as many decimal places in the quotient as those in the dividend *exceed* those in the divisor. The quotient is .65625.

Subtraction of Decimals—Align the decimal points in the minuend and the subtrahend as shown for addition, and proceed as explained in subtraction of whole numbers. The decimal point in the remainder is placed in exact alignment with those decimal points above the line.

Example—Subtract 27.267 from 167.02.

The solution:

$$
\begin{array}{r}
167.020 \\
-\ 27.267 \\
\hline
139.753
\end{array}
$$

Note that it is necessary to add a zero to the decimal 167.02, in order to make the subtraction, but this does not change its value— $\frac{20}{1000}$ is the same value as $\frac{2}{100}$.

Multiplication of Decimals—Proceed as in multiplication of whole numbers, and count off as many decimal places in the product as there are in *both* the multiplier and multiplicand.

Example—Multiply 1.76 by .06.

The solution:

$$
\begin{array}{r}
1.76 \\
\times\ .06 \\
\hline
.1056
\end{array}
$$

Compound Numbers

A compound number expresses units of two or more denominations of the same kind, such as 5 yards, 1 foot, and 4 inches. The process of changing the denomination in which a quantity is expressed without changing its value is called reduction. Thus, 1 yard and 2 inches = 38 inches, 25 inches = 2 feet and 1 inch, etc., are examples of reduction. Problems of reduction occur and are explained with the various measures and weights.

Reduction Descending—To reduce a compound number to a lower denomination, multiply the largest units in the given number by the number of units in the next lower denomination, and add to the product the units of that denomination in the given number. Continue this process until the original number is reduced as far as desired. For an explanation of this rule, see the following example.

Example—Reduce the quantity 6 yards, 2 feet, 7 inches to inches.

$$
\begin{array}{rl}
& 6 \text{ yards} \\
\text{Multiply.} \ldots \times 3 & \\
\hline
& 18 \text{ feet} \\
\text{Add.} \ldots \ldots + 2 & \\
\hline
& 20 \text{ feet} \\
\text{Multiply.} \ldots \times 12 & \\
\hline
& 240 \text{ inches} \\
\text{Add.} \ldots \ldots + 7 & \\
\hline
\text{Total.} \ldots \ldots \ldots & 247 \text{ inches}
\end{array}
$$

Reduction Ascending—To reduce a number of small units to units of larger denominations, divide the number by the number of units in a unit of the next higher denomination. The quotient is in the higher denomination and the remainder, if any, is in the lower. Continue this process until the number is reduced as far as is desired.

Example—Reduce 378 inches to a quantity of yards, feet, and inches.

The solution:

$$
\begin{array}{l}
12 \ ) \ 378 \\
\hline
 3 \ )\overline{31} \text{ feet, 6 inches remainder} \\
 \overline{10} \text{ yards, 1 foot remainder}
\end{array}
$$

Therefore, 378 inches = 10 yards, 1 foot, 6 inches.

Ratios

By definition, a ratio is the relation of one number to another as obtained by dividing the first number by the second. Thus, the ratio of 2 to 4 is expressed as 2 : 4; the symbol : is read "to" in the case of a ratio and "is to" in the case of a proportion. It is equivalent to "divided by," hence:

$$2 : 4 = \tfrac{1}{2}$$

The first term of a ratio is the *antecedent*, and the second term is the *consequent*, thus:

$$\begin{array}{ccc} \text{antecedent} & & \text{consequent} \\ 2 & : & 4 \end{array}$$

Since a ratio is essentially a fraction, it follows that if both terms are multiplied or divided by the same number, the value of the ratio is not altered. Thus:

$$2 : 4 = 2 \times 2 : 4 \times 2 = 2 \div 2 : 4 \div 2$$

Two quantities of different kinds cannot form the terms of a ratio. Thus, no ratio can exist between $5 and 1 day, but a ratio can exist between $5 and $2 or between 1 day and 10 days.

Proportion

When two ratios are equal, the four terms form a proportion. A proportion is therefore expressed by using the sign = or : : between two ratios, thus:

$$\text{(expressed)}\ 4 : 8 : : 2 : 4$$
$$\text{(read)}\ 4\ \text{is to}\ 8\ \text{as}\ 2\ \text{is to}\ 4$$

The same proportion is also expressed as follows:

$$^4/_8 = ^2/_4$$

Table 2. Fractions of an Inch and Decimal Equivalents

			$\frac{1}{64}$	.015625
		$\frac{1}{32}$		.031250
			$\frac{3}{64}$	.046875
	$\frac{1}{16}$			.062500
			$\frac{5}{64}$	.078125
		$\frac{3}{32}$		.093750
			$\frac{7}{64}$	.109375
$\frac{1}{8}$				.125000
			$\frac{9}{64}$	.140625
		$\frac{5}{32}$		.156250
			$\frac{11}{64}$	.171875
	$\frac{3}{16}$			.187500
			$\frac{13}{64}$	.203125
		$\frac{7}{32}$		.218750
			$\frac{15}{64}$	.234375
$\frac{1}{4}$				.250000
			$\frac{17}{64}$	.265625
		$\frac{9}{32}$		.281250
			$\frac{19}{64}$	.296875
	$\frac{5}{16}$			.312500
			$\frac{21}{64}$	.328125
		$\frac{11}{32}$		.343750
			$\frac{23}{64}$	.359375
$\frac{3}{8}$				.375000
			$\frac{25}{64}$	.390625
		$\frac{13}{32}$		.406250
			$\frac{27}{64}$	.421875
	$\frac{7}{16}$			.437500
			$\frac{29}{64}$	.453125
		$\frac{15}{32}$		.468750
			$\frac{31}{64}$	.484375
$\frac{1}{2}$				.500000
			$\frac{33}{64}$	.515625
		$\frac{17}{32}$		.531250
			$\frac{35}{64}$	.546875
	$\frac{9}{16}$			.562500
			$\frac{37}{64}$	.578125
		$\frac{19}{32}$		.593750
			$\frac{39}{64}$	.609375
$\frac{5}{8}$				.625000
			$\frac{41}{64}$	.640625

Table 2. Fractions of an Inch and Decimal Equivalents (Cont'd)

1/8	1/16	1/32	1/64	Decimal
		21/32		.656250
			43/64	.671875
	11/16			.687500
			45/64	.703125
		23/32		.718750
			47/64	.734375
3/4				.750000
			49/64	.765625
		25/32		.781250
			51/64	.796875
	13/16			.812500
			53/64	.828125
		27/32		.843750
			55/64	.859375
7/8				.875000
			57/64	.890625
		29/32		.906250
			59/64	.921875
	15/16			.937500
			61/64	.953125
		31/32		.968750
			63/64	.984375
				1.000000

The first and last terms of a proportion are called the *extremes,* and the middle terms are called the *means,* thus:

$$4 : 8 : : 2 : 4$$

The product of the extremes equals the product of the means. Thus, in proportion

$$4 : 8 = 2 : 4$$
$$4 \times 4 = 8 \times 2$$

Since the equation is not altered by dividing both sides by the same number, the value of any term can be obtained as follows:

$$\frac{4 \times 4}{4} = \frac{8 \times 2}{4}$$

$$4 = 2 \times 2 = 4$$

"Rule of Three"

When three terms of a proportion are given, the method of finding the fourth term is called the "rule of three."

Example—If 5 bundles of shingles cost $100, what will 25 bundles cost?

Let X represent the unknown term in the proportion, and, remembering that each ratio must be made up of like quantities,

$$5 \text{ bundles} : 25 \text{ bundles} = 100 \text{ ($)} : X \text{ ($)}$$

Multiplying the extremes by the means,

$$5 \times X = 25 \times 100$$

$$X = \frac{25 \times 100}{5} = \$500$$

Percentage

By definition, percentage means the rate per one hundred, or the proportion in one hundred parts. Therefore $1/100$ of a number is called 1 percent, $2/100$, 2 percent, etc. The symbol % is read as percent; thus 1%, 2%, etc. Carefully note the following explanation with respect to the symbol %. The notation 5% means $5/100$, which, when reduced to a decimal (as is necessary when making a calculation), becomes .05, but .05% has a quite different value; .05% means $.05/100$, which, when reduced to a decimal, becomes .0005, that is, $5/100$ of 1%.

If the decimal has more than two places, the figures that follow the hundredths place signify parts of 1%.

Example—If the list price of shingles is $90 per 1000, what is the net cost for 1000 shingles with a 5% discount for cash?

Reduce % rate to a decimal.
5% = 5/100 = .05

Multiply decimal by list price.
$90 × .05 = $4.50

Subtract product obtained from list price.
$90 − $4.50 = $85.50

Powers of Numbers (Involution)

The word "involution" means the multiplication of a quantity by itself any number of times, and a "power" is the product arising from this multiplication. Involution, then, is the process of raising a number to a given power. The "square" of a number is its second power: the "cube," its third power, etc. Thus:

$$\text{square of } 2 = 2 \times 2 = 4$$

$$\text{cube of } 2 = 2 \times 2 \times 2 = 8$$

The power to which a number is raised is indicated by a small "superior" figure called an *exponent*. Thus, in Fig. 1, the exponent indicates the number of times the number, or "root," has been multiplied by itself.

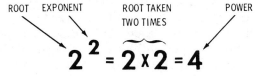

Fig. 1. The "root," "exponent," and "power"
of a number.

Roots of Numbers (Evolution)

The word "evolution" means the operation of extracting a root. The root is a factor that is repeated to produce a power. Thus, in the equation $2 \times 2 \times 2 = 8$, 2 is the root from which the power 8 is produced. This number is indicated by the symbol $\sqrt{}$, called the radical sign, which, when placed over a number, means that the root of that number is to be extracted. Thus:

$\sqrt{4}$ *means that the square root of 4 is to be extracted*

27

The *index* of the root is a small figure that is placed over the radical sign that denotes what root is to be taken. Thus, $^3\sqrt{9}$ indicates the cube root of 9; $^4\sqrt{16}$ indicates the extraction of the fourth root of 16. When there is no index given, the radical sign alone always means the *square root* is to be extracted from the number under the radical sign.

Sometimes the number under the radical sign is to be raised to a power before extracting the root, as:

$$\sqrt[3]{4^3} = \sqrt[3]{4 \times 4 \times 4} = \sqrt[3]{64}$$

Example—Extract the square root of 186,624.

$$\begin{array}{r} \sqrt{18'66'24} \quad 432 \\ 16 \\ \hline 83\sqrt{266} \\ 249 \\ \hline 862\sqrt{1724} \\ 1724 \\ \hline \end{array}$$

From the decimal point, count off the given number into periods of two places each. Begin with the last period counted off (18). The largest square that can be divided into 18 is 4; put this down in the quotient, and put the square (16) under the 18. Write down the remainder (2), and bring down the next period (66). Multiply 4 (in the quotient) by 2 for the first number of the next divisor; 8 goes into 26 three times. Place 3 after 4 in the quotient and also after 8 in the divisor. Multiply the 83 by 3, placing the product 249 under 266, and subtract, obtaining the remainder 17. Bring down the last period (24), and proceed as before, obtaining 432 as the square root of 186,624.

Extracting the cube root of a number is a more complicated though similar process, as indicated by the following procedure:

1. Separate the number into groups of three figures each, beginning at the decimal point.
2. Find the greatest cube that can be divided into the left-hand group, and write its root for the first figure of the required root.

3. Cube this root, subtract the result from the left-hand group, and annex the next group to the remainder for a dividend.
4. For a partial divisor, take three times the square of the root already found, considered as hundreds, and divide the dividend by it. The quotient (or the quotient diminished) will be (or be close to) the second figure of the root.
5. To this partial divisor, add three times the product of the first figure of the root, considered as tens, by the second figure, and to this add the square of the second figure. This sum will be the complete divisor.
6. Multiply the complete divisor by the second figure of the root, subtract the product from the dividend, and annex the next group to the remainder for a new dividend.
7. Proceed in this manner until all the groups have been annexed. The result will be the cube root required, as shown in the following example.

Example—Extract the cube root of the number 50,653. The solution:

$$\sqrt[3]{50'653.}\quad(\,37$$

$$\begin{array}{r} 27 \\ \hline \end{array}$$

$$\begin{array}{rr} & 23\ 653 \\ 2700 & \\ 630 & 23\ 653 \\ \underline{49} & \underline{} \\ 3379 & \end{array}$$

Therefore, the cube root of 50,653 is 37.

MEASURES

To *measure* is the act or process of determining the extent, quantity, degree, capacity, dimension, volume, etc., of a substance by comparing it with some fixed standard, which is usually fixed by law. A measure may relate to any of these standards. There are many kinds of measures, and practically all of them are standard, but standards vary in different countries. The measures mentioned in this text are all U.S. standards unless designated otherwise. The study of measurements is sometimes called *mensuration*.

Among the many kinds of measures are the following:

1. Linear—measures of length.
2. Square—used to measure areas.
3. Cubic—used to measure volume, or volumetric contents.
4. Weight—many systems of weights are standard.
5. Time—almost standardized all over the world.
6. Circular or angular—the same all over the world.

Linear Measure

Long Measure

12 inches	= 1 foot		
3 feet	= 1 yard	= 36 inches
5½ yards	= 1 rod	= 16½ feet
40 rods	= 1 furlong	= 660 feet
8 furlongs	= 1 mile	= 5280 feet
3 miles	= 1 league (land)	

(The furlong is practically never used, except at race tracks and in some athletic events.)

Land Surveyor's Measure

7.92 inches	= 1 link		
100 links	= 1 chain	=	66 feet
10 chains	= 1 furlong	=	660 feet
80 chains	= 1 mile	=	5280 feet

The use of the surveyor's chain, or Gunter's chain, was abandoned in the late 1800's and was superseded by the steel tape which is much more accurate; the chain (meaning 66 feet) is still used by the U.S. General Land Office, however, when surveying very old deeds. The standard surveyor's tape is often called, from habit, a chain. It is 100 feet long and is graduated in feet except for the last foot, which is divided into tenths and hundredths of a foot.

Nautical Measure (U.S. Navy)

6 feet = 1 fathom
120 fathoms = 1 cable length
The International Nautical Mile (adopted in 1954) =
   6076.1033 feet
3 nautical miles = 1 marine league

The "knot" is a measure of speed, *not* of length, and is equivalent to 1 nautical mile per hour. A speed of 16 knots is equal to 16 nautical miles per hour.

Square Measure

Square measure is used to measure areas. In most, but not all cases, linear units are used to measure the two dimensions, length and width, and their product is the area in square units. Expressed as an equation,

$$\text{length} \times \text{width} = \text{area}$$

The two dimensions, length and width, must be measured in the same units, but any unit of linear measurement may be used. If inches are multiplied by inches, the result will be in square inches; if feet are multiplied by feet, the result will be in square feet, etc.

For the small areas commonly found in everyday life, such as table tops or shelves, the unit most commonly used is the square inch. Plywood and lumber are commonly sold by the square foot. Carpets and other floor coverings and materials and ceilings are measured in square yards. The carpenter measures roofing by the "square" of 10 × 10 feet, or 100 square feet. Tracts of land are usually measured in acres or, for large areas, in square miles.

Square Measure

144 square inches = 1 square foot
9 square feet = 1 square yard

30¼ square yards = 1 square rod = 272.25 square feet
160 square rods = 1 acre = 4840 square yards or 43,560 square feet
640 acres = 1 square mile = 3,097,600 square yards
36 square miles = 1 township

Cubic Measure

Cubic measure is used to determine or appraise volumes. Three dimensions are involved—length, width, and height—and their product is volume. Expressed as an equation,

$$\text{length} \times \text{width} \times \text{height} = \text{volume}$$

As with square measure, the usual linear units—inches, feet, and yards—are ordinarily used to measure these three dimensions. Most small measurements of capacity, such as small shipping cases or small cabinets, are measured in cubic inches. The contents of buildings, their "cubage," are ordinarily expressed in cubic feet. Earthwork, either excavated and loose or in place, is expressed in cubic yards.

Cubic Measures of Volume

1728 cubic inches = 1 cubic foot
27 cubic feet = 1 cubic yard

Dry Measure—Quantities of loose, granular materials, such as grains, some fruits, and certain vegetables, are measured in arbitrary units, that, in turn, are defined by means of cubic measures of volume, usually in cubic inches. Their value is sometimes, but not always, fixed by law.

Dry Measure (U.S.)

2 pints = 1 quart = 67.2 cubic inches
8 quarts = 1 peck = 537.61 cubic inches
4 pecks = 1 bushel = 2150.42 cubic inches

Dry Measure (British and Canadian)

1 gallon = .5 peck = 277.42 cubic inches
4 pecks = 1 bushel = 2219.23 cubic inches

The British dry quart is apparently not often used; it is equal to 69.35 cubic inches, or 1.032 U.S. dry quarts.

The weight, rather than the volume, of grains is the standard fixed by the U.S. government:

1 bushel of wheat = 60 pounds
1 bushel of barley = 48 pounds
1 bushel of oats = 32 pounds
1 bushel of rye = 56 pounds
1 bushel of corn (shelled) = 56 pounds

Board or Lumber Measure—Timbers and logs are measured in board or lumber measure. The board foot is 1 foot wide, 1 foot long, and 1 inch thick, thereby containing 144 cubic inches. In the retail market, all lumber which is less than one inch thick is called one inch. At the sawmills, the full sizes govern the thickness of the saw kerfs; usually about ¼ inch is allowed for and accounted as sawing loss. Actual finished (dressed) sizes of common lumber, the dimension and timbers for pine are as follows:

The standard dressed thickness of 1-inch boards is ¾ inch.
The standard thickness of 2-inch dimension boards is 1½ inches.
The standard dressed widths of lumber 2 inches thick and less are ½ inch less for widths under 8 inches and ¾ inch less for 8-inch widths and wider.
The standard dressed widths and thicknesses for lumber and timbers are ½ inch less both ways under 8 inches wide and ¾ inch for 8-inch widths and over. So a 2″ × 8″ would be 1½″ × 7¼″. A 2″ × 10″ would be 1½″ × 9¼″.

Liquid Measure—Liquid measure is used to measure various liquids such as oils, liquors, molasses, and water.

Liquid Measure

4 gills = 1 pint = 28.875 cubic inches
2 pints = 1 quart = 57.75 cubic inches
4 quarts = 1 gallon = 231 cubic inches

There is no legal standard barrel in the U.S. By custom, a barrel of water is understood to be 31½ gallons. The British barrel is generally 36 Imperial gallons. Crude oil is often disposed of at the wells in barrels of 50 gallons, while refined oils are marketed in barrels of 48 gallons. Owing to this lack of uniformity, it is safest to specify "barrels of 50 gallons," or something of that nature, to avoid misunderstanding. The barrel is sometimes used as a dry measure unit of varying value. For Portland cement, 4 bags = 1 barrel = 4 cubic feet = 376 pounds.

Measures of Weight

The simplest definition of weight is that it is the force with which a body is attracted toward the earth. It is a quantity of heaviness. There are three systems, or standards, of weights used in the United States. They are:

1. Avoirdupois—used for almost all ordinary purposes
2. Troy—used in weighing precious metals and jewels
3. Apothecaries—used by pharmacists when compounding drugs

Avoirdupois Weights

16 drams = 1 ounce
16 ounces = 1 pound
100 pounds = 1 hundredweight
20 hundredweights = 1 ton

In England, the following weights are in common usage:

14 pounds = 1 stone
112 pounds = 1 hundredweight
20 hundredweight = 1 ton = 2240 pounds

The 2240-pound ton is sometimes used in the United States for weighing coal at the mines and at customs houses for evaluating shipments from England.

Troy Weights

3.086 grains = 1 carat
24 grains = 1 pennyweight
20 pennyweights = 1 ounce
12 ounces = 1 pound

Apothecaries Weights

20 grains = 1 scruple
3 scruples = 1 dram
8 drams = 1 ounce
12 ounces = 1 pound

This standard of weights is fast becoming obsolete, although pharmacists must be familiar with it. Manufacturing pharmacists and chemists are rapidly changing to the metric weights, using the metric *gram* as a basis instead of the apothecaries' scruple; 1 scruple = 1.296 grams.

Time Measure

Time is defined as measurable duration. It is the period during which an action or process continues. The basis, or standard, used in our ordinary determination of time is the *mean solar day*, beginning and ending at mean midnight. The word "mean" as used here simply means average; the direct ray of the sun does not move in an exact and uniform path around the equator.

Time Measure

60 seconds = 1 minute
60 minutes = 1 hour
24 hours = 1 day
7 days = 1 week
30 days (commonly) = 1 month

365 days	=	1 year
10 years	=	1 decade
100 years	=	1 century
1000 years	=	1 millennium

The length of an *astronomical* year is 365 days, 5 hours, 48 minutes, and 45.51 seconds, or approximately 365¼ days. This makes it necessary to add 1 day every 4 years, thus making the "leap" year 366 days.

Circular Measure

This measure is used in astronomy, land surveying, navigation, and in measuring angles of all kinds. Circles of all sizes are divisible into degrees, minutes, and seconds. Note that a degree is *not* a measurement of length. It is $1/360$ of the circumference of a circle with any radius.

Circular Measure

60 seconds	=	1 minute
60 minutes	=	1 degree
360 degrees	=	1 circle

The Metric System

The base, or fundamental, unit in the metric system is the meter. The meter is defined as the distance between two scribed marks on a standard bar made of platinum-iridium kept in the vaults of the International Bureau of Weights and Measures, near Paris, France. Of course, many other standard meter bars have been made from the measurement on this bar. It is permissible and official to use this measurement in the United States, and, in fact, the yard, the basis for the English system of measurement, has been defined as exactly $3600/3937$ meter, or 1 meter = 39.37 inches.

The advantage, and immeasurably greater convenience, of the metric system over the English system of units lies in the fact that it is expressed in tenths, thereby readily allowing the use of decimals. However, the American public is accustomed to the English units, and as recent experience indicates, the system should continue for a long time. The metric system is, of course, in common use all over the world with the exception of some English-speaking peoples. The meter is used like the yard to measure cloth and short distances.

Units of other denominations are named by prefixing to the word "meter" the Latin numerals for the lower denominations and the Greek numerals for the higher denominations, as shown in the following chart:

Lower denomination	*Higher denomination*
Deci = 1/10	Deka = 10
Centi = 1/100	Hecto = 100
Milli = 1/1000	Kilo = 1000
Micro = 1/1,000,000	Myria = 10,000
	Mega = 1,000,000

Therefore, 1 decimeter = $^1/_{10}$ of a meter, 1 millimeter = $^1/_{1000}$ of a meter, 1 kilometer = 1000 meters, etc. From this explanation of the metric prefixes, the linear table that follows can easily be understood.

Metric Table of Linear Measure

Metric Denomination		Meter	U.S. value
	1 millimeter	= .001	= .0394 in.
10 millimeters =	1 centimeter	= .01	= .3937 in.
10 centimeters =	1 decimeter	= .1	= 3.937 in.
10 decimeters =	1 meter	= 1.	= 39.3707 in.
			= 3.28 ft.
10 meters =	1 dekameter	= 10.	= 32.809 ft.
10 dekameters =	1 hectometer	= 100.	= 328.09 ft.
10 hectometers =	1 kilometer	= 1000.	= .62138 mi.
10 kilometers =	1 myriameter	= 10,000.	= 6.2138 mi.

The kilometer is commonly used for measuring long distances. The square meter is the unit used for measuring ordinary surfaces, such as flooring or ceilings.

Metric Table of Square Measure

100 sq. millimeters
    (sq. mm.)   = 1 sq. centimeter   = .155+ sq. in.
100 sq. centimeters
    (sq. cm.)   = 1 sq. decimeter   = 15.5+ sq. in.
100 sq. decimeters
    (sq. dm.)   = 1 sq. meter (sq. m.)= 1.196+ sq. yd.

The acre is the unit of land measure and is defined as a square whose side is 10 meters, equal to a square dekameter, or 119.6 square yards.

Metric Table of Land Measure

1 centiare (ca)	= 1 sq. meter	= 1.196 sq. yd.
100 centiares (ca.)	= 1 are	= 119.6 sq. yd.
100 ares (A.)	= 1 hectare	= 2.471 acres
100 hectares (ha.)	= 1 sq. kilometer	= .3861 sq. mi.

The cubic meter is the unit used for measuring ordinary solids, such as excavations or embankments.

Metric Table of Cubic Measure

1000 cu. millimeters
    (cu. mm.)   = 1 cu. centimeter   = .061+ cu. in.
1000 cu. centimeters
    (cu. cm.)   = 1 cu. decimeter   = 61.026+ cu. in.
1000 cu. decimeters
    (cu. dm.)   = 1 cu. meter   = 35.316+ cu. ft.

The liter is the unit of capacity, both of liquid and of dry measures, and is equivalent to a vessel whose volume is equal to a cube whose edge is one-tenth of a meter, equal to 1.0567 quarts liquid measure, and .9081 quart dry measure.

Metric Table of Capacity

10 milliliters (ml.)	= 1 centiliter	= .0338 fluid ounce
10 centiliters (cl.)	= 1 deciliter	= .1025 cubic inch
10 deciliters (dl.)	= 1 liter	= 1.0567 liquid quart
10 liters (l.)	= 1 dekaliter	= 2.64 gallons
10 dekaliters (dl.)	= 1 hectoliter	= 26.418 gallons
10 hectoliters (hl.)	= 1 kiloliter	= 264.18 gallons
10 kiloliters (kl.)	= 1 myrialiter (ml.)	

1 myrialiter = 10 cu. meters

  = 283.72 + bu.= 2641.7 + gal.

1 kiloliter = 1 cu. meter

  = 28.372 + bu.= 264.17 gal.

1 hectoliter = $^1/_{10}$ cu. meter

  = 2.8372 + bu.= 26.417 gal.

1 decaliter = 10 cu. dm.

  = 9.08 quarts = 2.6417 gal.

1 liter = 1 cu. dm.

  = .908 quart = 1.0567 qt. liquid

1 deciliter = $^1/_{10}$ cu. dm.

  = 6.1022 cu. in.= .845 gal.

1 milliliter = 10 cu. cm.

  = .6102 cu. in. = .338 fluid oz.

1 centiliter = 1 cu. cm.

  = .061 cu. in. = .27 fluid dr.

The hectoliter is the unit used for measuring liquids, grain, fruit, and roots in large quantities. The gram is the unit of weight equal to the weight of a cube of distilled water, the edge of which is $^1/_{100}$ of a meter and is equal to 15.432 troy grains.

Metric Table of Weight Measure

10 milligrams (mg.)	= 1 centigram	= .15432 + gr. troy
10 centigrams (cg.)	= 1 decigram	= 1.54324 + gr. troy
10 decigrams (dg.)	= 1 gram	= 15.43248 + gr. troy
10 grams (g.)	= 1 dekagram	= .35273 + oz. avoir.
10 dekagrams (Dg.)	= 1 hectogram	= 3.52739 + oz. avoir.

10 hectograms (hg.)	= 1 kilogram	= 2.20462 + lb. avoir.
10 kilograms (kg.)	= 1 myriagram	= 22.04621 + lb. avoir.
10 myriagrams (Mg.)	= 1 quintal	= 220.46212 + lb. avoir.
10 quintals	= 1 ton	= 2204.62125 + lb. avoir.

GEOMETRY

By definition, geometry is that branch of mathematics that deals with space and figures in space. In other words, it is the science of the mutual relations of points, lines, angles, surfaces, and solids, which are considered as having no properties except those arising from extension and difference of situation.

Lines

There are two kinds of lines—straight and curved. A straight line is the shortest distance between two points. A curved line is one which changes its direction at every point. Two lines are said to be parallel when they have the same direction. A horizontal line is one parallel to the horizon or surface of the earth. A line is perpendicular with another line when they are at right angles to each other. These definitions are illustrated in Fig. 2.

Angles

An angle is the difference in direction between two lines proceeding from the same point (called the vertex). Angles are said to be right (90 degrees) when formed by two perpendicular lines, Fig. 3A, acute (less than 90 degrees) when less than a right angle, Fig. 3B, and obtuse (more than 90 degrees) when greater than a right angle, Fig. 3C. All angles except right (or 90-degree) angles are called oblique angles.

Angles are usually measured in degrees (circular measure). The *complement* of an angle is the difference between 90 degrees and the angle; the *supplement* of the angle is the difference between the angle and 180 degrees. These relations are shown in Fig. 3D.

Plane Figures

The term "plane figures" means a plane surface bounded by straight or curved lines, and a plane, or plane surface, is one in

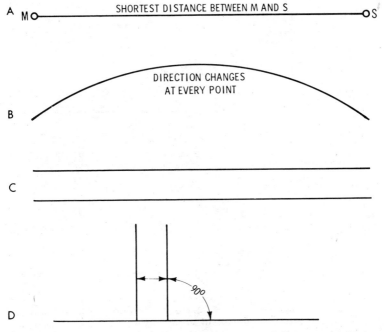

Fig. 2. Various lines; A. Straight; B. Curved; C. Parallel; D. Perpendicular.

which any straight line joining any two points lies wholly in the surface. Fig. 4 defines a plane surface. There is a great variety of plane figures, which are known as polygons when their sides are straight lines. The sum of the sides is called the *perimeter*. A regular polygon has all its sides and angles equal. Plane figures of three sides are known as triangles, Fig. 5, and plane figures of four sides are quadrilaterals. Fig. 6 shows examples of these; Fig. 8 details its structure. Various plane figures are formed by curved sides and are known as circles, ellipses, etc., as shown in Fig. 7.

Solids

Solids have three dimensions—length, width, and thickness. The bounding planes are called the *faces*, and the intersections are called the *edges*. A prism, as shown in Fig. 9, is a solid whose ends consist of equal and parallel polygons and whose

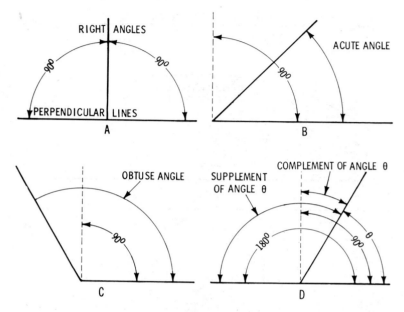

Fig. 3. Various angles; A. Right; B. Acute; C. Obtuse; D. Complement and supplement of an angle.

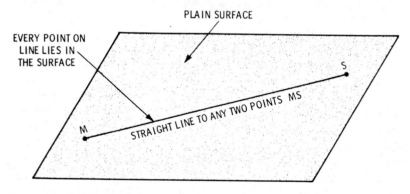

Fig. 4. A plane surface means that every point on a straight line joining any two points in the surface lies in the surface.

sides are parallelograms. The altitude of a prism is the perpendicular distance of its opposite sides or bases. A parallelopipedon is a prism which is bounded by six parallelograms; the

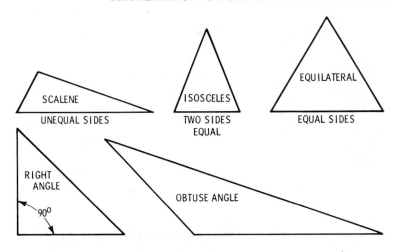

Fig. 5. Various triangles; a triangle is a polygon having three sides and three angles.

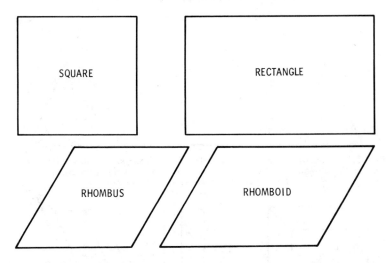

Fig. 6. Various quadrilaterals; all opposite sides of a quadrilateral are equal.

opposite parallelograms are parallel and equal. A cube is a parallelopipedon whose faces are equal. One important solid is the cylinder, which is a body bounded by a uniformly curved sur-

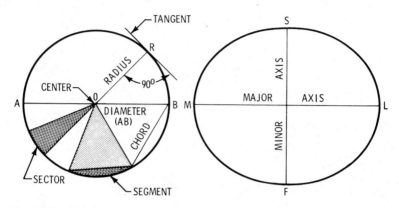

Fig. 7. Curved figures. A circle is a plane figure bounded by a uniformly curved line, every point of which is equidistant from the center point O; OR is a radius, and AB is a diameter. An ellipse is a curved figure enclosed by a curved line which is such that the sum of the distances between any point on the circumference and the two foci is invariable; ML is the major axis, and SF is the minor axis.

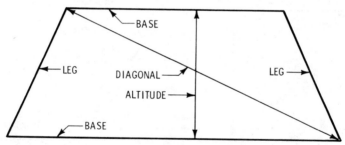

Fig. 8. The parallel sides of a quadrilateral (four-sided polygon) are the bases; the distance between the bases is the altitude, and a line joining two opposite vertices is a diagonal.

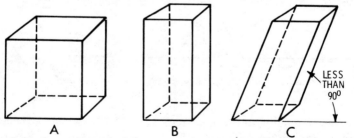

Fig. 9. Various prisms, A. Cube, or equilateral parallelopipedon; B. Parallelopipedon; C. Oblique parallelopipedon.

face and having its ends equal and forming parallel circles, as shown in Fig. 10. There are numerous other solids having curved surfaces, such as cones and spheres.

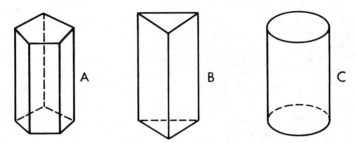

Fig. 10. Various solids; A. Pentagonal prism; B. Triangular prism; C. Cylinder.

Geometrical Problems

The following problems illustrate the method in which various geometrical figures are constructed, and they should be solved by the use of pencil, dividers, compass, and scale. Many of these problems are commonly encountered in carpentry with layout work; therefore, experience in working them out will be of value to carpenters and woodworkers.

Problem 1—To bisect, or divide into two equal parts, a straight line or arc of a circle.

In Fig. 11, from the ends A and B, as centers, describe arcs

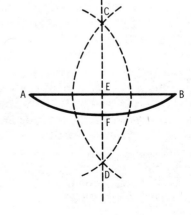

Fig. 11. To bisect a straight line or arc of a circle.

cutting each other at C and D, and draw line CD, which cuts the line at E, or the arc at F.

Problem 2—To draw a perpendicular to a straight line, or a radial line to an arc.

In Fig. 11, the line CD is perpendicular to AB; also, the line CD is radial to the arc AB.

Problem 3—To erect a perpendicular to a straight line from a given point in that line.

In Fig. 12, with any radius from any given point A, in the line BC describe arcs cutting the line at B and C. Next, with a longer radius describe arcs with B and C as centers, intersecting at D, and draw the perpendicular DA.

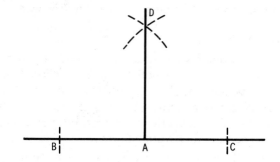

Fig. 12. To erect a perpendicular to a straight line from a given point on that line.

Second Method—In Fig. 13, from any point F above BC, describe a circle passing through the given point A and cutting the given line at D; draw DF, and extend it to cut the circle at E; draw the perpendicular AE.

Third Method (boat builders' layout method)—In Fig. 14, let MS be the given line and A, the given point. From A, measure off a distance AB (4 feet). With centers A and B and radii of 3 and 5 feet, respectively, describe arcs L and F intersecting at C. Draw a line through A and C, which will be the perpendicular required. This method is used extensively by carpenters when squaring the corners of buildings, but they ordinarily use multiples of 3, 4, and 5, such as 6, 8, and 10, or 12, 16, and 20.

Fourth Method—In Fig. 15, from A, describe an arc EC, and

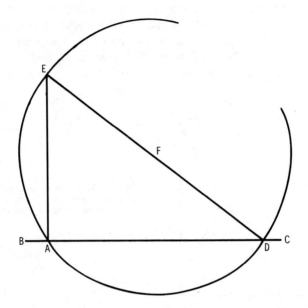

Fig. 13. To erect a perpendicular to a straight line from a given point on that line, second method.

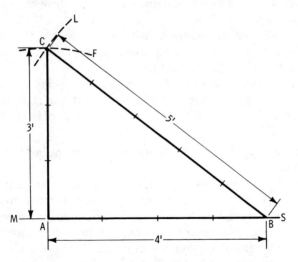

Fig. 14. To erect a perpendicular to a straight line from a given point on that line, third method.

47

from E with the same radius describe the arc AC, cutting the other at C; through C, draw a line ECD; lay off CD equal to CE, and through D, draw the perpendicular AD. The triangle produced is exactly 60 degrees at E, 30 degrees at D, and 90 degrees at A. The hypotenuse ED is exactly twice the length of the base EA.

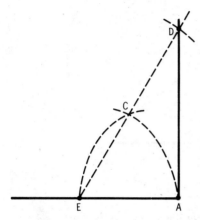

Fig. 15. To erect a perpendicular to a straight line from a given point on that line, fourth method.

Problem 4—To erect a perpendicular to a straight line from any point outside the line.

In Fig. 16, from the point A, with a sufficient radius cut the given line at F and G, and from these points describe arcs cutting at E. Draw the perpendicular AE.

Second Method—In Fig. 17, from any two points B and C at some distance apart in the given line and with the radii BA and CA, respectively, describe arcs cutting at A and D. Draw the perpendicular AD.

Problem 5—To draw a line parallel to a given line through a given point.

In Fig. 18, with C as the center, describe an arc tangent to the given line AB; the radius will then equal the distance from the given point to the given line. Take a point B on the given line remote from C, and describe an arc. Draw a line through C, tangent to this arc at D, and it will be parallel to the given line AB.

Second Method—In Fig. 19, from A, the given point, describe

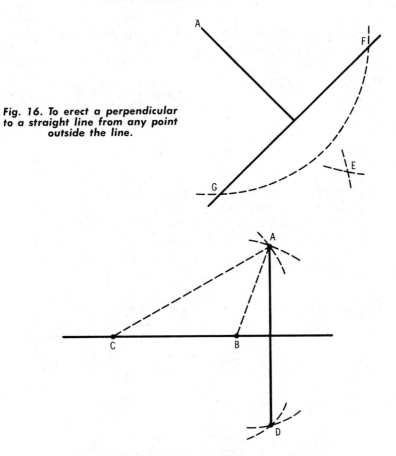

Fig. 16. To erect a perpendicular to a straight line from any point outside the line.

Fig. 17. To erect a perpendicular to a straight line from any point outside the line, second method.

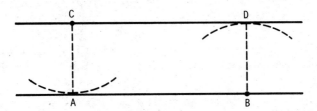

Fig. 18. To draw a line parallel to a given line through a given point.

the arc FD, cutting the given line at F; from F, with the same radius, describe the arc EA, and lay off FD equal to EA. Draw the parallel line through the points AD.

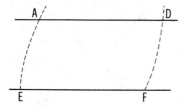

Fig. 19. To draw a line parallel to a given line through a given point, second method.

Problem 6—To divide a line into a number of equal parts.

In Fig. 20, assuming line AB is to be divided into five equal parts, draw a diagonal line AC of five units in length. Join BC at 5 and through the points 1, 2, 3, 4, draw lines 1L, 2a, etc., parallel to BC. AC will then be divided into five equal parts, AL, La, ar, rf, and fB.

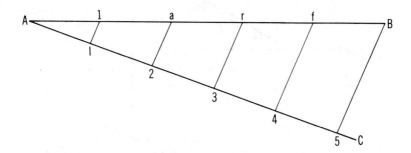

Fig. 20. To divide a line into a number of equal parts.

Problem 7—To draw an angle equal to a given angle on a straight line. In Fig. 21, let A be the given angle, and FG the line. With any radius from the points A and F, describe arcs DE and IH cutting the sides of angle A and line FG. Lay off arc IH equal to arc DE, and draw line FH. Angle F is then equal to A, as required.

Problem 8—To bisect an angle.

In Fig. 22, let ACB be the angle; with the center of the angle at C, describe an arc cutting the sides at A and B. Using A and

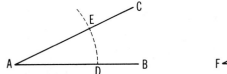 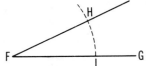

Fig. 21. To draw an angle equal to a given angle on a straight line.

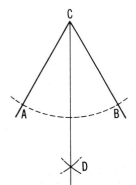

Fig. 22. To bisect an angle.

B as centers, describe arcs which intersect at D. A line through C and D will divide the angle into two equal parts.

Problem 9—To find the center of a circle.

In Fig. 23, draw any chord MS. With M and S as centers, and with any radius, describe arcs L F and L' F', and draw a line through their intersection, giving a diameter AB. Applying the same construction with centers A and B, describe arcs ef and e'f'. A line drawn through the intersections of these arcs will cut line AB at O, the center of the circle.

Problem 10—To describe an arc of a circle with a given radius through two given points.

In Fig. 24, take the given points A and B as centers, and, with the given radius, describe arcs which intersect at C; from C, with the same radius, describe an arc AB, as required.

Second Method—In Fig. 25, for a circle or an arc, select three points ABC in the circumference which are well apart; with the same given radius, describe arcs from these three points that

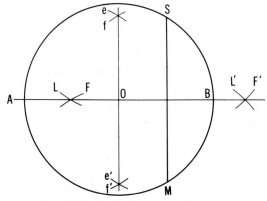

Fig. 23. To find the center of a circle.

Fig. 24. To describe an arc of a circle with a given radius through two given points.

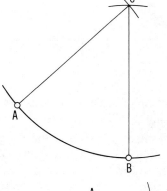

Fig. 25. To describe an arc of a circle with a given radius through two given points, second method.

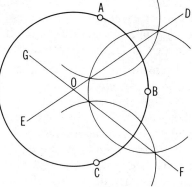

intersect each other, and draw two lines, DE and FG, through their intersections. The point where these lines intersect is the center of the circle or arc.

Problem 11—To describe a circle passing through three given points.

In Fig. 25, let A, B, and C be the given points, and proceed as in the last problem to find the center O from which the circle may be described. This problem is useful in such work as laying out an object of large diameter, such as an arch, when the span and rise are given.

Problem 12—To draw a tangent to a circle from a given point in the circumference.

In Fig. 26, from A, lay off equal segments AB and AD; join line BD, and draw line AE parallel to BD for the tangent.

Problem 13—To draw tangents to a circle from points outside the circle.

In Fig. 27, from A, and with the radius AC, describe an arc BCD; from C, with a radius equal to the diameter of the circle, intersect the arc at BD; join BC and CD, which intersect the circle at E and F, and draw the tangents AE and AF.

Problem 14—To describe a series of circles tangent to two inclined lines and tangent to each other.

In Fig. 28, bisect the inclination of the given lines AB and CD by the line NO. From a point P in this line, draw the perpendicular PB to the line AB, and on P, describe the circle BD, touching the lines and the center line at E. From E, draw EF perpendicular to the center line intersecting AB at F, and from F, describe an arc EG intersecting AB at G. Draw GH parallel to BP, thus

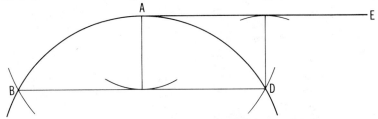

Fig. 26. To draw a tangent to a circle from a given point in the circumference.

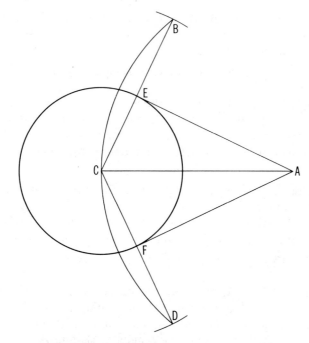

Fig. 27. To draw tangents to a circle from points outside the circle.

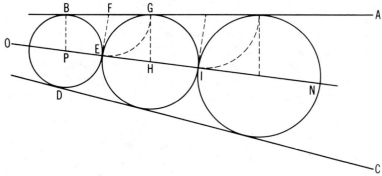

Fig. 28. To describe a series of circles tangent to two inclined lines and tangent to each other.

producing H, the center of the next circle, to be described with the radius HE, and so on for the next circle IN.

Problem 15—To construct an equilateral triangle on a given base.

In Fig. 29, with A and B as centers and a radius equal to AB, describe arcs 1 and f. At their intersection C, draw lines CA and CB, which are the sides of the required triangle. If the sides are to be unequal, the process is the same, taking as the radii the lengths of the two sides to be drawn.

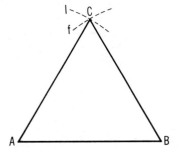

Fig. 29. To construct an equilateral triangle on a given base.

Problem 16—To construct a square on a given base.

In Fig. 30, with end points A and B of the base as centers and a radius equal to AB, describe arcs which intersect at C; on C, describe arcs which intersect the others at D and E, and on D and E, intersect these arcs F and G. Draw AE and BG, and join the intersections HI to form the square AHIB.

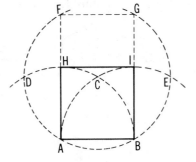

Fig. 30. To construct a square or a rectangle on a given base.

Problem 17—To construct a rectangle on a given base.

In Fig. 30, let AB be the given base. Erect a perpendicular at A and at B equal to the altitude of the rectangle, and join their ends F and G by line FG; AFGB is the rectangle required.

Problem 18—To construct a parallelogram given the sides and an angle.

In Fig. 31, draw side DE equal to the given length A, and lay off the other side DF, equal to the other length B, thus forming the given angle C. From E, with DF as the radius, describe an arc, and from F, with the radius DE, intersect the arc at G. Draw FG and EG. The remaining sides may also be drawn as parallels to DE and DF.

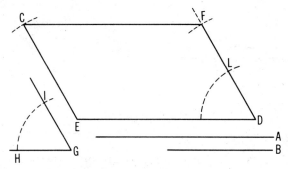

Fig. 31. To construct a parallelogram given the sides and an angle.

Problem 19—To draw a circle around a triangle.

In Fig. 32, bisect two sides AB and AC of the triangle at E and F, and from these points draw perpendiculars intersecting at K. From K, with radius KA or KC, describe the circle ABC.

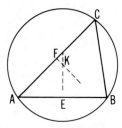

Fig. 32. To draw a circle around a triangle

Problem 20—To circumscribe and inscribe a circle about a square.

In Fig. 33, draw the diagonals AB and CD intersecting at E. With a radius EA, circumscribe the circle. To inscribe a circle,

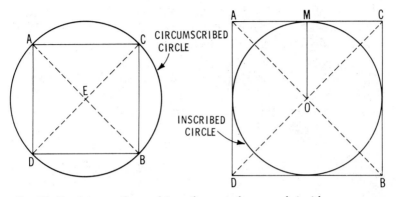

Fig. 33. *To circumscribe and inscribe a circle around, inside a square.*

draw a perpendicular from the center (as just found) to one side of the square, as line OM. With radius OM, inscribe the circle.

Problem 21—To circumscribe a square around a circle.

In Fig. 34, draw diameters MS and LF at right angles to each

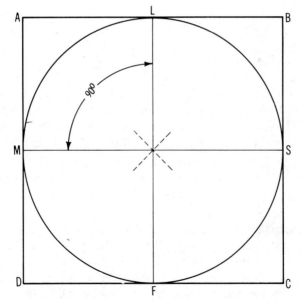

Fig. 34. *To circumscribe a square about a circle.*

other. At points M, L, S, and F, where these diameters intersect the circle, draw tangents, that is, lines perpendicular to the diameters, obtaining the sides of the circumscribed square ABCD.

Problem 22—To inscribe a circle in a triangle.

In Fig. 35, bisect two angles A and C of the triangle with lines that intersect at D; from D, draw a perpendicular DE to any side. With DE as the radius, describe a circle.

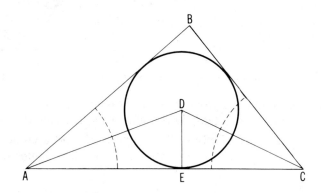

Fig. 35. To inscribe a circle in a triangle.

Problem 23—To inscribe a pentagon in a circle.

In Fig. 36, draw two diameters AC and BD at right angles intersecting at O; bisect AO at E, and from E, with radius EB, AC at F; from B, with radius BF, intersect the circumference at G and H, and with the same radius, step round the circle to I and K; join the points thus found to form the pentagon BGIKH.

Problem 23A—To inscribe a five-pointed star in a circle.

In Fig. 37, proceed as explained for the inscribed pentagon in Problem 23. Then, connect point B with points K and I, point H with points G and I, etc. The star is mathematically correct.

Problem 24—To construct a hexagon from a given straight line.

In Fig. 38, from A and B, the ends of the given line, describe arcs intersecting at g; from g, with the radius gA, describe a circle. With the same radius, lay off arcs AG, GF, BD, and DE. Join the points thus found to form the hexagon.

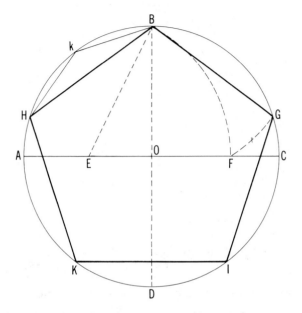

Fig. 36. To inscribe a pentagon in a circle.

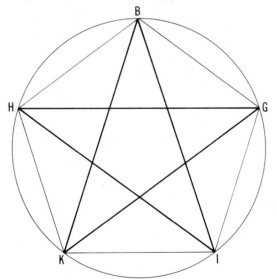

Fig. 37. To inscribe a five-pointed star in a circle.

59

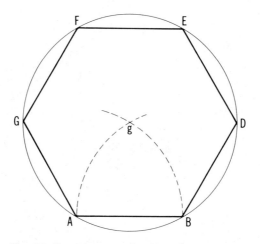

Fig. 38. To construct a hexagon from a given straight line.

Problem 25—To inscribe a hexagon in a circle.

In Fig. 39, draw a diameter ACB; from A and B, as centers with the radius of the circle AC, intersect the circumference at D, E, F, and G, and draw lines AD, DE, etc., to form the hexa-

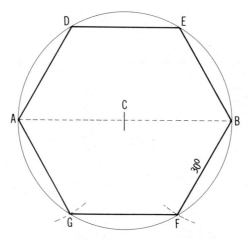

Fig. 39. To inscribe a hexagon in a circle.

gon. The points D, E, etc., may also be found by stepping off the radius (with the dividers) six times around the circle.

Problem 26—To describe an octagon on a given straight line.

In Fig. 40, extend the given line AB both ways, and draw perpendiculars AE and BF; bisect the external angles A and B by lines AH and BC, which are made equal to line AB. Draw CD and HG parallel to AE and equal to line AB. Draw CD and HG parallel to AE and equal to line AB; with G and D as centers, and with the radius equal to AB; intersect the perpendiculars at E and F, and draw line EF to complete the hexagon.

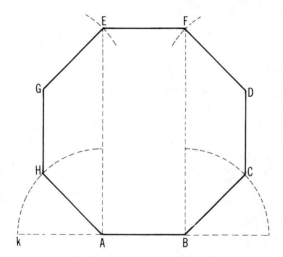

Fig. 40. To describe an octagon on a given straight line.

Problem 27—To inscribe an octagon in a square.

In Fig. 41, draw the diagonals of the square intersecting at e; from the corners A, B, C, D, with Ae as the radius, describe arcs intersecting the sides of the square at g, h, etc., and join the points found to complete the octagon.

Problem 28—To inscribe an octagon in a circle.

In Fig. 42, draw two diameters AC and BD at right angles; bisect the arcs AB, BC, etc., at e, f, etc., to form the octagon.

Problem 29—To circumscribe an octagon about a circle.

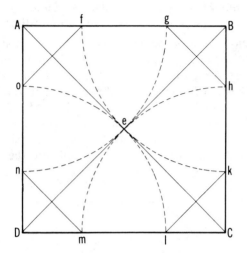

Fig. 41. To inscribe an octagon in a square.

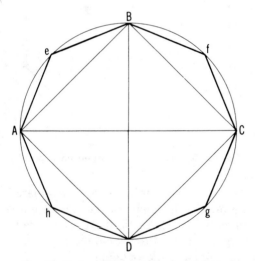

Fig. 42. To inscribe an octagon in a circle.

In Fig. 43, describe a square about the given circle AB; draw perpendiculars hk, etc., to the diagonals, touching the circle, to form the octagon. The points h, k, etc., may be found by cutting the sides from the corners.

62

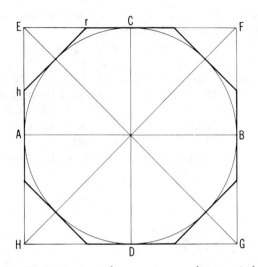

Fig. 43. To circumscribe an octagon about a circle.

Problem 30—To describe an ellipse when the two axes are given.

In Fig. 44, draw the major and minor axes AB and CD, respectively, at right angles intersecting at E. On C, with AE as the radius, intersect the axis AB at F and G, the *foci*; insert pins through the axis at F and G, and loop a thread or cord on them equal in length to the axis AB, so that when stretched, it reaches extremity C of the *conjugate axis*, as shown in dotted lines.

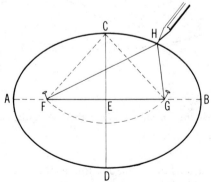

Fig. 44. To describe an ellipse when the two axes are given.

Place a pencil inside the cord, as at H, and, by guiding the pencil in this manner, describe the ellipse.

Second Method—Along the edge of a piece of paper, mark off a distance ac equal to AC, one-half the major axis, and from the same point a distance ab equal to CD, one-half the minor axis, as shown in Fig. 45. Place the paper so as to bring point b on the line AB, or major axis, and point c on the line DE, or minor axis. Lay off the position of point a. By shifting the paper so that point b travels on the major axis and point c travels on the minor axis, any number of points in the curve may be found through which the curve may be traced.

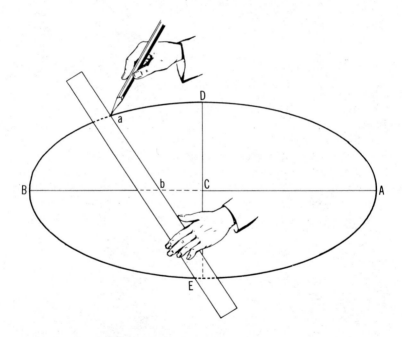

Fig. 45. To describe an ellipse given the two axes, second method.

Mensuration

As mentioned earlier, mensuration is the act, art, or process of measuring. It is that branch of mathematics that deals with finding the length of lines, the area of surfaces, and the volume

Table 3. Decimals of a Foot and Inches

Inch	0″	1″	2″	3″	4″	5″	6″	7″	8″	9″	10″	11″
0	.0000	.0833	.1677	.2500	.3333	.4167	.5000	.5833	.6667	.7500	.8333	.9167
1-16	.0052	.0885	.1719	.2552	.3385	.4219	.5052	.5885	.6719	.7552	.8385	.9219
1-8	.0104	.0937	.1771	.2604	.3437	.4271	.5104	.5937	.6771	.7604	.8437	.9271
3-16	.0156	.0990	.1823	.2656	.3490	.4323	.5156	.5990	.6823	.7656	.8490	.9323
1-4	.0208	.1042	.1875	.2708	.3542	.4375	.5208	.6042	.6875	.7708	.8542	.9375
5-16	.0260	.1094	.1927	.2760	.3594	.4427	.5260	.6094	.6927	.7760	.8594	.9427
3-8	.0312	.1146	.1979	.2812	.3646	.4479	.5312	.6146	.6979	.7812	.8646	.9479
7-16	.0365	.1198	.2031	.2865	.3698	.4531	.5365	.6198	.7031	.7865	.8698	.9531
1-2	.0417	.1250	.2083	.2917	.3750	.4583	.5417	.6250	.7083	.7917	.8750	.9583
9-16	.0469	.1302	.2135	.2969	.3802	.4635	.5469	.6302	.7135	.7969	.8802	.9635
5-8	.0521	.1354	.2188	.3021	.3854	.4688	.5521	.6354	.7188	.8021	.8854	.9688
11-16	.0573	.1406	.2240	.3073	.3906	.4740	.5573	.6406	.7240	.8073	.8906	.9740
3-4	.0625	.1458	.2292	.3125	.3958	.4792	.5625	.6458	.7292	.8125	.8958	.9792
13-16	.0677	.1510	.2344	.3177	.4010	.4844	.5677	.6510	.7344	.8177	.9010	.9844
7-8	.0729	.1562	.2396	.3229	.4062	.4896	.5729	.6562	.7396	.8229	.9062	.9896
15-16	.0781	.1615	.2448	.3281	.4115	.4948	.5781	.6615	.7448	.8281	.9115	.9948

of solids. Therefore, the problems that follow will be divided into three groups, as:

1. Measurement of lines.
   a. One dimension—length.
2. Measurement of surfaces (areas).
   a. Two dimensions—length and width.
3. Measurement of solids (volumes).
   a. Three dimensions—length, width, and thickness.

Measurement of Lines—Length.

Problem 1—To find the length of any side of a right triangle given the other two sides.

Rule: The length of the hypotenuse equals the square root of the sum of the squares of the two legs; the length of either leg equals the square root of the difference of the square of the hypotenuse and the square of the other leg.

Example—The two legs of a right triangle measure 3 feet and 4 feet. Find the length of the hypotenuse. If the length of the

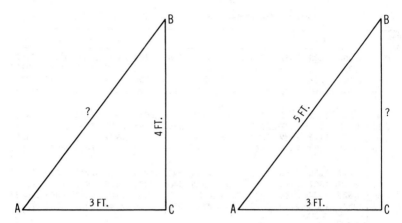

Fig. 46. To find the length of any side of a right triangle given the other two sides.

hypotenuse and one leg are 5 feet and 4 feet, respectively, what is the length of the other leg?

In Fig. 46A,

$$AB = \sqrt{3^2 + 4^2} = \sqrt{25} = 5 \; feet$$

In Fig. 46B,

$$BC = \sqrt{5^2 - 3^2} = \sqrt{25 - 9} = \sqrt{16} = 4 \; feet$$

Problem 2—To find the length of the circumference of a circle. *Rule:* Multiply the diameter by 3.1416.

Example—What length of molding strip is required for a circular window that is 5 feet in diameter?

$$5 \times 3.1416 = 15.7 \; feet$$

Since the carpenter does not ordinarily measure feet in tenths, .7 should be reduced to inches; it corresponds to 8½ inches from Table 3. That is, the length of molding required is 15 feet 8½ inches.

Problem 3—To find the length of the arc of a circle. *Rule: Arc* = .017453 × radius × central angle.

Example—If the radius of a circle is 2 feet, what is the length of a 60° arc?

Solution:

2 × .017453 × 60 = 2.094, or approximately 2 feet 1⅛ inches

Problem 4—To find the rise of an arc.
Rule:

$$Rise\ of\ an\ arc = \sqrt{(4 \times radius^2)} - length$$

Example—If the radius of a circle is 2 feet, what is the rise at the center of a 2-foot chord?

Solution:

$$\tfrac{1}{2}\ \sqrt{(4 \times 2^2)} - 2 = \tfrac{1}{2}\ \sqrt{14} = 1.87\ feet = 1\ foot\ 10\tfrac{1}{2}\ inches$$

Measurement of Surfaces—Area.

Problem 5—To find the area of a square.
Rule: Multiply the base by the height.

Example—What is the area of a square whose side is 5 feet (as shown in Fig. 47)?

$$5 \times 5 = 25\ square\ feet$$

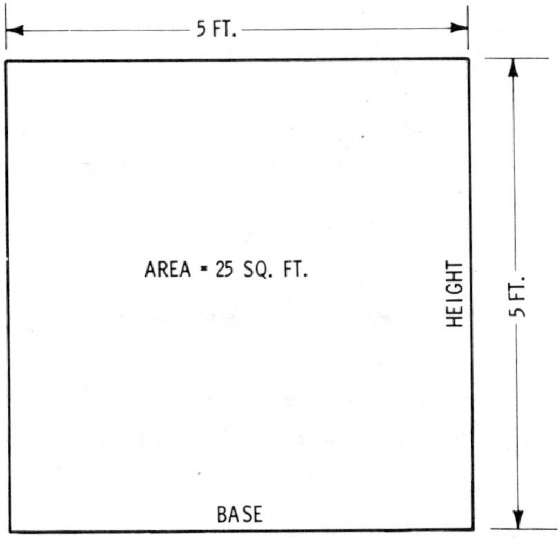

Fig. 47. **To find the area of a square.**

Problem 6—To find the area of a rectangle.

Rule: Multiply the base by the height (i.e., width by length).

Example—What is the floor area of a porch 5 feet wide and 12 feet long (as in Fig. 48)?

5 × 12 = 60 square feet

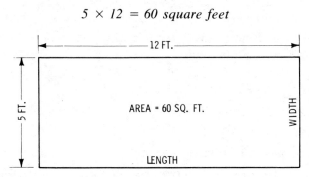

Fig. 48. To find the area of a rectangle.

Problem 7—To find the area of a parallelogram.

Rule: Multiply the base by the perpendicular height.

Example—What is the area of the 5′ × 12′ parallelogram shown in Fig. 49?

5 × 12 = 60 square feet

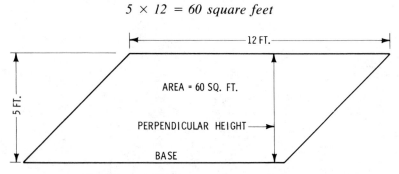

Fig. 49. To find the area of a parallelogram.

Problem 8—To find the area of a triangle.

Rule: Multiply the base by one-half the altitude.

Example—How many square feet of sheathing are required to cover a church steeple having four triangular sides (as shown in Fig. 50)?

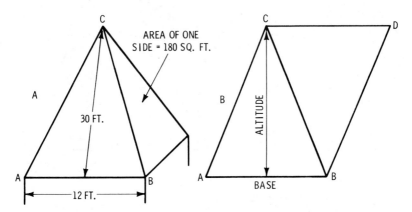

Fig. 50. To find the area of a triangle (equal to ½ area of parallelogram ABDC).

Problem 9—To find the area of a trapezoid.

Rule: Multiply one-half the sum of the two parallel sides by the perpendicular distance between them.

Example—What is the area of the trapezoid shown in Fig. 51?

LA and FR are the parallel sides, and MS is the perpendicular distance between them. Therefore,

$$area = \text{½} \ (LA + FR) \times MS$$
$$area = \text{½} \ (8 + 12) \times 6 = 60 \ square \ feet$$

Problem 10—To find the area of a trapezium.

Rule: Draw a diagonal, dividing the figure into triangles; measure the diagonal and the altitudes, and find the area of the triangles; the sum of these areas is then the area of the trapezium.

Example—What is the area of the trapezium shown in Fig. 52? (Draw diagonal LR and altitudes AM and FS.)

area of triangle ALR $= \text{½} \ (12 \times 9) = 54 \ square \ feet$

69

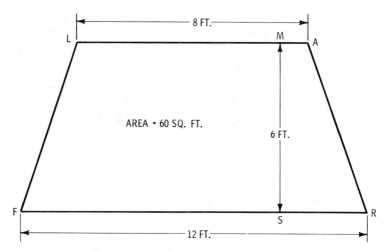

Fig. 51. To find the area of a trapezoid.

area of triangle LRF   = ½ (12 × 6) = 36 square feet
area of trapezium LARF = ALR + LRF = 36 + 54 = 90 sq. ft.

Problem 11—To find the area of any irregular polygon.
Rule: Draw diagonals, dividing the figure into triangles, and find the sum of the areas of these triangles.

Problem 12—To find the area of any regular polygon, such as shown in Fig. 53, when the length of only one side is given.
Rule: Multiply the square of the sides by the figure for "area when side = 1" opposite the particular polygon in Table 4.

Example—What is the area of an octagon (8-sided polygon) whose sides are 4 feet in length?
In Table 4 under 8 find 4.828. Multiply this by the square of one side.

$$4.828 \times 4^2 = 77.25 \ square \ feet$$

Problem 13—To find the area of a circle (Fig. 54).
Rule: Multiply the square of the diameter by .7854.

Example—How many square feet of floor surface are there in a 10 foot circular floor?

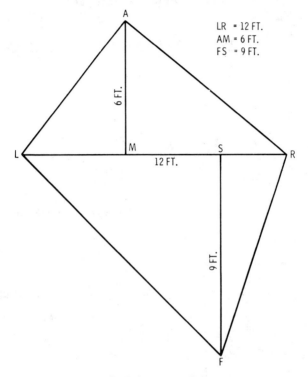

LR = 12 FT.
AM = 6 FT.
FS = 9 FT.

A

6 FT.

L   M   S   R
        12 FT.

9 FT.

F

Fig. 52. To find the area of a trapezium.

10² × .7854 = 78.54 square feet

Problem 14—To find the area of a sector of a circle.
Rule: Multiply the arc of the sector by one-half the radius.

Example—How much tin is required to cover a 60° section of a 10-foot circular deck?

length of 60° arc = ⁶⁰/₃₆₀ of 3.1416 × 10 = 5.24 feet
tin required for 60° sector = 5.24 × ½ × 5 = 13.1 square feet

Problem 15—To find the area of a segment of a circle.

71

Table 4. Regular Polygons

Number of sides	3	4	5	6	7	8	9	10	11	12
Area when side = 1.............	.433	1.0	1.721	2.598	3.634	4.828	6.181	7.694	9.366	11.196

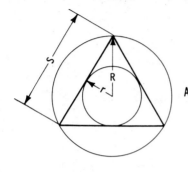

Steel square cut to miter sides at 30^0

$$R = 2r, \text{ or } .577 \, S$$
$$\text{AREA} = .433 \, S^2$$
$$= 1.299 \, R^2$$
$$= 5.196 \, r^2$$
$$= \frac{(R + r) \, S}{2}$$

A. Equilateral triangle (3 sides).

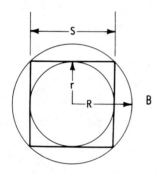

Steel square cut to miter sides at 45^0

$$R = .707 \, S, \text{ or } 1.414 \, r$$
$$\text{AREA} = S^2$$
$$= 2R^2$$
$$= 4r^2$$

B. Square (4 sides).

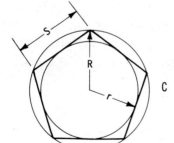

Steel square cut to miter sides at 36^0

$$R = .851 \, S, \text{ or } 1.236 \, r$$
$$\text{AREA} = 1.72 \, S^2$$
$$= 2.378 \, R^2$$
$$= 3.633 \, r^2$$

C. Pentagon (5 sides).

Fig. 53. Regular

Rule: Find the area of the sector which has the same arc, and also find the area of the triangle formed by the radii and chord; take the sum of these areas if the segment is greater than 180°; take the difference if the segment is less than 180°.

Steel square cut to miter sides at 30⁰

R = S, or 1.155 r
AREA = 2.598 S²
    = 2.598 R²
    = 3.464 r²

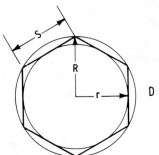

D. Hexagon (6 sides).

Steel square cut to miter corners at 25⁰ 43'

R = 1.152 S, or 1.11 r
AREA = 3.634 S²
    = 2.736 R²
    = 3.371 r²

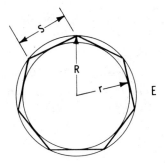

E. Heptagon (7 sides).

Steel square cut to miter corners at 22⁰ 30'

R = 1.307S or 1.082 r
AREA = 4.828 S²
    = 2.828 R²
    = 3.314 r²

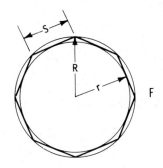

F. Octagon (8 sides).

polygons.

73

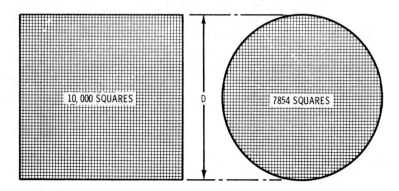

Fig. 54. The decimal .7854 is used to find the area of a circle. If a square is divided into 10,000 equal parts (small squares), then a circle with a diameter D equal to one side of the large square will contain 7854 small squares; therefore, if the area of the large square is 1 square inch, then the area of the circle will be 7854/ 10,000, or .7854 square inch.

Problem 16—To find the area of a ring.

Rule: Take the difference between the areas of the two circles.

Problem 17—To find the area of an ellipse.

Rule: Multiply the product of the two diameters by .7854.

Example—What is the area of an ellipse whose two diameters are 10 inches and 6 inches?

$$10 \times 6 \times .7854 = 47.12 \ square \ inches$$

Problem 18—To find the circular area of a cylinder.

Rule: Multiply 3.1416 by the diameter and by the height.

Example—How many square feet of lumber are required for the sides of a cylindrical tank (Fig. 55) which is 8 feet in diameter and 12 feet high? How many 4″ × 12′ pieces will be required?

$$cylindrical \ surface = 3.1416 \times 8 \times 12 = 302 \ square \ feet$$

$$circumference \ of \ tank = 3.1416 \times 8 = 25.1 \ feet$$

$$number \ of \ 4'' \times 12' \ pieces = \frac{25.1 \times 12}{4} = 25.1 \times 3 = 75.3$$

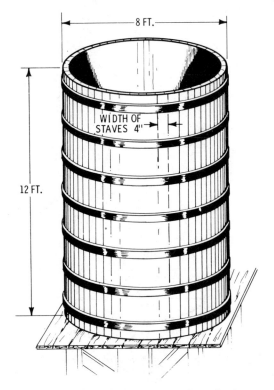

Fig. 55. To find the area of a cylinder.

Problem 19—To find the area of a cone (Fig. 56).

Rule: Multiply 3.1416 by the diameter of the base and by one-half the slant height.

Example—A conical spire with a base 10 feet in diameter and an altitude of 20 feet is to be covered. Find the area of the surface to be covered.

$$slant\ height\ =\ \sqrt{5^2\ +\ 20^2}\ =\ \sqrt{425}\ =\ 20.62\ feet$$

$$circumference\ of\ base\ =\ 3.1416\ \times\ 10\ =\ 31.416\ feet$$

$$area\ of\ conical\ surface\ =\ 31.416\ \times\ \frac{1}{2}\ \times\ 20.62\ =\ 324\ square\ ft.$$

Problem 20—To find the area of the frustum of a cone (Fig. 57).

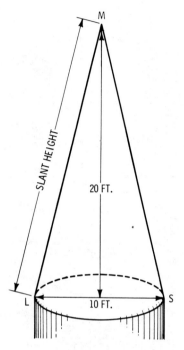

M

SLANT HEIGHT

20 FT.

L   10 FT.   S

**Fig. 56. To find the surface area
of a cone.**

Rule: Multiply one-half the slant height by the sum of the circumference.

Example—A tank is 12 feet in diameter at the base, 10 feet at the top, and 8 feet high. What is the area of the slant surface?

circumference of 10-foot diameter $= 3.1416 \times 10 = 31.416$ feet

circumference of 12-foot diameter $= 3.1416 \times 12 = 37.7$ feet

sum of circumferences $= 69.1$ feet

slant height $= \sqrt{1^2 + 8^2} = \sqrt{65} = 8.12$

slant surface $=$ sum of circumferences $\times \frac{1}{2}$ slant height

slant surface $= 69.1 \times \frac{1}{2} \times 8.12 = 280$ square feet

Measurement of Solids—Volume

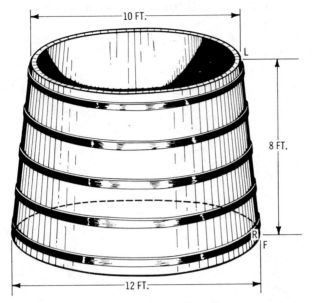

Fig. 57. To find the area of the frustum of a cone.

Problem 21—To find the volume of a rectangular solid.
Rule: Multiply the length, width, and thickness together.

Example—What is the volume of a 4″ × 8″ × 12′ timber? (Before applying the rule, reduce all dimensions to feet.)

$$4'' = \text{}^1\!/_3 \text{ foot}$$
$$8'' = \text{}^2\!/_3 \text{ foot}$$

volume of timber = ¹/₃ × ²/₃ × 12 = 2.67 cubic feet

If the timber were a piece of oak weighing 48 pounds per cubic foot, the total weight would be

$$48 \times 2.67 = 128 \text{ pounds}$$

Problem 22—To find the volume of a rectangular wedge.
Rule: Find the area of one of the triangular ends, and multiply the area by the distance between the ends.

77

Example—An attic has the shape of a rectangular wedge. What volume storage capacity would there be for the proportions shown in Fig. 58? In the illustration, the boundary of the attic is LARFMS.

area of triangular end MLA $= 20 \times {}^{10}/_2 = 100$ square feet

volume of attic $= 100 \times 40 = 4000$ cubic feet

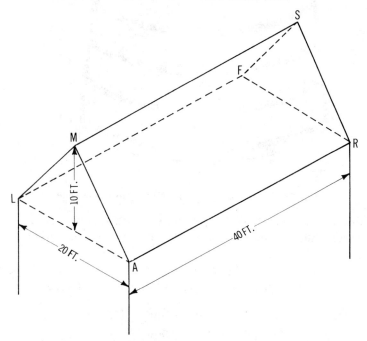

Fig. 58. To find the volume of a rectangular wedge.

TRIGONOMETRY

Trigonometry is that branch of mathematics that deals with the relations that exist between the sides and angles of triangles, and more especially with those of the methods of calculating the required parts of triangles from given parts. The only branch of trigonometry useful to the carpenter and builder is plane trigonometry, where the lines in the triangles are straight and where they all lie in the same plane.

There are six elements, or parts, in every triangle—three sides and three angles. The sum of the three angles, no matter what the lengths of the sides, will always be equal to 180 degrees.

When any three of the six parts are given, provided one or more of them are sides, the other three are calculable. The angles are measured in circular measure—in degrees (°), minutes ('), and seconds (''). The term *degree* has no numerical value; in trigonometry it simply means 1/360 of a circle, nothing more.

To the student of trigonometry, any two radii that divide a circle into anything more than 0° or less than 360° form an angle. The first 90° division is called the *first quadrant*. Angles in this quadrant are the *acute angles* (Fig. 59A) mentioned earlier in this chapter. Angles from 90° to 180° are in the *second quadrant*. These are the *obtuse angles* (Fig. 59B) mentioned. Angles from 180° to 270° lie in the *third quadrant,* and angles from 270° to 360° lie in the *fourth quadrant*. These quadrants are represented pictorially in Fig. 60. Only angles in the first and second quadrants, from 0° to 180°, will be discussed in this section. Note that a straight line may be considered as an angle of 180°. Trigonometry is actually based on geometry, but it makes use of many algebraic operations that can be used by carpenters and builders.

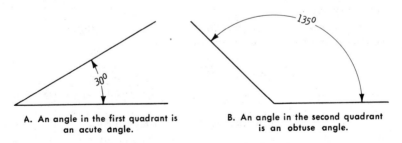

A. An angle in the first quadrant is an acute angle.

B. An angle in the second quadrant is an obtuse angle.

Fig. 59. Acute and obtuse angles.

Trigonometric Functions

In mathematics, a *function* means a quantity that necessarily changes because of a change in another number with which it is connected in some way. In trigonometry, it is probably less con-

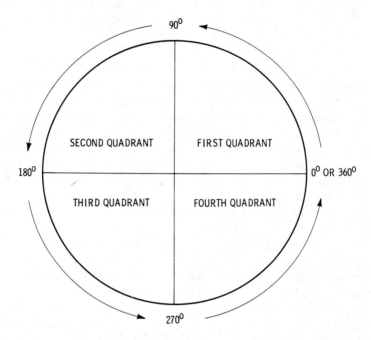

Fig. 60. The four quadrants of a circle.

fusing to call the trigonometric functions simply *ratios*, which they truly are.

Refer to Fig. 61 for an explanation of the following. There are six trigonometric ratios commonly used:

$$\text{Sine of angle A} = \frac{\text{opposite side}}{\text{hypotenuse}} \text{ or } \frac{BC}{AB}$$

$$\text{Cosine of angle A} = \frac{\text{adjacent side}}{\text{hypotenuse}} \text{ or } \frac{AC}{AB}$$

$$\text{Tangent of angle A} = \frac{\text{opposite side}}{\text{adjacent side}} \text{ or } \frac{BC}{AC}$$

$$\text{Cotangent of angle A} = \frac{\text{adjacent side}}{\text{opposite side}} \text{ or } \frac{AC}{BC}$$

$$\text{Secant of angle A} = \frac{\text{hypotenuse}}{\text{adjacent side}} \text{ or } \frac{AB}{AC}$$

$$\text{Cosecant of angle A} = \frac{\text{hypotenuse}}{\text{opposite side}} \text{ or } \frac{AB}{BC}$$

Note that these last three functions are only *reciprocals* of the sine, cosine, and tangent, respectively, or

$$\text{cosecant} = \frac{1}{\text{sine}}$$

$$\text{secant} = \frac{1}{\text{cosine}}$$

$$\text{cotangent} = \frac{1}{\text{tangent}}$$

If a proposition calls for multiplication by the sine of an angle, the same result will be obtained by dividing by the cosecant. It is convenient to do this in many calculations.

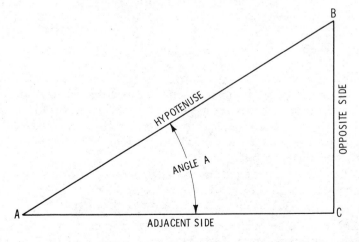

Fig. 61. A right triangle illustrates the application of trigonometric ratios which are commonly used.

It is impossible in a discussion of this type to give a comprehensive table of the trigonometric ratios, although an adequate but limited number of trigonometric functions are presented in Table 5. Anyone who would like to follow up the information given here is advised to obtain a book of five- or six-place tables.

As an example of how trigonometric ratios are used to solve one of the carpenter's most common problems, determining the length of rafters given the rise and run, refer to Fig. 62. The slope of the roof, in degrees, may be determined by dividing the opposite side 12 feet, by the adjacent side, 18 feet. This is the tangent of the angle A and is equal to $^{12}/_{18}$, or .6667. From Table 5, angle A is determined to be 33° 42'. The length of the rafter may be determined by the ratio:

$$\text{secant} = \frac{\text{hypotenuse}}{\text{adjacent side}}$$

or the hypotenuse (the length of the rafter) is equal to

secant 33°42' × adjacent side

The secant of 33°42' is equal to 1.2020. Therefore, the calculation for the length of the rafter is

1.2020 × 18 = 21.64 feet = 21 feet 7³/₁₆ inches

Since the opposite side is known to be 12 feet, the calculation could just as easily be made by using the cosecant function.

The slopes, in degrees, for all regular roof pitches are given in Table 6; these pitches range from 12 × 1 to 12 × 12, and the three main trigonometric ratios—sine, cosine, and tangent—are provided for each pitch.

Other typical examples of how trigonometric ratios can aid carpenters are shown in the following problems.

Problem 1—A grillwork consisting of radial and vertical members is to be built in a semicircular opening with a radius of 6 feet, as shown in Fig. 63. Find the lengths of the vertical pieces MS and LF.

Table 5. Natural Trigonometric Functions

Degree	Sine	Cosine	Tangent	Secant	Degree	Sine	Cosine	Tangent	Secant
0	.00000	1.0000	.00000	1.0999	46	.7193	.6947	1.0355	1.4395
1	.01745	.9998	.01745	1.0001	47	.7314	.6820	1.0724	1.4663
2	.03490	.9994	.03492	1.0006	48	.7431	.6691	1.1106	1.4945
3	.05234	.9986	.05241	1.0014	49	.7547	.6561	1.1504	1.5242
4	.06976	.9976	.06993	1.0024	50	.7660	.6428	1.1918	1.5557
5	.08716	.9962	.08749	1.0038	51	.7771	.6293	1.2349	1.5890
6	.10453	.9945	.10510	1.0055	52	.7880	.6157	1.2799	1.6243
7	.12187	.9925	.12278	1.0075	53	.7986	.6018	1.3270	1.6616
8	.1392	.9903	.1405	1.0098	54	.8090	.5878	1.3764	1.7013
9	.1564	.9877	.1584	1.0125	55	.8192	.5736	1.4281	1.7434
10	.1736	.9848	.1763	1.0154	56	.8290	.5592	1.4826	1.7883
11	.1908	.9816	.1944	1.0187	57	.8387	.5446	1.5399	1.8361
12	.2079	.9781	.2126	1.0223	58	.8480	.5299	1.6003	1.8871
13	.2250	.9744	.2309	1.0263	59	.8572	.5150	1.6643	1.9416
14	.2419	.9703	.2493	1.0306	60	.8660	.5000	1.7321	2.0000
15	.2588	.9659	.2679	1.0353	61	.8746	.4848	1.8040	2.0627
16	.2756	.9613	.2867	1.0403	62	.8829	.4695	1.8807	2.1300
17	.2924	.9563	.3057	1.0457	63	.8910	.4540	1.9626	2.2027
18	.3090	.9511	.3249	1.0515	64	.8988	.4384	2.0503	2.2812
19	.3256	.9455	.3443	1.0576	65	.9063	.4226	2.1445	2.3662
20	.3420	.9397	.3640	1.0642	66	.9135	.4067	2.2460	2.4586
21	.3584	.9336	.3839	1.0711	67	.9205	.3907	2.3559	2.5598
22	.3746	.9272	.4040	.1.0785	68	.9272	.3746	2.4751	2.6695
23	.3907	.9205	.4245	1.0864	69	.9336	.3584	2.6051	2.7904
24	.4067	.9135	.4452	1.0946	70	.9397	.3420	2.7475	2.9238
25	.4226	.9063	.4663	1.1034	71	.9455	.3256	2.9042	3.0715
26	.4384	.8988	.4877	1.1126	72	.9511	.3090	3.0777	3.2361
27	.4540	.8910	.5095	1.1223	73	.9563	.2924	3.2709	3.4203
28	.4695	.8829	.5317	1.1326	74	.9613	.2756	3.4874	3.6279
29	.4848	.8746	.5543	1.1433	75	.9659	.2588	3.7321	3.8637
30	.5000	.8660	.5774	1.1547	76	.9703	.2419	4.0108	4.1336
31	.5150	.8572	.6009	1.1663	77	.9744	.2250	4.3315	4.4454
32	.5299	.8480	.6249	1.1792	78	.9781	.2079	4.7046	4.8097
33	.5446	.8387	.6494	1.1924	79	.9816	.1908	5.1446	5.2408
34	.5592	.8290	.6745	1.2062	80	.9848	.1736	5.6713	5.7588
35	.5736	.8192	.7002	1.2208	81	.9877	.1564	6.3138	6.3924
36	.5878	.8090	.7265	1.2361	82	.9903	.1392	7.1154	7.1853
37	.6018	.7986	.7536	1.2521	83	.9925	.12187	8.1443	8.2055
38	.6157	.7880	.7813	1.2690	84	.9945	.10453	9.5144	9.5668
39	.6293	.7771	.8098	1.2867	85	.9962	.08716	11.4301	11.474
40	.6428	.7660	.8391	1.3054	86	.9976	.06976	14.3007	14.335
41	.6561	.7547	.8693	1.3250	87	.9986	.05234	19.0811	19.107
42	.6691	.7431	.9004	1.3456	88	.9994	.03490	28.6363	28.654
43	.6820	.7314	.9325	1.3673	89	.9998	.01745	57.2900	57.299
44	.6947	.7193	.9657	1.3902	90	1.0000	Inf.	Inf.	Inf.
45	.7071	.7071	1.0000	1.4142	—	——	——	——	——

For triangle OMS, the hypotenuse is known to be 6 feet, and angle O is 30°. Line MS is the opposite side of the triangle, and

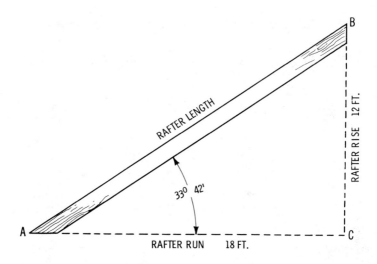

Fig. 62. *Trigonometric ratios may be used to determine the lengths of rafters for a roof.*

Table 6. Roof Pitches in Degrees and Minutes
(Measured from the horizontal)

Pitch	Sine	Cosine	Tangent
12 x 1 = 4° 46′	.083098	.996541	.083386
12 x 2 = 9° 28′	.164474	.986381	.166745
12 x 3 = 14° 2′	.242486	.970155	.249946
12 x 4 = 18° 26′	.316201	.948692	.333302
12 x 5 = 22° 37′	.384564	.923098	.416601
12 x 6 = 26° 34′	.444635	.895712	.496404
12 x 7 = 30° 15′	.503774	.863836	.583183
12 x 8 = 33° 41′	.554602	.832115	.666497
12 x 9 = 36° 53′	.600188	.799859	.750366
12 x 10 = 39° 46′	.639663	.768656	.832183
12 x 11 = 42° 31′	.675805	.737081	.916866
12 x 12 = 45° 00′	.707107	.707107	1.000000

opposite side = 30°, or $\dfrac{\text{opposite side}}{\text{hypotenuse}}$ = sine 30° × hypotenuse. (sine 30° = .500). This is the calculation:

$$\text{opposite side} = .500 \times 6 = 3 \text{ feet}$$

For triangle OLF, the hypotenuse is 6 feet, and angle O is 60°.

Line LF is the opposite side, and $\dfrac{\text{opposite side}}{\text{hypotenuse}} = 60°$,

or opposite side = 60° × hypotenuse. (sine 60° = .866)
This is the calculation:

opposite side = .866 × 6 = 5.196 feet = 5 feet 2³/₈ inches

Problem 2—When laying out the grillwork in Fig. 63, how far must the members LF and MS be spaced from the center O to be vertical?

The hypotenuse is known to be 6 feet and the length of adjacent side OF is to be found.

$$\frac{\text{adjacent side}}{\text{hypotenuse}} = \cos 60°, \text{ or}$$

adjacent side = cos 60° × hypotenuse. (cos 60° = .500) This is the calculation:

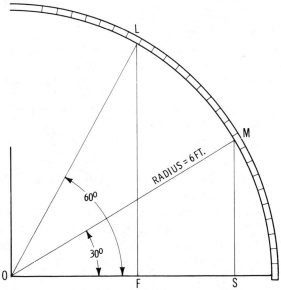

Fig. 63. The method of finding the length of vertical pieces in grillwork with the aid of trigonometric relations.

$$\text{adjacent side OF} = .500 \times 6 = 3 \text{ feet}$$

For the length of the adjacent side OS, $\dfrac{\text{adjacent side}}{\text{hypotenuse}} = \cos 30°$, or adjacent side $= \cos 30° \times$ hypotenuse. (cos 30° = .866) This is the calculation:

$$\text{adjacent side OS} = .866 \times 6 = 5.196 \text{ feet} = 5 \text{ feet } 2\tfrac{3}{8} \text{ inches}$$

Problem 3—A bridge is to be constructed from the top of a building to an opening in the roof of an adjacent building, as in Fig. 64. If the rise OF to the point of entry L is 15 feet and the pitch of the roof is ½, what length beams FL are required?

From Table 6, ½ pitch, or 12″ × 12″, is 45°. The adjacent side OF is known to be 15 feet. The required length of the opposite side = adjacent side × tan 45°. This is the calculation:

$$\text{opposite side FL} = 15 \times 1.00 = 15 \text{ feet}$$

Problem 4—When estimating the amount of roofing material necessary to cover the side of the roof from O to L in Fig. 64, what is the distance from O to L?

It is required to find the hypotenuse with the adjacent side and included angle being given. $\dfrac{\text{hypotenuse}}{\text{adjacent side}} = \text{secant angle O}$, or

$$\text{hypotenuse} = 1.4142 \times 15 = 21.213 \text{ feet} = 21 \text{ feet } 2\tfrac{9}{16} \text{ inches}.$$

SUMMARY

All the sciences are based on arithmetic and the ability to use it. Arithmetic is the art of calculating by using numbers. A number is a total amount, or aggregate, of units. By computing the units, we arrive at a certain number or total. By the same token, a unit means a single article, often a definite group adopted as a standard of measurement, such as dozen, ton, foot, bushel, or mile.

Fractions indicate that a number or unit has been divided into a certain number of equal parts, and shows how many of these

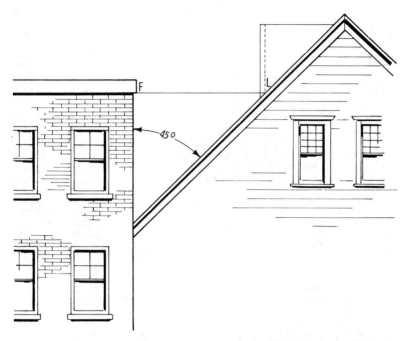

Fig. 64. *The method of finding the distance from one side of a building to a given point on an adjacent roof by employing trigonometric relations.*

parts are to be considered. Two forms of fractions are in common usage—the decimal and the common fraction. The common fraction is written by using two numbers, one written over or alongside the other with a line between them, the lower (or second) number being called the denominator, and the upper (or first) number being called the numerator.

Geometry is a branch of mathematics that deals with space and figures in space. It is the science of the mutual relations of points, lines, angles, surfaces, and solids, which are considered as having no properties except those arising from extension and difference of situation. There are two kinds of lines—straight and curved. A straight line is the shortest distance between two points. A curved line is one that changes its direction at every point.

Trigonometry is the branch of mathematics that deals with the

Table 7. Functions of Numbers

No.	Square	Cube	Square Root	Cubic Root	Logarithm	1000 x Reciprocal	No. = Diameter	
							Circum.	Area
1	1	1	1.0000	1.0000	0.00000	1000.000	3.142	0.7854
2	4	8	1.4142	1.2599	0.30103	500.000	6.283	3.1416
3	9	27	1.7321	1.4422	0.47712	333.333	9.425	7.0686
4	16	64	2.0000	1.5874	0.60206	250.000	12.566	12.5664
5	25	125	2.2361	1.7100	0.69897	200.000	15.708	19.6350
6	36	216	2.4495	1.8171	0.77815	166.667	18.850	28.2743
7	49	343	2.6458	1.9129	0.84510	142.857	21.991	38.4845
8	64	512	2.8284	2.0000	0.90309	125.000	25.133	50.2655
9	81	729	3.0000	2.0801	0.95424	111.111	28.274	63.6173
10	100	1000	3.1623	2.1544	1.00000	100.000	31.416	78.5398
11	121	1331	3.3166	2.2240	1.04139	90.9091	34.558	95.0332
12	144	1728	3.4641	2.2894	1.07918	83.3333	37.699	113.097
13	169	2197	3.6056	2.3513	1.11394	76.9231	40.841	132.732
14	196	2744	3.7417	2.4101	1.14613	71.4286	43.982	153.938
15	225	3375	3.8730	2.4662	1.17609	66.6667	47.124	176.715
16	256	4096	4.0000	2.5198	1.20412	62.5000	50.265	201.062
17	289	4913	4.1231	2.5713	1.23045	58.8235	53.407	226.980
18	324	5832	4.2426	2.6207	1.25527	55.5556	56.549	254.469
19	361	6859	4.3589	2.6684	1.27875	52.6316	59.690	283.529
20	400	8000	4.4721	2.7144	1.30103	50.0000	62.832	314.159
21	441	9261	4.5826	2.7589	1.32222	47.6190	65.973	346.361
22	484	10648	4.6904	2.8020	1.34242	45.4545	69.115	380.133
23	529	12167	4.7958	2.8439	1.36173	43.4783	72.257	415.476
24	576	13824	4.8990	2.8845	1.38021	41.6667	75.398	452.389
25	625	15625	5.0000	2.9240	1.39794	40.0000	78.540	490.874
26	676	17576	5.0990	2.9625	1.41497	38.4615	81.681	530.929
27	729	19683	5.1962	3.0000	1.43136	37.0370	84,823	572.555
28	784	21952	5.2915	3.0366	1.44716	35.7143	87.965	615.752
29	841	24389	5.3852	3.0723	1.46240	34.4828	91.106	660.520
30	900	27000	5.4772	3.1072	1.47712	33.3333	94.248	706.858
31	961	29791	5.5678	3.1414	1.49136	32.2581	97.389	754.768
32	1024	32768	5.6569	3.1748	1.50515	31.2500	100.531	804.248
33	1089	35937	5.7446	3.2075	1.51851	30.3030	103.673	855.299
34	1156	39304	5.8310	3.2396	1.53148	29.4118	106.814	907.920
35	1225	42875	5.9161	3.2711	1.54407	28.5714	109.956	962.113
36	1296	46656	6.0000	3.3019	1.55630	27.7778	113.097	1017.88
37	1369	50653	6.0828	3.3322	1.56820	27.0270	116.239	1075.21
38	1444	54872	6.1644	3.3620	1.57978	26.3158	119.381	1134.11
39	1521	59319	6.2450	3.3912	1.59106	25.6410	122.522	1194.59
40	1600	64000	6.3246	3.4200	1.60206	25.0000	125.66	1256.64
41	1681	68921	6.4031	3.4482	1.61278	24.3902	128.81	1320.25
42	1764	74088	6.4807	3.4760	1.62325	23.8095	131.95	1385.44
43	1849	79507	6.5574	3.5034	1.63347	23.2558	135.09	1452.20
44	1936	85184	6.6332	3.5303	1.64345	22.7273	138.23	1520.53
45	2025	91125	6.7082	3.5569	1.65321	22.2222	141.37	1590.43

Table 7. Functions of Numbers (Cont'd)

No.	Square	Cube	Square Root	Cubic Root	Logarithm	1000 x Reciprocal	No. = Diameter Circum.	Area
46	2116	97336	6.7823	3.5830	1.66276	21.7391	144.51	1661.90
47	2209	103823	6.8557	3.6088	1.67210	21.2766	147.65	1734.94
48	2304	110592	6.9282	3.6342	1.68124	20.8333	150.80	1809.56
49	2401	117649	7.0000	3.6593	1.69020	20.4082	153.94	1885.74
50	2500	125000	7.0711	3.6840	1.69897	20.0000	157.08	1963.50
51	2601	132651	7.1414	3.7084	1.70757	19.6078	160.22	2042.82
52	2704	140608	7.2111	3.7325	1.71600	19.2308	163.36	2123.72
53	2809	148877	7.2801	3.7563	1.72428	18.8679	166.50	2206.18
54	2916	157464	7.3485	3.7798	1.73239	18.5185	169.65	2290.22
55	3025	166375	7.4162	3.8030	1.74036	18.1818	172.79	2375.83
56	3136	175616	7.4833	3.8259	1.74819	17.8571	175.93	2463.01
57	3249	185193	7.5498	3.8485	1.75587	17.5439	179.07	2551.76
58	3364	195112	7.6158	3.8709	1.76343	17.2414	182.21	2642.08
59	3481	205379	7.6811	3.8930	1.77085	16.9492	185.35	2733.97
60	3600	216000	7.7460	3.9149	1.77815	16.6667	188.50	2827.43
61	3721	226981	7.8102	3.9365	1.78533	16.3934	191.64	2922.47
62	3844	238328	7.8740	3.9579	1.79239	16.1290	194.78	3019.07
63	3969	250047	7.9373	3.9791	1.79934	15.8730	197.92	3117.25
64	4096	262144	8.0000	4.0000	1.80618	15.6250	201.06	3216.99
65	4225	274625	8.0623	4.0207	1.81291	15.3846	204.20	3318.31
66	4356	287496	8.1240	4.0412	1.81954	15.1515	207.35	3421.19
67	4489	300763	8.1854	4.0615	1.82607	14.9254	210.49	3525.65
68	4624	314432	8.2462	4.0817	1.83251	14.7059	213.63	3631.68
69	4761	328509	8.3066	4.1016	1.83885	14.4928	216.77	3739.28
70	4900	343000	8.3666	4.1213	1.84510	14.2857	219.91	3848.45
71	5041	357911	8.4261	4.1408	1.85126	14.0845	223.05	3959.19
72	5184	373248	8.4853	4.1602	1.85733	13.8889	226.19	4071.50
73	5329	389017	8.5440	4.1793	1.86332	13.6986	229.34	4185.39
74	5476	405224	8.6023	4.1983	1.86923	13.5135	232.48	4300.84
75	5625	421875	8.6603	4.2172	1.87506	13.3333	235.62	4417.86
76	5776	438976	8.7178	4.2358	1.88081	13.1579	238.76	4536.46
77	5929	456533	8.7750	4.2543	1.88649	12.9870	241.90	4656.63
78	6084	474552	8.8318	4.2727	1.89209	12.8205	245.04	4778.36
79	6241	493039	8.8882	4.2908	1.89763	12.6582	248.19	4901.67
80	6400	512000	8.9443	4.3089	1.90309	12.5000	251.33	5026.55
81	6561	531441	9.0000	4.3267	1.90849	12.3457	254.47	5153.00
82	6724	551368	9.0554	4.3445	1.91381	12.1951	257.61	5281.02
83	6889	571787	9.1104	4.3621	1.91908	12.0482	260.75	5410.61
84	7056	592704	9.1652	4.3795	1.92428	11.9048	263.89	5541.77
85	7225	614125	9.2195	4.3968	1.92942	11.7647	267.04	5674.50
86	7396	636056	9.2736	4.4140	1.93450	11.6279	270.18	5808.80
87	7569	658503	9.3274	4.4310	1.93952	11.4943	273.32	5944.68
88	7744	681472	9.3808	4.4480	1.94448	11.3636	276.46	6082.12
89	7921	704969	9.4340	4.4647	1.94939	11.2360	279.60	6221.14

Table 7. Functions of Numbers (Cont'd)

No.	Square	Cube	Square Root	Cubic Root	Logarithm	1000 x Reciprocal	No. = Diameter	
							Circum.	Area
90	8100	729000	9.4868	4.4814	1.95424	11.1111	282.74	6361.73
91	8281	753571	9.5394	4.4979	1.95904	10.9890	285.88	6503.88
92	8464	778688	9.5917	4.5144	1.96379	10.8696	289.03	6647.61
93	8649	804357	9.6437	4.5307	1.96848	10.7527	292.17	6792.91
94	8836	830584	9.6954	4.5468	1.97313	10.6383	295.31	6939.78
95	9025	857375	9.7468	4.5629	1.97772	10.5263	298.45	7088.22
96	9216	884736	9.7980	4.5789	1.98227	10.4167	301.59	7238.23
97	9409	912673	9.8489	4.5947	1.98677	10.3093	304.73	7389.81
98	9604	941192	9.8995	4.6104	1.99123	10.2041	307.88	7542.96
99	9801	970299	9.9499	4.6261	1.99564	10.1010	311.02	7697.69

relations that exist between the sides and angles of triangles, especially the methods of calculating the required parts of triangles from given parts. There are six elements, or parts, in every triangle—three sides and three angles. The sum of the three angles, no matter what the lengths of the sides, will always be equal to 180 degrees.

REVIEW QUESTIONS

1. What is the definition of arithmetic?
2. What are even numbers?
3. What are odd numbers?
4. What are fractions? How are they used?
5. What is trigonometry and how is it used in carpentry?

CHAPTER 2

Surveying

By definition, "surveying" means the art or science of determining the area and configuration of portions of the surface of the earth. There are two general divisions of surveying that may be classified with respect to the nature of the measurements taken as:

1. Leveling.
2. Measurement of angles (transit work).

Leveling, in surveying, is the operation of determing the comparative levels of different points of land for the purpose of laying out a grade or building site, etc., by sighting through a leveling instrument at one point to a leveling staff at another point, as shown in Fig. 1.

THE LEVEL

This instrument, as shown in Fig. 2, is employed to determine the difference in elevation between points. A common form is known as the wye level, so called because its shape resembles the letter Y. It consists of a telescope mounted on two supports which from their shape are called Y's. The cross bar supporting the telescope is attached to a vertical spindle, which allows it to be turned in a horizontal plane. Directly beneath the telescope and attached parallel to it is a spirit level by means of which the line of collimation of the telescope may be rendered horizontal. The line of collimation is the line that would connect the intersection of the cross hairs with the optical center of the objective.

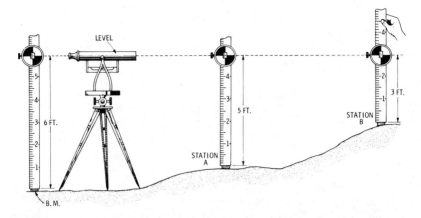

Fig. 1. The terms "backsight" and "foresight" do not necessarily mean backward and forward; readings taken on a point of known elevation, such as a bench mark or a turning point, are called backsights, whereas readings taken on a point of unknown elevation are termed foresights. In the illustration, the backsight (to the bench mark) is +6 feet 0 inches, and the foresight to station A is −5 feet 0 inches. The difference in the two elevations is 6 feet − 5 feet = 1 foot. If the reading at station A had been greater than the 6-foot HI (height of instrument), the calculation would have shown a negative result, thereby indicating that station A was lower than the bench mark. The elevation at station B is calculated in the same manner: 6 − 3 = 3 feet. Therefore, the elevations from any number of points can be obtained in the same way, if they can be seen from the same position of the instrument; if they cannot, a new HI must be used.

Courtesy David White Instruments Division of Realist, Inc.

Fig. 2. A typical builder's level.

Construction of the Wye Level

In construction, a circular plate is screwed to a tripod, and to this is attached a similar plate parallel to the first and connected with it by a ball-and-socket joint. Four screws (sometimes only three), called foot or plate screws, hold these plates apart by resting on the lower one and passing through the other. A vertical spindle in the center of the plates supports a rod, bar, or beam and is used to revolve the instrument. The beam is horizontal and carries at its ends two vertical standards or supports of equal size terminated by two forks of the general form of the letter Y. The inside of the Y's is Y-shaped, with an open bottom to prevent an accumulation of dirt. The top of the Y's may be closed by semicircular straps or bridles called clips, which are hinged on one side and pinned on the other. The pins are tapered to permit fastening of the telescope. It is *never* clamped tightly.

The tops of the Y's and the corresponding clips are called the rings or collars and should be of equal diameter. A telescope is placed on the rings which support a spirit level. A clamping screw just above the upper plate serves to secure the instrument in any position desired. A tangent screw, also above the upper plate, provides slow-motion, or vernier, adjustment to the instrument.

The Telescope—The "objective," or "object glass" (so called because it faces the object looked at), is a compound lens that is made to correct spherical and chromatic aberrations of single lenses; it gathers light and forms an image at a point in the tube where cross hairs are placed. The ocular, or eye, piece is also a compound lens through which the operator looks to see a magnified view of the image. In the best precision instruments, often foreign-made, the image is often *inverted*. A good instrument man quickly becomes accustomed to the inverted image, but most American-made instruments have an *erecting* image, which shows the object right side up. Tangent screws may be used to give motion to the tubes carrying the objective and ocular.

The Cross Hairs—These are made of platinum-drawn wires or "spider's threads" attached to a ring within the telescope at the spot where the image is formed. The ring is secured by four capstan-headed screws which pass through the telescope tube.

There are commonly two hairs, one horizontal and the other vertical, with their intersection in the axis of the telescope.

Bubble Level—The spirit level attached to the telescope can be raised vertically by means of altitude screws at the rear end, and it may be moved laterally to a limited extent by means of azimuth screws at the forward end.

The Supports—These form the Y's and are supported by the bar to which they are fastened by two nuts, one above and one below. These nuts may be moved to provide an adjustment, to move the scope in a horizontal direction.

Lines of the Level

There are three principal lines of a level:
1. Vertical axis.
2. Bubble line.
3. Line of collimation.

The Vertical Axis—This passes through the center of the spindle.

Bubble Line—The metallic supports of the spirit level are equal, and the tangent at their top or bottom is horizontal when the bubble is centered. This tangent is the bubble line.

Line of Collimation—The line that would connect the intersection of the cross hairs with the optical center of the objective is the line of collimation.

Relations Between the Lines of a Level—The following relations must be obtained:

1st Relation—The bubble line and the line of collimation must be parallel.

2nd Relation—The plane described by the bubble line should be horizontal, that is, perpendicular to the vertical axis. These conditions are generally satisfied in a new level, but exposure and use may alter these relations; therefore there is the necessity of adjusting the instrument occasionally.

Adjustments of the Wye Level

Levels and transits are expensive, precision instruments and should be treated as such. Although a passable job of leveling may be done by a relatively inexperienced man, it is questionable if a major job of adjusting should be attempted by a novice. A perfect job of adjustment is difficult, even for an experienced adjuster, and there are few instruments in perfect adjustment. For precision work, the adjustment should be checked constantly. The first relation given above cannot be established directly but requires three adjustments.

First Adjustment—*Making the line of collimation parallel to the bottom element of the collars, or collimating the instrument.* Clamp the instrument, and unclip the collars. Sight at a distant point (as far as distinct), bringing the horizontal cross hair on it. Carefully turn the telescope in the collars by one-half a revolution around its axis, and sight again. If the horizontal cross hair is still on the sighted point, the telescope is collimated with regard to that cross hair; if it is off the point, bring it halfway back by means of the capstan-headed screws and the rest of the way by the plate screws. Repeat the operation over another point. Collimate it with regard to the other cross hair. Leave the screws at a snug bearing.

Second Adjustment—*Setting the bubble line in a plane with the bottom element of the collars.* Unclip the telescope, and clamp the instrument over a pair of plate screws. Center the bubble by means of the plate screws. Carefully and slowly turn the telescope in the collars in a small arc to the right, then to the left. If the bubble moves from center, bring it back by means of the azimuth or side screws.

Third Adjustment—*Setting the bubble line parallel to the bottom element of the collars.* Unclip the telescope, and clamp the instrument over a pair of plate screws. Center the bubble by means of the plate screws. Carefully take the telescope up, replacing it carefully in the Y's in the opposite direction, that is, the objective sighting in the direction where the eye piece originally was. If the bubble has moved, bring it back halfway by means of the altitude or foot screws of the spirit level and the rest of the way by the plate screws. Repeat in another direction until the adjustment is satisfactory.

The second relation is established by making the bubble line stay in the center of the graduation during a complete revolution of the instrument around its spindle.

Fourth Adjustment—*Making the axis of the instrument (not of the telescope) vertical.* Pin the clips; clamp and center the bubble over a pair of plate screws. Reverse the telescope over the same pair of plate screws; bring the bubble halfway back (if it has moved) by means of the plate screws.

Fifth Adjustment—*Making the bubble remain centered during a full revolution of the instrument.* Center the bubble, and revolve the instrument horizontally by a one-half revolution. If the bubble moves, correct it halfway by means of the support screws (at the foot of the Y's). If the rings become worn and unequal, use the two-peg method of the dumpy level.

The dumpy level, so called because of its compactness, is shown in Fig. 3. It is used mostly in England, although it is used to some extent in the United States because of the better stabil-

Fig. 3. A dumpy level.

ity of its adjustments over the wye level. The dumpy level differs from the wye level mainly in that the telescope of the dumpy level is permanently attached to the supports or uprights, but these uprights are adjustable. The two-peg adjustment method is as follows:

Drive two stakes (pegs) several hundred feet apart. Set the instrument approximately halfway between them. Level up and sight the rod, which is held in succession on each stake. The difference in the readings is the true difference of the elevation of the stakes, even if the instrument is not in proper adjustment. To test the instrument, set it near one of the stakes (the highest one, for instance); level up and sight the rod held on the other stake. Subtract the height of the instrument from the reading; the difference should be equal to the difference of elevation of the stakes as previously found. If these differences are not equal, set the target halfway between these readings, sight on it, and center the bubble by means of the altitude screws. Repeat the operation until satisfaction is obtained.

Centering the Objective and Ocular—These adjustments are made permanently by the manufacturer. Usually, four screws hold the tubes carrying the glasses; their heads pass through the outside tube where, after permanent adjustment, they are covered by a metallic ring.

Parallax—This is the apparent motion of the cross hairs on the object sighted when the eye is moved slightly. It shows the imperfect focusing of the ocular over the cross hairs. To correct this condition, hold a white surface, such as that of a piece of paper, slightly in front of the objective, and move the ocular tube in and out until the cross hairs are perfectly defined.

Leveling Rod

This instrument, used in leveling, is usually 6½ feet high, graduated to hundredths of a foot and provided with a sliding target. The rod is made in two parts, arranged so that its length can be extended to 12 feet. Precision rods are of one-piece construction and have no target. Builders' rods may be graduated in feet, inches, and eighths of an inch, with a vernier reading in 64ths of an inch. A sliding disc, called a target, is provided with a vernier for extremely accurate work, reading to thousandths of a foot.

In use, the rod is held in a vertical position with its lower end resting on the point, the elevation of which is desired; the target is then moved up and down until its center coincides with the cross hairs in the telescope of the level. The reading of the elevation is made from the rod on a line corresponding with the center line of the target. There are various kinds of rods; some are designed to be read by the rodman, while others can be read through the telescope of the level.

Methods of Leveling

The simplest type of leveling is to find the difference in level between two points that are visible from a third point, the difference in level being less than the length of the leveling rod, as in Fig. 4. Set up and level the instrument at some point approximately halfway between the two points. Have the rodman hold the rod vertically on one of the points, and move the target up and down until its center coincides with the cross hairs of the

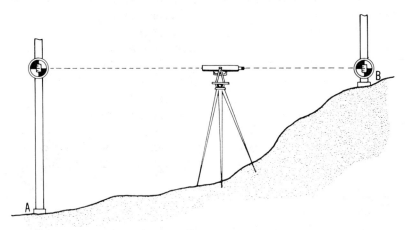

Fig. 4. Leveling between two points whose difference in level is less than the length of the rod.

level. Take a reading; this is the HI, or height of the instrument above the bench mark A. Turn the telescope on its spindle, have the rod held on the other point, and take a similar reading at B. The difference in level is equal to the difference in the readings.

If the difference in level is greater than the length of the rod, the method shown in Fig. 5 is used. Divide the distance between the two points into sections of such length that the difference in level between the dividing points A, B, and C, called stations, are less than the length of the rod. Set up and level between A and B, and measure the distance Aa, which is called backsight. Then, reverse the telescope, and take reading Bb, which is called foresight. Next, set up and level between B and C, and take readings Bb' and Cc. Repeat the operation between C and D, taking readings Cc' and Dd. The difference in level between stations A and D is equal to the sum of the differences between the intermediate stations; that is, this difference equals (Aa − Bb) + (Bb' − Cc) − (Cc' − Dd), or (Aa + Bb' + Cc') − (Bb + Cc + Dd).

Usually one wants to find the relative elevations of several points, as in grading work, in which case it is necessary to keep more elaborate notes and to measure distances between the stations. The method employed for this type of leveling is shown in Fig. 6, and the field notes are recorded as shown in Table 1.

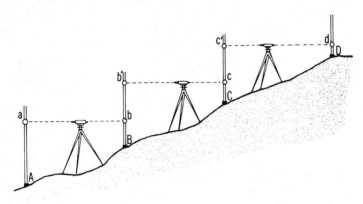

Fig. 5. *Leveling between points whose difference in level is greater than the length of the rod.*

Table 1. Field Notes
(Corresponding to the operations illustrated in Fig. 6)

Station	Distance	Backsight	Height of Instrument	Foresight	Elevation	Remarks
A	0	4.2	104.2	....	100.0	
B	100	....	....	10.1	94.1	Bench
C	60	....	....	7.3	96.9	mark,
D	50	....	....	5.8	98.4	top of
T	....	4.1	99.1	9.2	95.1	hydrant
E	70	6.8	....	....	92.3	Turning
F	110	....	....	9.5	89.6	point
G	80	....	....	11.5	87.6	

Assume a datum or reference line below the elevation of the lowest station, and refer all elevations to this line. Start at some permanently fixed point, such as a mark on a building or the top of a hydrant; this is called a bench mark. Let A in Fig. 6 be the bench mark, and assume a datum line 100 feet below the level of A. Start with the instrument between A and B, and take a backsight on A. The distance Aa is found to be 4.2 feet, which, when added to 100 feet, gives the height of the instrument. Next, take foresights on B, C, and D, and record these readings in the proper column. Readings Bb, Cc, etc., subtracted from the height of the instrument, will give the elevations at B, C, etc. This is done, and the results are recorded in the proper column of field notes. The ground falls away so rapidly beyond D that it is necessary to set up the level farther along and, therefore, establish a new height of instrument. This is done by holding the rod at some convenient point, such as at T, called the *turning point,* and taking a foresight, which measures the distance Tt (9.2 feet). The level is then set up in its second position between E and F, and a backsight is taken on the rod in the same position, which gives the distance Tt' (4.1 feet). The distance t't then equals 9.2 − 4.1 = 5.1 feet, and this is subtracted from the previous height of instrument, thus giving the new HI, which is 104.2 − 5.1 = 99.1 feet. A backsight is now taken on E, and foresights are taken on F and G. These are recorded in the proper columns, and the elevations are found by subtracting these distances from the new HI. The horizontal distances between the stations are measured with a tape and recorded in the second column. When plotting a cross section from notes kept in this manner, the datum line is drawn first, and perpendiculars are erected at points corresponding to the different stations. The proper elevations are then indicated on these vertical lines, and a contour line is drawn through the points so marked.

Directions for Using Level

Note carefully the following mode of procedure in leveling:

1. Center the bubble over one pair of plate screws, then over the other pair. Plate screws should have a snug bearing. When looking at the bubble or at the cross hairs, the eyes should look naturally, that is, without strain. (Try to observe with both eyes open.)
2. Adjust the eye piece to the cross hairs for parallax.
3. Turn the instrument toward the target (it is better to level up facing the target).
4. Look again at the bubble.
5. Sight the target, and have it set right by motions according to a prearranged code with the rodman.
6. Look again at the bubble.
7. Read the rod or direct the target from the intersection of the cross hairs only.
8. Approve the target when absolutely sure.
9. Have the height of the target called out by the rodman.
10. Enter this height in the field book.
11. Quickly make needed calculations.

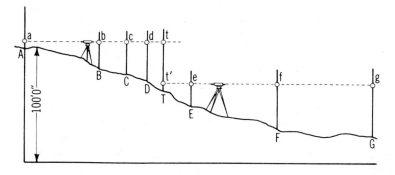

Fig. 6. Finding the relative elevations of several points in rough terrain.

101

12. Briskly motion the rodman to a new station or to stay for a turning point and backsight, and move yourself to another position.

The following additional hints will also be found useful:

Guarding against the sun—Draw the telescope shade, or use an umbrella or a hat.

Length of sights—Avoid sights too short and too long; 250 to 350 feet should be the limit of the sights.

Equal sights—The length of the backsight should practically be the same as the length of the foresight; this may be approximated by pacing, or by sighting with the stadia cross hairs in the telescope.

Long sights—When sights longer than the maximum allowable in one direction only are unavoidable, correction should be made for curvature.

Leveling up or down a steep slope—The leveler, after some practice, will place his instrument so as to take a reading near the top or the botttom of the rod (as the case may be), thus gaining vertical distance, but this produces unequal sights. He may also follow a zig-zag course.

Leveling across a large body of water—*1. A running stream.* Drive a stake to the water surface on each side of the stream and in a direction normal to the flow, although the line may not run so. Take a foresight reading on the first, a backsight reading on the second, and continue to and along the line. The elevations of the two stakes may be assumed equal. *2. Across a pond.* If a pond or lake is too wide to ensure a good sighting across, use essentially the same method as for a stream. Drive stakes on each side and to the water surface; take a foresight reading on the first and a backsight reading on the second.

Across a wall—Take a foresight reading on the rod set on a stake, driven to the natural surface on the first side of the wall. Measure the height of the wall above the stake, and enter it as a backsight reading. Drive a stake to the natural surface on the second side of the wall, measure the height of the wall on that side above the stake, and enter it as a foresight reading. Set the rod on the stake, and take a sight on it, which will be a backsight reading. Continue using this method until the leveling has been completed.

In underbrush — If it cannot be cut down on the line of sight, find a high place or provide one by piling logs, rocks, etc., to set the instrument on.

Through swamp — Push the legs of the tripod down as far as possible. The leveler lies on his side. Two men may be necessary at the level. If the ground is still unsafe, drive stakes or piles to support the instrument.

Elevations to be taken at road crossings — Take elevations both ways for some distance.

Elevations to be taken at river crossings — Take elevations of high-water marks and flood marks, with the dates of same. Question residents for these dates and also for dates and data of extreme low water.

Proper length of sights — This will depend on the distance at which the rod appears distinct and on the precision required. Under ordinary conditions, sights should not exceed 300 feet where elevations are required to the nearest .01 foot, and even at a much shorter distance, the boiling of the air may prevent a precision reading of this degree.

Correction for refraction and earth curvature — A level line is a curved line at which every point is perpendicular to the direction of gravity, and the line of sight of a leveling instrument is tangent to this curve. This makes it necessary to take this curve into account in some leveling operations. If reasonable care is used to make the lengths of backsights and foresights approximately equal, this aberration is self-correcting, but in extremely long lines, it is approximately 2 inches in one-half mile, or about $\frac{2}{3} d^2$, in feet, where d is equal to the distance, in miles. This correction is usually combined with that for refraction. The combined correction is 547 d^2, and it is *negative*.

Trigonometric Leveling

Finding the difference in elevation of two points by means of the horizontal distance between them and the vertical angle is called trigonometric leveling. It is used chiefly in determining the elevation of triangulation stations and in obtaining the elevation of a plane-table station from any visible triangulation point of known elevation. In triangulation work, the vertical angles are usually measured at the same time the horizontal angles are measured, so as to obtain the elevations of triangulation points as well as their horizontal positions. The vertical angle is measured to some definite point on the signal whose height above the center mark of the station was determined when the signal was erected; the height of the instrument above its station should be measured and. recorded. In the most exact work, the angles are measured with a special vertical circle instrument. In less precise work, an ordinary Theodolite, whose vertical arc reads by verniers to 30 seconds or to 20 seconds, may be used, but with such instruments only single readings can be made. The best results with such an instrument are obtained by taking the average of several independent readings, one-half of which are taken with the telescope direct and the other half with the telescope inverted. In every case, the index correction, or reading of the vertical arc when the telescope is level, must be recorded.

THE TRANSIT

This instrument is designed and used for measuring both horizontal and vertical angles. It consists of a telescope mounted in standards which are attached to a horizontal plate, called the limb. Inside the limb, and concentric with it, is another plate, called the vernier plate. The lower plate or limb turns on a vertical spindle or axis which fits into a socket in the tripod head. By means of a clamp and a tangent screw, it may be fastened in any position and made to move slowly through a small arc. The circumference of this plate is usually graduated in divisions of either one-half or one-third of 1 degree, and in the common form of transit, these divisions are numbered from one point on the limb in both directions around to the opposite point, which is 180 degrees. The graduation is generally concealed beneath the plate above it, except at the verniers. This upper plate is the vernier plate, which turns on a spindle fitted into a socket in the lower plate. It is also provided with a clamp by means of which it can be held in any position, and with a tangent screw by which it can be turned through a small arc. A vernier is a device for reading smaller divisions on the scales than could otherwise be read.

The transit is generally provided with a compass so that the bearing of any given line with the magnetic meridian may be determined, if desired. It also has a spirit level attached to the telescope, so that it may be brought to a horizontal position and made to serve as a level. A typical transit is shown in Fig. 7.

Fig. 7. A typical transit.

Construction of the Transit

The general features of the transit construction are shown in Fig. 8; referring to the figure, these are briefly as follows:

Parallel Plates—There are two plates, one upper and one

Fig. 8. The transit. In the illustration, A represents the lower plate; B, the upper plate; C, the central dome; D, the divided limb; E, the spindle; F, the foot screws; G, foot-screw cups; H, the vernier plate; J, the compass circle; K, the clamp-screw vernier plate to divided limb; L, the tangent screw; M and N, spirit levels; O, standards or supports; P, the horizontal shaft; Q, the vertical arc; R, the objective; S, the ocular; T, the telescope; U, racks and pinions; V, the adjustable cross-hair ring; v, the divided-limb vernier; v', the vertical-arc vernier; X, the spirit level; Y, the gradienter; and Z, the scaled index.

lower. The lower plate A is generally formed with two parts. The outside part is a flat ring and is screwed to the tripod head. The inside part is another flat ring of a diameter larger than the opening in the outside part and has a central dome C, which is perforated on the top. The inside part is movable and rests on the under side of the outside part. The upper plate B is generally made in the form of a central nut, with four arms at right angles (or three at 120°). The upper plate carries an inverted conical shell, the lower portion of which passes through the perforation in the dome of the inside part of the lower plate, where it expands into a spherical shape and thus forms a ball joint with the lower plate. This spherical member is perforated in the center to allow the passage of a plumb-bob string.

Foot Screws—The two plates are connected by four (sometimes only three) foot screws F in order (1) to clamp the lower and upper plates, making them fast with each other and with the inverted shell, and (2) to serve in leveling the instrument. The screws pass through the ends of the arms of the upper plate and are surmounted by dust caps. Their feet fit into small cups G, which rest on the top surface of the lower plate to avoid wear.

Shifting Center—Since these cups, as well as the central part of the lower plate, may be moved (after slightly loosening the foot screws), a slight motion may be given to the instrument to better set it over a given point of the ground. This arrangement is called a shifting center.

Outer Spindle—A second conical shell fits and may revolve in the conical shell attached to the upper plate. It is the outer spindle, and it carries projections to form attachments with the other parts of the transit.

Divided Limb—The upper portion of the outer spindle terminates in a horizontal disc of plate D, the limb of which is divided into 360°, subdivided into one-half, one-third, or one-quarter of 1 degree. Every ten degrees are numbered, either from 0° to 360° or from 0° to 180°, either way; the degree marks are a little longer than the subdivisions, and every fifth degree has a mark slightly longer yet.

Lower Motion—The outer spindle and the divided limb are also called the lower motion.

Inner Spindle—A solid inverted cone fits into the outer spindle and may revolve in it; it is the inner spindle, and, like the outer one, it is provided with some projections for similar purposes.

Vernier Plate—The upper portion of the inner spindle projects farther than the divided limb and also carries a horizontal disc H, which moves in a plane parallel to the divided limb (which it covers), except for two rectangular openings in opposite directions through which the divisions of the limb may be seen. These openings each carry a vernier v by means of which the subdivisions of degrees are again divided. Some verniers read to 1 minute, others to 0.5 minute, and some to 10 seconds. To facilitate the reading of the vernier, the openings are sometimes fitted with a reflector and a magnifying glass.

Upper Motion—The inner spindle and vernier plate H are also called the upper motion. The vernier plate carries a compass circle, shown at J.

Compass Circle—This consists of a circular box, the bottom of which carries at its center a sharp pivot of hard metal (hard steel or iridium) on which a magnetic needle approximately 5 inches long is balanced by an agate cup fixed in the middle of its length, as shown in Fig. 9. The needle is strongly magnetized; its north end is distinguished by color or ornamentation, and its balance is regulated by a small coil of fine wire wound around one arm, which can be shifted. The limb, which is formed by the edge of the sides of the box, is divided into 360° with half degrees shown; they are numbered from two zeros marked at the ends of a diameter to 90° right and left. The bottom of the box is marked with two rectangular diameters corresponding to the graduations 0° and 90° of the vernier and two other diameters at 45° to the first. The forward end of the diameter marked 0° is designated by the letter N, and the rear end is designated by the letter S, corresponding to north and south. The ends of the transverse diameter marked 90° are designated by the letters E on the left and W on the right, corresponding to east and west. Note that this designation is the reverse of the standard mariner's compass. Since the telescope is fixed to sight from south to north, the compass indicates the direction of the sighting. When set to an ordinary surveyor's compass, the forward end of the frame carries a vernier and a tangent screw to read fractions smaller than ½ degree.

Controlling Clamps—A screw K permits clamping of the vernier plate H to the divided limb D. Another screw attached to the upper plate permits clamping of the divided limb to the upper plate.

Tangent Screws—One tangent, or slow-motion, screw L accompanies each clamp screw. It is used to complete the clamping at the exact spot where the clamp is to be made.

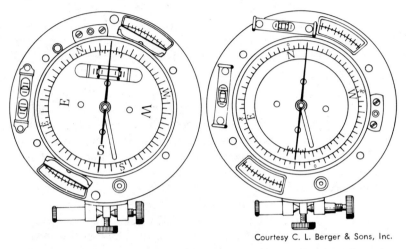

Courtesy C. L. Berger & Sons, Inc.

Fig. 9. Two typical compass boxes. The compass circles are graduated to ½ degrees and numbered in quadrants. The variation plate is provided so that the magnetic declination may be set accurately; the cardinal points shift with the graduated circle.

Spirit Levels—The spirit levels are attached to the vernier plate—one level M in front (north point of the box), the other N on the side—thus forming an angle of 90°.

Standards—The vernier plate carries two vertical standards or supports O, which are shaped like an inverted V and placed one on each side. The center of their legs is just opposite the 90° graduation of the compass box. They are made equal.

Horizontal Axis—The standards carry between and on the top of them a movable horizontal axis P.

Vertical Circle—To the horizontal axis is attached, by means of a clamp screw, a vertical circle or arc Q, which is divided like the horizontal circle, and which in its vertical motion just touches a circular vernier v' carried by the left standard together with a slow-motion screw.

Telescope—In the middle of the horizontal axis and perpendicular to it is attached a telescope T of a description similar to that of the engineer's level, with an objective R and an ocular S, racks and pinions U for their motions, and an adjustable cross-hairs ring V, with ordinary and stadia hairs.

Telescope Level—An adjustable spirit level X is also attached to the under part of the telescope, as in the engineer's level. This permits the transit to also be used as a leveling instrument, if necessary.

Motions of the Telescope—The telescope can function over the full range of the horizon and can measure any horizontal angle. Also, since the telescope is on a horizontal axis endowed with free motion, it may move in a vertical plane carrying with it the vertical arc, and it can therefore measure vertical angles. In the horizontal motion, the vertical cross hair of the telescope is brought exactly on the point sighted by means of the slow-motion screw L, carried by the vernier plate H. In the vertical motion, the horizontal cross hair of the telescope is brought exactly on the point sighted by means of the slow-motion screw carried on the inside of the left hand support and by moving the vertical circle.

Lines of a Transit

The following are the principal lines of a transit:
1. Vertical axis.
2. Horizontal axis.
3. Plate level line.
4. Attached level line.
5. Line of collimation.

Vertical Axis—The vertical line that passes through the center of the spindle E.

Horizontal Axis—The axis P of the shaft by which the telescope rests on the supports; it must be made horizontal.

Plate Level Line—The top or bottom lines of the plate level case N. These are level when the bubble is centered.

Attached Level Line—The level line of the bubble level X attached to the telescope; it is employed only when the instrument is used as an engineer's level.

Line of Collimation—The line determined by the optical center of the objective and the intersection of the cross hairs.

Relations Between the Lines of a Transit—The following relations must be obtained:

1. The plate levels must be perpendicular to the vertical axis.
2. The line of collimation must be perpendicular to the horizontal axis.
3. The horizontal axis must be perpendicular to the vertical axis.
4. The attached level line and the line of collimation must be parallel.
5. The zero of the vertical circle must correspond to the zero of the vernier when the telescope is horizontal.

Adjustments of the Transit

The following are the necessary adjustments of the transit.

First Adjustment—*Making the axis of the spindle vertical and the planes of the plates perpendicular to it.* Set one level over a pair of plate screws; the other level will thus be set over the other pair. Level up both levels by means of the plate screws. Turn the vernier plate around by a one-half revolution. If the bubbles remain centered during the motion, the vernier plate is in adjustment; if they have moved, bring them halfway back by means of the adjusting screws and the rest of the way by means of the foot screws. Repeat the operation, and determine if the bubbles remain centered when revolving the divided circle; if they do not, the plates are not parallel, and the transit must be sent to the manufacturer for repairs.

Second Adjustment—*Collimating the telescope.* Set up the transit in the center of open and practically level ground. Carefully level the instrument. Drive a stake or pin approximately 200 or 300 feet away; measure the distance. Take a sight on that point, and clamp the plates. Revolve the telescope vertically (in altitude) by one-half a revolution, thus reversing the line of sight. Measure in the new direction the same distance as first measured, and drive a pin. Unclamp and revolve the vernier plate by one-half a horizontal revolution. Sight again at the first

111

point, and clamp. Again, revolve the telescope vertically by
one-half a revolution. If the line of sight falls on the pin, the
telescope is collimated; if not, drive a new pin on the last sight at
the same distance as before, and drive another pin at one-fourth
the distance between the first pin and the second. Move the vertical cross hair by means of the capstan-headed screw and an
adjusting pin, until the intersection of the cross hairs covers the
last pin set. Repeat the operation to be certain of collimation.

Third Adjustment—*Adjusting the horizontal axis so that the
line of collimation will move in a vertical plane.* Level up carefully and sight on a high, well-defined point, such as a corner of
a chimney, and clamp. Slowly move the telescope down until it
sights the ground, and drive a pin there. Unclamp; revolve the
vernier plate one-half a revolution, and revolve the telescope
vertically one-half a revolution, thereby reversing the line of
sight. Look again at the high point, and clamp. Slowly move the
telescope down until it sights the ground. If the intersection of
the cross hairs covers the pin, the horizontal axis is in adjustment; if not, correct halfway by means of a support-adjusting
screw and the rest of the way by means of the plate screws.
Repeat the operation, and verify the adjustment.

Fourth Adjustment—*Making the line of collimation horizontal
when the bubble of the attached level is centered.* Drive two
stakes 300 or 400 feet apart, and set up the instrument approximately halfway between these stakes. Level up and take
readings on the rod held successively on the two stakes; the
difference between the readings is the difference of elevation of
the stakes. Next, set the transit over one of the stakes, level up
and take a reading of the rod held on the other stake; measure
the height of the instrument. The difference between this and the
last rod reading should equal the difference of elevation as previously determined; if it does not, correct the error halfway by
means of the attached level-adjusting screw. Repeat the operation, and verify the adjustment.

Fifth Adjustment—*Making the vernier of the vertical circle
read zero when the bubble of the attached level is centered.*
Level up the instrument. Sight on a well-defined point, and take
note of the reading on the vertical circle. Turn the vernier plate

one-half a revolution, and also turn the telescope vertically one-half a revolution; again, sight on the same point. Read and record the reading on the vertical circle. One-half the difference of the two readings is the index error, which may be corrected by moving either the vernier or the vertical circle, or the error may be noted and applied as a correction to all measurements of vertical angles.

It will sometimes be necessary to adjust the compass. When the adjustment is required, it may be accomplished by using the following procedure:

First Adjustment—*Straighten the needle.* Examine to see if the ends of the needle are set on opposite divisions; if not, fix the pivot so that they will. Revolve the box by one-half a revolution; if the needle does not set on opposite divisions, bend both ends by one-half the difference.

Second Adjustment—Place the pivot in the center of the plate. If the needle is straight, move the pivot until the needle sets on opposite divisions at points such as 0°, 45°, and 90°.

Instructions for Using the Transit

The transit requires various adjustments, as explained in the preceding section. To center the transit over a stake, rest one leg of the tripod on the ground, then grasp the other legs and place the instrument as nearly over the stake as possible. Then attach the plumb bob, and center it accurately by means of the shifting head. Avoid having the plates too much out of level, because this will result in unnecessary straining of the leveling screws and plates. Once the instrument has been centered over the stake, level it up by the spirit levels on the horizontal plate. To do this, turn the instrument on its vertical axis until the bubble tubes are parallel to a pair of diagonally opposite plate screws. Then, stand facing the instrument, and grasp the screws between the thumb and forefinger; turn the thumbscrew in the direction the bubble must move. When adjusting the screws, turn both thumbscrews in or out, never in the same direction. Adjusting one level will disturb the other, but each must be adjusted alternately until both bubbles remain constant.

The method of measuring a horizontal angle is shown in Fig.

10. The process of laying off a given angle is similar to that of measuring an angle. The transit is set up at the vertex of the angle, the vernier is clamped at zero, and the telescope is pointed at the target, thereby marking the direction of the fixed line. The limb is now clamped, the vernier is unclamped, and the vernier plate is turned through the desired angle and clamped. A stake should now be driven in line with the vertical cross hair in the telescope, thus establishing the two sides of the angle. When laying out the foundations of buildings, a corner stake is first located by measurement, then the direction of one of the walls is laid out by driving a second stake. This direction may be determined by local conditions, such as the shape of the lot or the relation to other buildings. If the building is to be an extension to, or in line with, another building, the direction can be obtained by sighting along the building wall and driving two stakes in line with it. If it is to make a given angle with another building, this angle can be laid off as shown in Fig. 11.

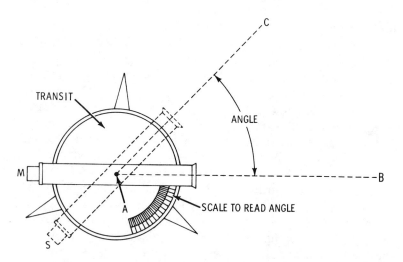

Fig. 10. The general principle of transit work. The transit is placed over the apex A of the angle CAB which is to be measured. The telescope is sighted to stake B (position M), and a reading is taken; it is then turned horizontally and sighted to stake C (position S), and another reading is taken. The difference between these readings gives angle CAB.

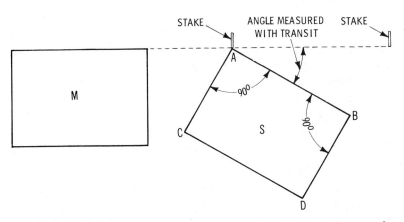

Fig. 11. The method of laying out a new building (S) at a given angle with an old building (M). After the corner and the direction of one wall are determined, a right angle may be laid off (if the building is rectangular), thus locating two of the sides (AB and AC). The length of side AB is then measured, thereby locating corner B. The transit is set up at B, and line BD is laid off at right angles to AB. AC and BD are then laid off by the proper length, and the four corners of the building are thus located. If the building had not been rectangular, the proper angles could have been laid off instead of right angles.

Gradienter

Some transits carry a device called a gradienter (Y in Fig. 8), which is attached to the horizontal axis by means of a clamp screw and inside of the right-hand support; it is designed and employed for the determination of grades and distances. It consists of an arm in the shape of an inverted Y with curved branches; to the extremities of this arm are attached an encased spiral spring and a nut through which moves a micrometer screw with a graduated head that revolves in front of a scaled index (Z in Fig. 8), which is also carried by the arm. The ends of the screw and the spring are on opposite sides of a shoulder that is carried by the right-hand support. The head is divided into tenths and hundredths, and every revolution moves it in front of the scale by one division, so that the scale gives the number of turns of the screw, and the graduated head gives the fraction of a turn.

In grading, if one revolution of the screw moves the cross hair a space of 1 foot on a rod held 100 feet away, the scope indicated by the telescope is 1 percent. To establish a grade, level up the telescope, clamp the arm of the gradienter, and turn the micrometer screw by as many divisions as are required in the grade. For instance, to set the gradienter at 2.35, move the head two complete turns plus 35 subdivisions. Measure the height of the telescope from the ground; set the rod at that height. Then hold the rod at any point on the line, raising it until the target is bisected by the cross hairs; the foot of the rod will then be on the grade.

Care of Instruments

With proper care, the usefulness of an instrument can be preserved for many years; therefore, the following suggestions on the care of instruments should be noted. The lenses of the telescope, particularly the object glass, should not be removed, since this will disturb the adjustment. If it is necessary to clean them, great care should be taken, and only soft, clean linen should be used. To retain the sensitivity of the compass needle, the delicate point on which it swings must be carefully guarded, and the instrument should not be carried without the needle being locked. When the needle is lowered, it should be brought gently on the center pin. The object slide seldom needs to be removed; when removal is necessary, the slide should be carefully protected from dust. Do not grease or oil the slide too freely; only a thin lubricant film is necessary. Any surplus of oil should be removed with a clean wiper. The centers, subject to considerable wear, require more frequent lubrication. After a thorough cleaning, they should be carefully oiled with a fine watch oil. All of the adjusting screws should be brought to a fine bearing, but they should never be tightened to such a degree that a strain is applied to the different parts; if this is done, the adjustment will be unreliable. When the instrument is carried on the tripod, all clamps should be tightened to prevent unnecessary wear on the centers.

THE STADIA

This is a device that is used for measuring distances, and it consists essentially of two extra parallel hairs in addition to the ordinary cross hairs of the transit or a level telescope, as shown in Fig. 12. The stadia hairs may be adjustable, or they may be fixed permanently on the diaphragm.

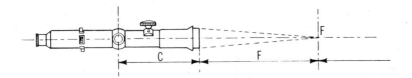

Fig. 12. *The principle of stadia operation. The fixed stadia hairs are set so that they will intercept 1 foot on a rod at a distance of 100 feet. Since the image of the cross hairs is projected to a point beyond the telescope objective equal to its focal length, the rays of light converge at that point, and measurements must begin from there. Therefore, a constant must be added to all stadia readings equal to the focal length of the object lens plus the distance from the face of the objective to the center of the instrument. This constant is the factor F + C; for transit telescopes; it is equal to approximately 1 foot.*

When using the stadia, distances are measured by observing through the telescope of a transit the space, on a graduated rod, included between two horizontal hairs, called stadia hairs. If the rod is held at different distances from the instrument, different intervals on the rod are included between the stadia hairs. The spaces on the rod are proportional to the distances from the instrument to the rod so that the intercepted space is a measure of the distance to the rod. This method of measurement furnishes a rapid means of measuring distances when filling in details of topographic and hydrographic surveys.

Most transits, all plane-table alidades, and some precision leveling instruments are fitted with stadia hairs. Stadia surveying has the advantage in that the intervening country does not have to be taped, and it provides a means of measuring inaccessible distances, such as across water and up steep hills and bluffs. It is well adapted to preliminary surveys for highways and railroads because the errors tend to be compensating rather than cumulative, but it should not be used for short distances, such as farms and city lots. In sights of 200 to 400 feet, it is possible to read a rod to the nearest hundredth of a foot, which represents one foot in distance. At 600 to 1200 feet, it is possible to read to the nearest hundredth of a yard, which represents 3 feet in distance. This is the precision to be expected in stadia measurements. The rod used is preferably a one-piece stadia rod, such as is shown at F in Fig. 13, but any standard leveling rod, except builders rods graduated in inches and sixteenths, may be used. When leveling with an instrument which is equipped with stadia hairs, care should be taken not to confuse the center leveling cross hair with either of the two outside stadia hairs. It has been done. Although it is by no means obsolete, stadia surveying has now to a great degree been superseded by aerial photography. Neither is a substitute for careful taping.

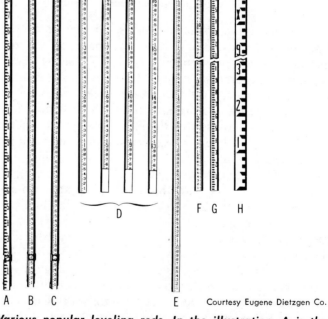

Courtesy Eugene Dietzgen Co.

Fig. 13. Various popular leveling rods. In the illustration, A is the Philadelphia rod, in English graduations; B, the California rod; C, the Philadelphia rod, in metric graduations; D, the Chicago rod; E, the architect's rod; F, the stadia rod, in English graduations; G, the stadia rod, in metric graduations; and H, the broad stadia rod.

For the vast majority of surveying purposes, the transit and levels described are more than sufficient. Three other devices can be even more useful, however.

The Theodolite (Fig. 14) is a transit that is more expensive but more accurate than a standard transit, and the Theodolite has more capacity. If you are doing readings over 500 feet, you may want to look into this.

Wild T16 Theodolite—Courtesy of Wild-Heerbrugg
Fig. 14. Wild T-16 Theodolite.

The automatic level (Fig. 15) is also a tool used where great precision is required. Another device, the electronic distance measurer (EDM), is good when great distances have to be read. It is a tool used on the sea and in other places—such as measuring from a point to a mountain—where there is no real point of reference. The electronic distance measurer and the Theodolite are often used together (Fig. 16). By the way, no one seems to know the origin of the term Theodolite.

Automatic level—Courtesy of Wild-Heerbrugg

Fig. 15. NA2 automatic level.

SUMMARY

Leveling, in surveying, is the operation of determining the comparative levels of different points of land for the purpose of laying out a grade or building site, by sighting through a leveling instrument at one point to a leveling staff at another point.

The transit is designed and used for measuring both horizontal and vertical angles. It is a telescope mounted in standards attached to a horizontal plate, called the limb. The transit is generally provided with a compass so that the bearing of any given line with the magnetic meridian may be determined. It also has a spirit level attached to the telescope so that it may be brought to a horizontal position and made to serve as a level.

A stadia is a device used for measuring distance. It consists essentially of two extra parallel hairs in addition to the ordinary cross hairs that are used in transit or level telescopes. When using the stadia, distances are measured by observing through the telescope of a transit the space, on a graduated rod, between the two horizontal hairs, called stadia hairs.

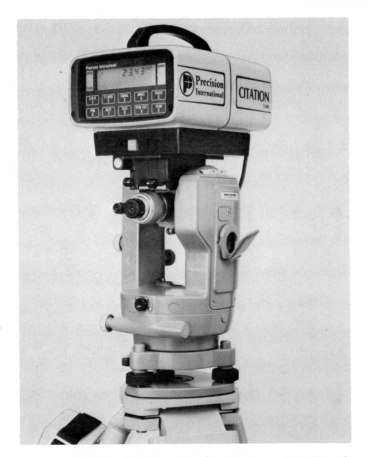

EDM Theodolite installation—Courtesy of Wild-Heerbrugg

Fig. 16. Typical EDM/Theodolite setup. Courtesy Wild Heerbrugg

REVIEW QUESTIONS

1. What are the three lines of the level?
2. What is a transit?
3. What are the fine lines of a transit?
4. Name the various leveling rods used for measuring distance.
5. Explain the terms "backsight" and "foresight" when used in leveling.

121

CHAPTER 3

Strength of Timbers

The various mechanical properties of woods have been investigated by exhaustive testing in many laboratories, most notably the Forest Products Laboratory of the U.S. Department of Agriculture at Madison, Wisconsin. In addition, much research has been done in civil and agricultural engineering laboratories at many state universities.

In the shop and in the field, the fitness of any species of wood for a given purpose depends on various properties. When treating the strength, stiffness, hardness, and other properties of wood, many technical terms are used. For an understanding of these terms, the following definitions are given.

DEFINITIONS

Bending forces—Forces that act on some members of a structural frame and tend to deform them by flexure.

Brittleness—Breaking easily and suddenly, usually with a comparatively smooth fracture; the opposite of *toughness,* sometimes incorrectly called *brashness,* which refers more to brittleness. Old and extremely dry wood is inclined to brashness; green or wet wood is tougher, though not as strong in most cases.

Compression—The effect of forces that tend to reduce the dimensions of a member, or to shorten it.

Deformation—A change of shape or dimension; disfigurement, such as the elongation of a structural member under tension.

Ductile—A term not applicable to wood; it is the property of a metal that allows it to be hammered thin or drawn into wires.

123

Elastic limit—The greatest stress that a substance can withstand and still recover completely when the force or strain is removed.

Factor of safety—The ratio between the stress at failure and allowable design stress. If the stress at failure in a bending beam is 4350 pounds per square inch, and the timber is stress-graded at 1450f, the safety factor is 4350/1450, or 3.

Force—In common parlance, a *pull* or a *push;* that which would change the state of a body at rest, or would change the course of a body in motion (Newton's Law).

Load—Pressure acting on a surface, usually caused by the action of gravity.

Member—A part of a structure, such as a column, beam, or brace, which usually is subjected to compression, tension, shear or bending.

Modulus, or coefficient, of elasticity—Stress, either tension or compression, divided by the elongation or contraction per unit of length. Inside the elastic limit, the modulus of elasticity is approximately constant for most materials. In wood, it varies greatly with different species, with moisture content, and even in pieces sawed from the same log; in other words, it is subject to considerable natural variation.

Modulus of rupture—The calculated fixed stress in a beam at the point of rupture. Since the elastic limit will have been passed at this point, it is not a true fiber stress, but it is a definite quantity, and the personal factor is not involved when obtaining it.

Permanent set—When a member, either metal or wood, is stressed beyond its elastic limit, or subjected to stresses that may be far below its elastic limit for extremely long periods of time, it may take on permanent deformation. Permanent set in timbers does not mean nor imply that the timbers have been weakened.

Resilience—A synonym for *elasticity*. The property that enables a substance to spring back when a deforming force is removed.

Shear—The effect of forces, external or internal, which causes bodies or parts of bodies to slide past each each other.

Strain—Alterations in the form of a member caused by forces acting on the member.

Strength—The power to resist forces, which may be tensile, compressive, or shearing, without breaking or yielding.

Stress—Distributed forces, such as pounds per square inch or tons per square foot. Within the elastic limit of materials, *stress* is approximately proportional to *strain*. This statement is called Hooke's Law.

Tenacity—A synonym for *tensile strength;* the power to resist tearing apart.

Tension—A force that tends to tear a body apart or elongate it.

Toughness—Strong but flexible; not brittle; nearly the same as *tenacity.*

Ultimate strength—The stress developed just before failure is evident.

Yield point—This property is not evident in timbers. In steels, it occurs after the elastic limit has been passed. In materials that show no defined yield point, it may be arbitrarily assumed or defined as the stress where a permanent set occurs.

As an example of the uses for these terms, the tie rod in a truss resists being pulled apart because of its *tensile strength.* The *stress* thus applied *strains* the rod, *deforming* or *elongating* it. It is *stretched* and a *contraction* of the area of its cross section results. If the *load* is not sufficient to *stress* the material past its *elastic limit,* the rod will return to its original length when the load is removed, depending on the duration of the load. If the *load* is heavy enough to stretch the rod past its *elastic limit,* it will not return to its original length when the *load* is removed, but it will remain *permanently set* if it is not pulled in two. The *elastic limit* is reached when *elongation* becomes proportionally greater than the *loading.* If the *load* is increased to the point where the rod breaks, or where its *tenacity* is overcome, it is said to be *ruptured*. The rod itself is called a *member* of the truss.

Tension

A tension test is made as indicated in Fig. 1. Although modern testing machines are by no means as simple as the apparatus shown, it serves well to show how such tests are made. The specimen is placed in the machine, gripped at each end, and the load is progressively increased until the material reaches its failure point. Usually the elongation is not of any significance unless it is desired to determine the modulus of elasticity. The allowable fiber stress indicated by modern stress-grading, such as 1200f or 1450f, apply equally to extreme fiber stress in bending and to tensile stresses.

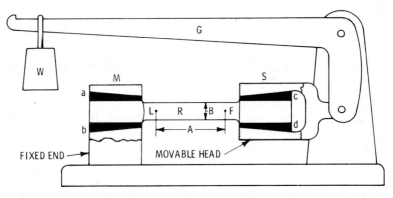

Fig. 1. The tension test. The specimen R is placed in the wedge grips a, b, c, and d, thus applying tension between the fixed end and the movable head of the machine. The movable head is connected to the scale lever G on which the weight W slides; this arrangement is similar to an ordinary weighing scale. Two center marks (L and F) are punched on the specimen at a standard distance (A) apart. When testing, the pull on the specimen is gradually increased by moving W to the left; dimensions A and B are then measured after each load increase.

Example—A truss member is subjected to a tensile force of 50,000 pounds. What size timber of No. 1 dense yellow pine (1600f grade) will be required?

This is the calculation:

$$\frac{50000}{1600} = 31.25 \text{ square inches cross section}$$

Therefore, either a standard-dressed 4″ × 10″ (3½″ × 9¼″) or a 6″ × 6″ (5½″ × 5½″) should be adequate.

Compression

A column supporting a load which tends to crush it is said to be in *compression*. Allowable compression parallel to the grain in stress-graded lumber is usually slightly less than the allowable bending and tensile stresses. For No. 1 dense timbers, 1600f grade, the compression stress is 1500 pounds per square inch, and for No. 2 dense, 1200f grade, it is 900 pounds per square inch. The builder need have no other concern than to see that the specified stresses are not exceeded. For loads applied across the grain, these stresses are much less; for the two grades mentioned above, the cross-grain stress is 455 pounds per square inch for both grades.

When making a compression test, as indicated in Fig. 2, a prepared specimen is placed between two plates, and a measured load is applied; the load is increased progressively until the failure point is reached. Actually, modern wood-compres-

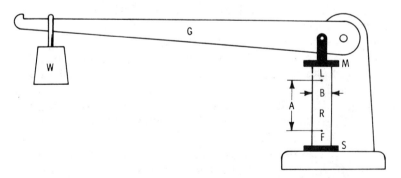

Fig. 2. The compression test. The specimen R is placed between two plates (M and S), and a compression stress of any desired intensity is applied by moving the weight W on the lever G. As the load is gradually increased, the changes in dimensions A and B are noted, and a final result can be obtained that will indicate the amount of compression which the specimen can withstand.

sion testing is not quite so simple. An instrument called a "compressometer" is pinned to the side of the specimen with sharp-pointed screws at points corresponding to points L and F in the illustration. It is fitted with a series of levers which are connected to a dial gauge, usually reading to .0001 inch. The stem of the dial gauge is depressed until it shows a positive reading, and compression in the specimen releases a part of the gauge. In this way, a sudden failure will release the gauge entirely, and jamming and ruining of the instrument is avoided. Usually at least one of the plates through which pressure is applied is a cast-iron hemisphere, thereby assuring an evenly distributed pressure over the entire cross section of the specimen.

WORKING STRESSES FOR COLUMNS

The amount of allowable loads on wood columns has been, and continues to be, a subject that is open to some discussion. The matter is complicated by the fact that columns of different lengths and diameters do not behave in the same manner under loadings. For the rather short column, failure will be caused by the actual crushing of the fibers of the wood, and the full compressive strength of the wood may thus be utilized. For a slightly longer column, failure may be caused by a sort of diagonal shearing action. For a long column, it will probably fail by bending sidewise and breaking. No one method can be adapted exactly for calculating allowable loads on columns of all lengths and slenderness ratios. Column formulas are numerous. Some are based on empirical data, or the results of actual testing. Only one, the Euler (pronounced *oiler*) formula seems to be based on purely mathematical calculations. It is of German origin, and, in its original form, it is so cumbersome that few designers in the U.S. care to use it. It assumes that a column will fail by *bending and breaking*. This is assured only if the column is long and comparatively slender; however, a *modified* Euler formula is greatly favored by present-day timber designers. It is written as follows:

$$\text{Allowable load per square inch of cross section} = \frac{.3E}{(l/d)^2}$$

where,

E = modulus of elasticity of the timber used,
l = unsupported length of the column, in inches,
d = least side, or diameter of a round column.

This formula is applicable only when the results of its use do not indicate a higher stress than the maximum allowable unit stresses as defined by the stress grade of the timber used. The ratio l/d in the above equation is sometimes called the slenderness ratio. As an example of the use of this formula, take the following problem:

How much of a load may safely be imposed on a 6″ × 6″ dressed yellow pine column which is 12 feet long?
The slenderness ratio, or l/d, of 6″ × 6″ columns 12 feet long is 144/6 = 24, and the modulus of elasticity of almost all good yellow pine is 1,760,000 pounds per square inch. This is the calculation:

$$\frac{.3 \times 1,760,000}{24 \times 24} = 917 \text{ pounds per square inch}$$

The cross-sectional area of standard 6″ × 6″ timbers is 30.25 square inches. Therefore, the total load allowable on the column will then be:

$$917 \times 30.25 = 27,739 \text{ pounds}$$

An important point with respect to timber in compression is that the ends should be cut exactly square so that there will be a full bearing surface; otherwise the timber will be subjected at the ends to more than the working stress (Fig. 3).

SHEARING STRESSES

Shearing stresses in wood are dangerous only in the direction parallel to the grain. It is almost impossible to shear the material across the grain until the specimen has *crushed*. The crushing strength, then, and not the shearing resistance of the wood, will govern the maximum stress that can be applied to the wood.

129

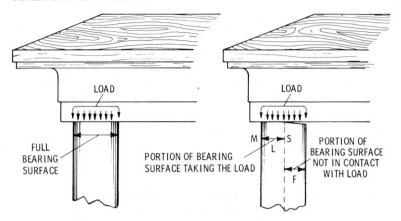

Fig. 3. *Good and poor column bearing surfaces illustrate the importance of squaring columns accurately when cutting them. The entire top of the column must be in contact with the load member so that the pressure per square inch of cross section on the column will correspond to the allowable working pressure for which the column was designed. If the portion MS of the bearing surface in contact is only ½ the entire surface, then the stress applied on the top of the column will be twice that of full contact, as shown by LF.*

The standard shearing test for woods with the grain was developed by the American Society for Testing Materials, and the procedure is standardized. The specimens are standard dimensions, shaped as shown in Fig. 4, in pairs, one with the notch at right angles to that in the other. The results of the tests on the two specimens are averaged, but usually they vary only slightly. The blocks are tested in a special shear tool, which is loaded in a universal testing machine, with the load applied at a rate of .024 inch per minute.

The results of testing different types of woods vary widely. To provide for this lack of uniformity, the shear allowances in stress-rated timbers may contain a reduction factor (safety factor) of as much as 10, or it may be as little as 2 or 3. This is necessary, because a piece which is below average in shearing resistance may appear anywhere.

The distinctions *across the grain* and *with the grain* should be carefully noted. Wet or green wood, in general, shears approximately one-fifth to one-half as easy as dry wood; a surface parallel to the rings (tangent) shears more easily than one parallel to

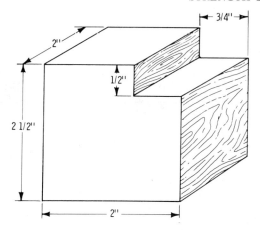

Fig. 4. The A.S.T.M. standard wood-shear test specimen.

the medullary rays. The lighter conifers and hardwoods offer less resistance than the heavier kinds, but the best pine shears one-third to one-half more readily than oak or hickory, thereby indicating that great shearing strength is characteristic of "tough" woods.

HORIZONTAL SHEARS

The types of shears discussed in the preceding section are called *external* shears because they are caused by forces that originate outside the body of the material, and for the most part they are evident and readily provided for. In addition, in every loaded beam, a system of *internal* stresses are set up. This may be explained by observing that every shearing force results from *two* forces which are *unbalanced*. They do not meet at the same point, and a *stress couple* is set up which can be met and held motionless only by another couple which acts in opposition to it. This is illustrated in Fig. 6; it represents a "particle" of indefinite size, but possibly infinitely small, that has been extracted from the body of a beam which has been stressed by bending. In Fig. 6A, the particle has been subjected to a vertical shearing force, or pair of forces, since there can be no action without an

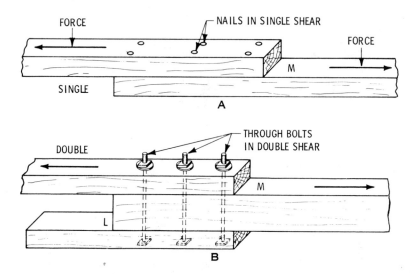

Fig. 5. Examples of single and double shear. In A, the nails are in single shear. This is the assumption made as a general rule when calculating the strength of nailed joints, but nails may be placed in double shear, similar to the bolts in B, if they are long enough to almost penetrate all three members; the nails in double shear will safely carry twice the load which could safely be placed on nails in single shear. However, most nailed joints are designed as if the nails were in single shear, though they may actually be in double shear. In B, the bolts are truly in double shear, but the joint is not twice as strong as a plain lapped joint if the center member is not at least as thick as the combined thicknesses of the outer members. The outer members are usually both the same thickness.

opposing and equal reaction. The particle is *unstable;* since the two forces do not meet at a common point, the particle tends to revolve in a counterclockwise direction. In Fig. 6B, a pair of horizontal forces is supplied; these forces represent another stress couple that balances or neutralizes the vertical shearing forces and are known as the *internal horizontal shears.* A reasonable deduction, therefore, is that at any point on the beam, there exist internal horizontal shears equal in intensity to the external vertical shears. It is the horizontal shears which are dangerous in wood beams, because timbers have a low resistance to shearing with the grain.

Fig. 6C shows how the four forces may be resolved into a single pair of concurrent forces which *do* meet at a common

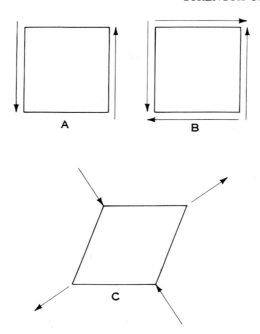

Fig. 6. The actions of vertical and horizontal shears.

point. These are not shearing forces but are the result of shearing forces. When the material has approximately the same resistance to shears in all directions, such as concrete or steel, this is what occurs. Each particle tends to elongate in one diagonal and forms the "diagonal tension" which is so dangerous in reinforced concrete beams. In fact, it is the most dangerous stress in such beams, and to resist it, elaborate web reinforcing and bent-up bars are provided at points where this stress is highest, usually near the ends of the beams. In I beams, diagonal tension results in buckling or wrinkling of the relatively thin webs. In wood beams, the forces are not resolved in this way, since wood is strong enough to resist the vertical components, but the horizontal components tend to split the beam, usually at or near the ends near the center of the height. Wood beams which are season checked at the ends, as many are, are low in resistance to such stresses.

If the depth of a wood beam is greater than one-tenth to one-twelfth of its span, horizontal shears, and not bending strength, often govern its ability to carry loads. Shears are usually not dangerous in wood beams unless they are relatively deep and heavily loaded.

TRANSVERSE OR BENDING STRESS

This is the kind of stress present on numerous building timbers, such as girders, joists, or rafters, that causes a deflection or bending between the points of support. What takes place when these or similar members are subjected to bending stress is considered under the subject of *beams* in this chapter.

STIFFNESS

By definition, stiffness is that quality possessed by a beam or other timber to resist the action of a bending force. The action of the bending force tends to change a beam from a straight to a curved form; that is, a *deflection* takes place. When a load is applied, the beam originally assumed to be straight and horizontal sags or bends downward between the supports. The amount of downward movement measured at a point midway between the supports is the amount of deflection. The action of beams subjected to bending forces is described as follows:

If a load of 100 pounds placed in the middle of a stick which is 2″ × 2″ and 4 feet long, supported at both ends bends or deflects this stick one-eighth of an inch (in the middle), then 200 pounds will bend it about one-fourth inch, 300 pounds, three-eighths inch, etc., the deflection varying directly as the load. This is in accordance with Hooke's Law, which states that stress is proportional to strain. Soon, however, a point is reached where an additional 100 pounds adds more than one-eighth inch to the deflection—the limit of elasticity has been exceeded. Taking another piece from the straight-grained and perfectly clear plank of the same depth and width but 8 feet long, the load of 100 pounds will deflect it by approximately 1 inch. Doubling the length reduces the stiffness eightfold. Stiffness, then, decreases as the cube of the length.

If AB in Fig. 7 is a piece of wood, and D is the deflection produced by a weight or load, then

$$\text{deflection (D)} = \frac{Pl^3}{48EI}$$

where,

P = the load, concentrated at the center of the span, in pounds,

l = the length of the span, in feet,

E = the modulus of elasticity of the material,

I = the moment of inertia (for rectangular beams = $\frac{bd^3}{12}$ where b = width and d height).

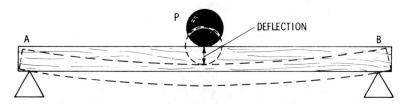

Fig. 7. A simple beam, loaded at the middle and supported at both ends, is used to illustrate the term "deflection."

The following rules, in conjunction with Figs. 8, 9, and 10, define the stiffness and strength of practically all types of wood beams.

1. For beams with a rectangular cross section, equal depths, and equal spans, their load-carrying capacity varies *directly* as their widths.
2. For beams with equal widths and equal spans, their strength varies directly as the square of their depth.
3. If depths and widths are the same, strengths vary *inversely* as the lengths of the spans.
4. Their stiffness, or resistance to deflection, will vary *inversely* as the *cubes* of their spans, other factors being equal.

135

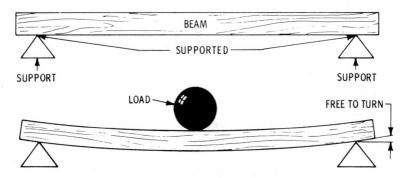

Fig. 8. A beam supported at the ends. The ends of the beam are free to follow any deflection, thus offering no resistance and rendering the beam less stiff than when the ends are fixed.

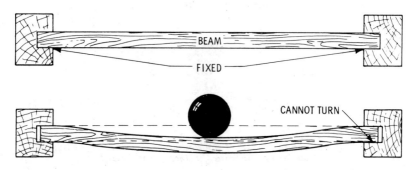

Fig. 9. A beam supported at the ends. The ends are gripped or embedded in some unyielding substance so that they cannot turn or follow the deflection of the beam under an applied load. The beam then deflects in a compound curve, thus adding extensively to its stiffness. Therefore, a beam with fixed ends will deflect less than one with supported ends.

5. Their stiffness will vary directly as the *cubes* of their depths, other factors being equal.
6. Other factors being equal, stiffness will vary *directly* as their widths.
7. If a beam is split horizontally, and the two halves are laid side by side, they will carry only *one-half* as much loading as the original beam.

These relations are not strictly true for I beams because of their irregular shapes, but they are approximately true for all

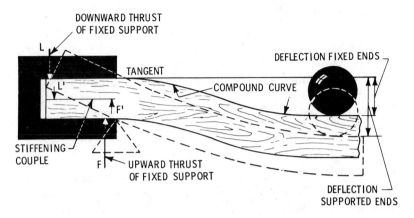

Fig. 10. *One end of a beam illustrating the stiffening effect of fixed ends as compared with supported ends. When the ends are fixed, the deflection of the beam will be resisted by an upward thrust, indicated by F, and a downward thrust, L; these thrusts form a resisting or stiffening couple which holds the portion of the beam embedded in the bearing in a horizontal position, thereby causing the beam to deflect in a compound curve, which increases its stiffness. The dotted lines show the excess deflection for the same load if the beam were simply supported at the ends.*

types of beams. It is usually most economical with materials to use as deep a beam as can conveniently be employed. Note that double 2″ × 4″ trimmers over window or door heads, if set edge up, are 8 times as strong and 32 times as stiff as when placed flatwise.

Both strength and stiffness are greater in dry timber than in green or wet wood of the same species. A piece of long-leaf yellow pine is 30% to 50% stronger and 30% stiffer when in an air-dry condition than when green. In general, both strength and stiffness are proportional to densities, or dry weights, although this is not invariably true. Edge-grain pieces are usually stronger and stiffer than those in which the tangent to the rings runs horizontally, but not appreciably so. There is little or no difference in the sapwood and heartwood of the same species, if the densities are the same. The tool handle of red heartwood is as serviceable as the handle of white sapwood, although white sapwood handles are still called "premium grade."

137

MODULUS OF ELASTICITY

Since it is desirable, and for many purposes essential, to know beforehand that a given piece with a given load will bend only by a given amount, the stiffness of wood is usually stated in a uniform manner under the term "modulus" (measure) of elasticity. For good grades of Douglas fir and yellow pine stress-rated, the modulus of elasticity is 1,760,000 pounds per square inch.

BEAMS

A beam is a single structural member, usually horizontal or nearly so, which carries a load or loads over a given space. At their supports, beams may be:

1. Freely supported merely means the beams are resting on their bearings.
2. Restrained, or partially fixed at their bearings. Although some designers choose to consider such restraint in their designs, the actual degree of restraint can never be accurately determined, so restrained beams are more often considered as being freely supported.
3. Fixed at their supports. In wood beams, this condition is rarely found; in steel frames, it is not unknown; and in reinforced concrete frames, it is quite common. Attempts to fix the ends of wood beams are rarely permanent. Building the ends of a beam, *any* beam, into a wall or casting it into concrete for a short distance does not fix the beams at their supports.

Allowable Loads on Wood Beams

The allowable loads on freely supported wood beams of any species are readily calculated if the timbers are stress rated and the allowable fiber-stress is known. For beams with a loading which is evenly distributed along its span, this is the equation to use:

$$W = \frac{f \times b \times d^2}{9 \times L}$$

where,

W = allowable evenly distributed loading, in pounds,
f = allowable fiber stress in pounds per square inch,
b = width of the beam, in inches,
d = depth of the beam, in inches,
L = length of the span, in feet.

Fig. 11 defines the dimensions of a beam—b, width, d, depth, and L, length.

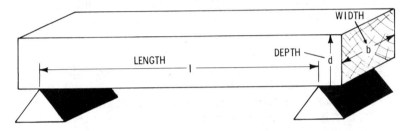

Fig. 11. A beam resting on knife-edge supports illustrates the terms length, width, and depth.

Problem—What will be the maximum allowable load on a beam whose nominal size is 6″ × 12″ and whose actual size is 5½″ × 11½″, with an 18 foot span? The timber is to be 1500f stress rated. This is the calculation:

$$\frac{1500 \times 5.5 \times 11.5 \times 11.5}{9 \times 18} = 6735 \ pounds$$

If the loading is to be concentrated at the center of the span, use one-half the load as calculated by the formula given; therefore, for the same timber as calculated, with the same span, the allowable concentrated load will be

$$\frac{6735}{2} = 3367 \ pounds$$

Breaking Loads on Wood Beams

Breaking loads are of no interest to the builder because the term is meaningless unless some explanation is made, since wood is extremely sensitive to the *duration* of loads. The load that would break a beam over a long period of time, for example, 10 years, will be only approximately $9/16$ of the load that would break it in a few minutes. The stresses specified in stress-rating lumber and timbers recognize this phenomenon. It is presumed that the full design loading will not be applied for more than 10 years during the life of the structure, and the time may be either cumulatively intermittent or continuous. It is also presumed that 90% of the full design loading may safely be applied for the full life of the structure. These presumptions make the use of stress-rated lumber quite conservative.

Example—What is the safe working load, concentrated at the center of the span, for a full-size 6″ × 10″ white oak timber with a 12-foot span, stress-rated 1900f, if it is laid flatwise (Fig. 12A)? If it is set edge up (Fig. 12B)?

This is the calculation for the timber laid flatwise:

$$\frac{1900 \times 10 \times 6 \times 6}{9 \times 12} = 6333$$

$$\frac{6333}{2} = 3167 \; pounds$$

For the timber set edge up:

$$\frac{1900 \times 6 \times 10 \times 10}{9 \times 12} = 10{,}555$$

$$\frac{10{,}555}{2} = 5278 \; pounds$$

Distributed Load

Instead of placing all the load in the middle of a beam, as in the example just given, the load may be regarded as being distributed; that is, the beam is uniformly loaded as in Fig. 13. Although this type of loading is actually a series of concentrated loads, it is often found in actual practice, and it is usually considered as being *uniformly* distributed.

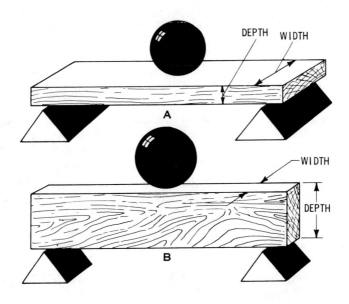

Fig. 12. The terms "width" and "depth" of a beam depend on the position of the beam. In A, the broad side is the width of the beam, whereas in B, which is the same beam turned over 90°, the narrow side is the width.

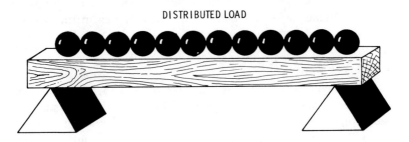

Fig. 13. A distributed load is indicated by the iron balls equally spaced along the beam between the supports.

Open-Web Steel Joists

One of the most invaluable of manufactured building parts are modern open-web steel joists. They are made by many firms, all to the same specifications but with slightly varying constructions. However, spans, depths, and carrying power have been standardized, prices are kept competitive, and there is little or no reason for the builder to prefer the products of one manufacturer to those of another. All of them employ electric welding to some extent, but the open webbing may be either expanded from a slitted I section, or it may be welded up from rods, bars, or light angles.

The standard open-web joists are usually obtainable in lengths of 4 to 32 feet, in increments of 6 inches, and in depths of 8 to 16 inches. In addition, many manufacturers can furnish long-span steel joists with depths of 18 to 32 inches, with top chords sloping in one direction or both directions to provide roof drainage, with spans up to 24 times their depths, or up to 64 feet. Considering the fact that an average of twelve types of joists are available for each span length, it is obviously impossible to give loading tables in a book of this sort, but they are available from the different manufacturers.

Open-web joists are valuable for many uses where their long spans permit large areas of floors, unobstructed by columns. Although they are entirely incombustible, they are quite vulnerable to fire, and where serious fire hazards exist, they must be effectively protected. They are termite- and rodent-proof, and they are also economical and easily and quickly erected. Pipes, wires, and conduits are readily run through their open webs. The progressive builder will find many other advantages in the use of open-web steel joists.

Cantilever Beams

A cantilever beam, as shown in Figs. 14 and 15, is firmly fixed at one end, or it is freely supported but with the end running back some distance to a support above it. The loading may be either distributed or concentrated at any point on the span. All beams which project beyond a support and which carry a load at the free end are classed as cantilevers. Stresses set up in the

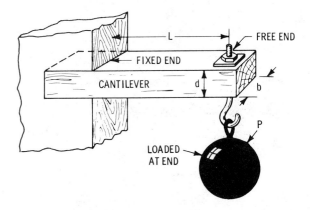

Fig. 14. A simple cantilever beam which is fixed at one end and free at the other; this beam is supporting a concentrated load at its free end.

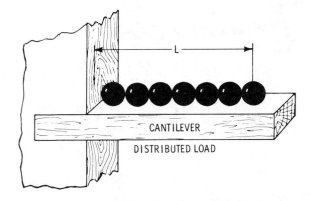

Fig. 15. A cantilever beam with an equally distributed load.

beam external to the outside support are the same as when the beam is rigidly fixed at the support. Fig. 16 illustrates the comparison between the working loads of variously supported beams, contrasting middle and distributed loads of beams supported at both ends with equal loads on cantilever beams. In the illustration, P=the concentrated loads, W=the evenly distributed load, f=the fiber stress, b=the width of the beam, d=the depth of the beam, and L=the length of the span.

143

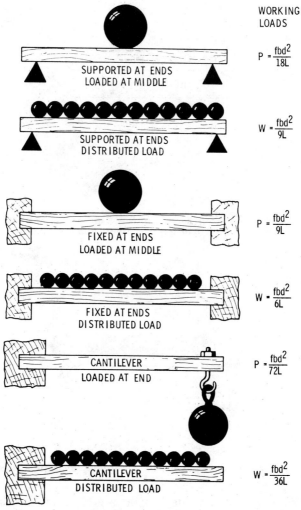

SUPPORTED AT ENDS
LOADED AT MIDDLE

$$P = \frac{fbd^2}{18L}$$

SUPPORTED AT ENDS
DISTRIBUTED LOAD

$$W = \frac{fbd^2}{9L}$$

FIXED AT ENDS
LOADED AT MIDDLE

$$P = \frac{fbd^2}{9L}$$

FIXED AT ENDS
DISTRIBUTED LOAD

$$W = \frac{fbd^2}{6L}$$

CANTILEVER
LOADED AT END

$$P = \frac{fbd^2}{72L}$$

CANTILEVER
DISTRIBUTED LOAD

$$W = \frac{fbd^2}{36L}$$

Fig. 16. The working loads for beams with different types of loads and different modes of support.

WIND LOADS ON ROOFS

Snow on roofs, if the roofs are of a slope that is low enough to permit the snow to lie in place, will weigh approximately 8 pounds per square foot per foot of depth when freshly fallen;

when wet, its weight will vary with the water content. A commonly used figure is 10 pounds per cubic foot. The snow load to provide for should be the depth of the heaviest snow on record multiplied by 10, but it should never be less than 20 pounds per square foot anywhere. If a roof is designed for much less than 20 pounds per square foot of live load, it will not be safe for men to work on.

In the past, there was considerable confusion regarding wind loads against sloping roofs, and some rather weird formulas were evolved to calculate their imaginary intensities, although no one had ever seen a roof blow *in,* and many persons have seen roofs blow *off.* In other words, wind loads are *negative;* that is, they create *suction.* This is now well recognized, and insurance companies are well informed on the subject.

In regions where hurricanes are not common the insurance companies recommend that an uplift allowance of 30 pounds per square foot be provided for, acting at right angles to the slope of the roof. This will include the slight *positive* pressure commonly found inside buildings during windstorms. If eaves are wide and overhanging, it is recommended that a gross lifting force of 45 pounds per square foot be provided for. If the weight of the roof itself is appreciable, it may be deducted from the gross uplift allowance. It should be recognized, however, that a maximum snow load and a maximum wind load can hardly occur at the same time and thus cannot be considered compensating.

STRUCTURAL STEEL

Few structures of any consequence are erected without the use of a certain amount of structural steel. Where great strength and rigidity are desired in a member of minimum cross-sectional area, a structural steel shape often fulfills the requirements without excessive cost or inconvenience. The more common forms of structural steel, shown in Fig. 17, are I beams, channels, and H beams used in columns. These are made in a variety of weights, and in the case of angles, they are designated by their size and flange thickness as 6 × 4½ inch L, or 10 × 8 inches— 45 pounds I, or 9 × 2½—20 pounds channel.

Where headroom is a consideration, steel beams often replace

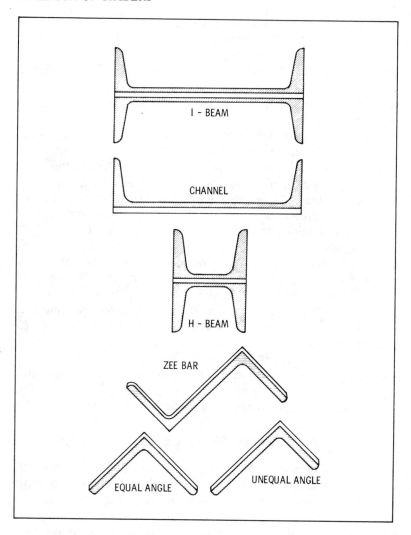

I - BEAM

CHANNEL

H - BEAM

ZEE BAR

EQUAL ANGLE

UNEQUAL ANGLE

Fig. 17. Various shapes of structural steel beams.

the considerably deeper wood girders. Steel angles are a great convenience in brick lintel construction. An H column fireproofed with tile or some other material provides a support of great strength and with a minimum of horizontal area. Steel shapes are also easily built into brick or stone walls, thereby affording great protection against collapse in case of fire. By riveting together two or more shapes, a variety of forms may be obtained which greatly strengthen the column, girders, or other built-up member. Angles are commonly riveted together back to back; cover plates are riveted to the flanges of beams to form girders and columns.

All important properties of structural steel, such as tensile strength, coefficients of expansion, etc., are known; their use as compression or tension members are governed by formulas in steel handbooks published by the rolling mills and are universally accepted and approved by engineers and building departments. All calculations for the use of steel should be determined in conjunction with steel handbooks and the building department regulations of the city in which such construction is employed.

When treated with an approved protective paint, steel is secure against the action of rust, and if the structural steel is fireproofed with concrete, brick, terra cotta, or some other suitable fireproofing enclosure, it is practically indestructible as well as fireproof and rustproof.

ALLOWABLE LOADS ON BEAMS

The tables of allowable loads for Wide Flange, American Standard, and Miscellaneous Shapes used as simple beams give the total allowable uniformly distributed loads in kips, for ordinary spans laterally supported, based on the stresses specified in the A.I.S.C. Standard Specification. The loads include the weight of the beam, which should be deducted to arrive at the net load that the beam will support. The tables are also applicable to simple beams that are laterally supported, carrying a single concentrated load at the center of the span. For this condition, the allowable concentrated load is one-half of the allowable uniformly distributed load for the same span.

It is assumed in all cases that the loads are applied normal to the X-X axis, as shown in the tables of properties of shapes published by the A.I.S.C., and that the beam deflects vertically in the plane of bending only. If the conditions of loading involve

147

forces outside this plane, the allowable loads must be determined from the general theory of texture, in accordance with the character of the load and its mode of application.

Shearing Stresses

With relatively short spans, the allowable loads for beams and channels may be limited by the shearing or buckling strength of the web, instead of by the maximum bending stress allowed in the flanges. This limit is indicated in the tables by solid cross lines. Loads shown above these lines will produce the maximum allowable shear on the beam web.

Crippling Values of Beam Webs

Beams should be designed so that the compression stress in the web at the toe of the fillet, resulting from reactions or concentrated loads, does not exceed 24 kips per square inch figured as follows, for webs without stiffeners:

$$\text{Maximum end reaction} = 24t\,(a + k)$$

$$\text{Maximum interior load} = 24t\,(a_1 + 2k)$$

where,

t = the thickness of the web, in inches,
k = the distance from the outer face of the flange to the web toe of the fillet, in inches,
a = the length of the bearing, in inches,
a_1 = the length of the concentrated load, in inches.

When the above values are exceeded, the webs of the beams should be reinforced, or the length of the bearing should be increased. Lack of proper lateral support for the top flanges of the beams at the reaction point so decreases the crippling strength of the webs as to render such practice inadmissible.

Lateral Deflection of Beams

The allowable loads given in the A.I.S.C. tables are calculated on the assumption that the compression flanges of the beams are

148

properly secured against yielding. These loads are, however, also allowable on the same span without side support, provided that the quantity *ld/bt* does not exceed 600. When *ld/bt* exceeds 600, the permissible unit stress must be reduced below 20,000 in accordance with the formula

$$f = \frac{12,000,000}{\frac{ld}{bt}}$$

This formula may be solved by the aid of tabulated values of *d/bt*. The allowable load must then be reduced below that tabulated for the span, in the same ratio as the value of *f* thus calculated is to 20,000. However, the selection of a beam for trial calculations may not be simple. It will usually be simplified by the use of the charts.

Vertical Deflection

Also given with the allowable loads are the deflections for beams of various spans carrying the tabulated allowable loads. These deflections are based on the nominal depth of the beam. The following formula may be used for calculating the maximum deflection of any symmetrical beam or girder which is uniformly loaded:

$$D = \frac{5Wl^3}{384\ E\ I}$$

where,

D = the deflection, in inches,
W = the total uniform load (including weight of beam), in pounds,
l = the span, in inches,
E = the modulus of elasticity, in pounds per square inch,
I = the stress, in pounds per square inch.

For E = 29,000,000 pounds per square inch, and flexural stress = 20,000 pounds per square inch, the formula reduces to approximately

$$D = \frac{0.02069\ L^2}{d}$$

where,

L = the span, in feet,
d = the depth of the beam, in inches.

The live-load deflection of floor beams carrying plastered ceilings should be limited to not more than 1/360 of the span length.

Reinforcing Bars

Standard concrete reinforcing bars are obtainable from most steel suppliers. The numbers given to bars No. 2 to No. 8 are nominal diameters in eighths of an inch. The No. 2 bar is $^2/_8$, or $^1/_4$ inch diameter round, the No. 8 bar is $^8/_8$, or 1 inch diameter. Bars No. 9, 10, and 11 are round bars with cross-sectional areas equivalent to square bars of 1, 1⅛, and 1¼ inch, respectively.

Most reinforcing bars are now rolled from new billet steel, but some are rolled from the balls of used railroad rails, sheared off, reheated, and rerolled. The rerolled bars are usually entirely satisfactory, but their use is forbidden in some specifications. The No. 2 bars are plain rounds, but the others all have standard deformed surfaces.

SUMMARY

In most shop work and in the field, the fitness of any species of wood for a given purpose depends on various properties. When treating the strength, stiffness, hardness, and other properties of wood, many factors must be considered. Stiffness is that quality possessed by a beam or other timber to resist the action of a bending force.

A beam is a single structural member, usually horizontal, that carries a load over a given space. The allowable loads on freely supported wood beams of any size can be calculated if the timber is stress rated and the allowable fiber-stress is known. In many designs, the load is distributed uniformly over the length of the beam. Although this type of loading is actually a series of concentrated loads, it is often found in actual practice, and is usually considered as being uniformly distributed.

Where great strength and rigidity is desired in a member of

minimum cross-sectional area, a structural steel shape often meets the requirements without excessive cost or inconvenience. All important properties of structural steel, such as tensile strength and coefficients of expansion, make it practically indestructible as well as fireproof.

REVIEW QUESTIONS

1. What is meant by brittleness, bending forces, compression, and elastic limit?
2. What is meant by working stresses?
3. Explain shearing stresses.
4. Why is it important in some cases to distribute the load on a beam between the supports?
5. What is a cantilever beam? Explain its purpose.

CHAPTER 4

Practical Drawing

By definition, the term mechanical drawing means drawing
done with the aid of drawing instruments as opposed to work
done freehand. The first subject to consider, then, is the drawing
instruments themselves and, then, how to use them.

DRAWING INSTRUMENTS

A draftsman should have good instruments; in fact, the best
are none too good and are easily rendered unfit for use unless
they are properly handled. Unfortunately, the advice given by
some instructors is to buy an inexpensive set of instruments for
use until you find out if you are gifted in the art of drafting. But
if an experienced draftsman cannot do good work with poor instruments, how can a beginner be expected to accomplish anything or determine if he has any talent for drawing?

There are many patterns and types of drawing instruments
available, and the beginning draftsman should purchase only the
best and most suitable equipment for his particular needs. The
advice of an experienced draftsman will be of great assistance to
the student who is about to buy these instruments. They are a
lifetime investment and, with reasonable care, should last in-
definitely.

The following list comprises everything needed for general
drafting work:

1 drawing board
1 set of instruments

1 T square
2 triangles (30° and 45°)
1 set of drawing scales
2 pencils (3H and 6H)
1 bottle of drawing ink
1 ink-and-pencil eraser
1 sponge eraser
1 pen holder and set of lettering pens
1 irregular curve
1 protractor

In some cases involving enlarging or reducing the size of drawings, proportional dividers are quite useful.

Drawing Board

A drawing board is usually made of a softwood or particleboard and should have a true edge (Fig. 1). Drawing boards are available in many different sizes, but in most cases a 20″ × 24″ board is large enough. To keep the drawing board surface free from dents and scratches, a vinyl drawing board top can be used. This covering offers excellent resiliency and leaves a smooth drawing surface at all times.

In some cases a drafting table (Fig. 2) is preferred over a

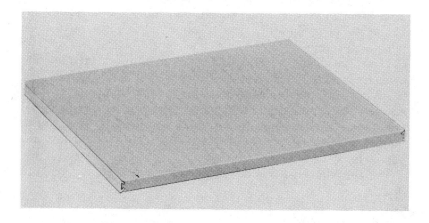

Fig. 1. A steel edge drawing board in wide use today.

drawing board. The table can be adjusted to any height, and may be tilted and locked at any desired angle. The top can be adjusted from horizontal to full easel position.

The most convenient method for fastening the paper to the drawing board is to use masking tape. It comes in convenient rolls, and small pieces may readily be torn off as required. Some brands of tape may be used several times; some only once. They may be pulled loose readily, but masking tape holds well, and neither the board nor the paper is damaged by holes.

Parallel Ruling Straightedge

The parallel ruling straightedge (Fig. 3) is an excellent alternative to the T square. The device is mounted over the entire or select portion of the drawing board; both ends are fastened to light metallic cords which run over a system of small pulleys in

Fig. 2. A typical drawing table; the table may be tilted and locked at any desired angle.

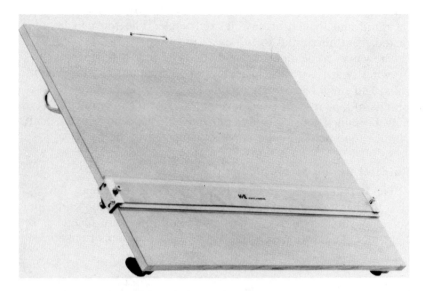

Fig. 3. A parallel straightedge attached to a drawing board.

such a manner that in no matter what position the straightedge is located, it is always parallel with the lower edge of the board.

Drafting Machines

A drafting machine is also popular in drafting rooms, for it can replace the T square, triangles, scale, and protractor (Fig. 4). Parallel motion is achieved by steel bands revolving around machined drums. The machine is controlled entirely by the left hand. Pressure can be applied to a control ring to change the setting on the protractor. The scale can automatically be snapped into any unit multiple of 15 degrees.

Set of Instruments

Drawing instruments are usually available in sets, that is, several instruments in a special case. For beginners and for general use, a good quality basic set containing the following instruments is all that is necessary:

1 compass
1 hair-spring dividers

Drawing board—Courtesy of Keuffel & Esser

Fig. 4. A typical drafting machine; this device can be used to take the place of a T square, the triangles, and the protractor, since all operations that can be performed with those tools can be done with the drafting machine.

3 spring bows (pencil, pen, and points)
1 extension bar
1 ruling pen

Fig. 5 shows a set comprising the above instruments of one popular pattern.

Compass—This instrument is designed and used for describing arcs or circles with either pencil or ink. It consists of two legs which are pivoted together so that they may be set to any desired radius. One leg carries an adjustable needle point, or center, and the other has a joint in which the pencil or pen arms may be secured. Each leg has a pivoted joint to permit adjustment of the ends, so that the end arms which carry the center

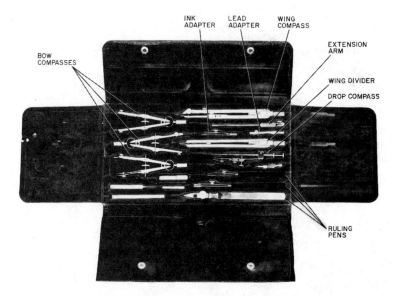

Fig. 5. A basic set of drawing instruments.

needle point and pen or pencil may be adjusted perpendicular to the paper for various radii. Fig. 6 shows a compass with pencil and pen arms and an extension bar.

The important requirement of good compasses is that their legs have the capability of movement to any radius without any spring back; cheap instruments may be springy, thus making it difficult to set them with precision.

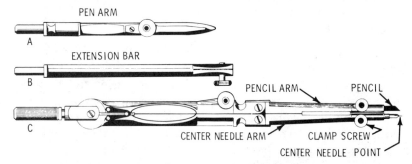

Fig. 6. The compass with a pencil arm may also be used with a pen arm or the extension bar to increase its versatility.

Hair-Spring Dividers—Compasses and dividers are quite similar; however, each has its own special use. Dividers consist of an instrument which has two legs that are pivoted at one end and provided with sharp needle points at the other, as shown in Fig. 7. They are used for spacing off distances. For precision, they are fitted with a hair-spring device that consists of an adjustable screw controlled by a steel spring in one leg. In operation, the legs are set to the approximate desired position and brought to the exact position by turning the adjusting screw.

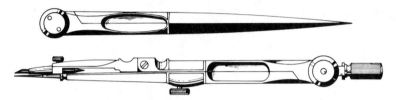

Fig. 7. The plain and the hair-spring dividers.

Spring Bows—These small compasses and dividers are made with two spring legs whose distance apart is regulated by a small through-bolt and thumbscrew. They are usually available in sets of three—pen bow, pencil bow, and dividers—as shown in Fig. 8. Spring bows are used for describing circles of small diameter and for minute spacing.

One most convenient instrument in this class is the drop-center compass. The needle point is located on a long stem; after the stem point is placed at the center of the desired circle, the instrument revolves around it. Circles of extremely small diameters (as small as .028) can thus be readily drawn.

Extension Bar—In order to extend the range of compasses, a lengthening or extension bar, as shown in Fig. 6B, is generally provided. This device greatly increases the diameters of circles which may be described by the compass.

Drawing or Ruling Pens—Not used as much as they once were, but still valuable for a line width other things won't make, are drawing or ruling pens (Fig. 9). The points are made of two steel blades that open and close as required for the thickness of lines by a regulating screw.

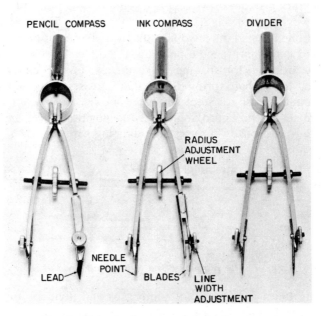

Fig. 8. The pencil compass, the ink compass, and the dividers.

Fig. 9. A typical ruling pen.

A good drawing pen should be made of properly tempered steel which is neither too soft nor hardened to brittleness. The nibs should be accurately set, both of the same length, and both equally firm when in contact with the drawing paper. The points should be so shaped that they are fine enough to admit absolute control of the contact of the pen in starting and ending lines, but otherwise they should be as broad and rounded as possible, in order to hold a convenient quantity of ink without dropping it. The lower (under) blade should be sufficiently firm to prevent the closing of the blades of the pen when using the pen against a straightedge. The spring of the pen, which separates the two blades, should be strong enough to hold the upper blade in its position, but not so strong that it would interfere with easy adjustment by the thumbscrew. The thread of the thumbscrew must be deeply and evenly cut so as not to strip. Fig. 9 presents side and end views of an ordinary ruling pen.

Technical pens have virtually replaced the old ruling pen. They have interchangeable pen points that range in size from very fine to very heavy. Probably the most commonly known technical pen is the Koh-i-Noor Rapidograph. It has gone through a number of permutations, the latest of which is that you buy the pen itself, then screw in place whichever size nib you need. Pens still come with permanent nibs attached, and you can get units for use with color (Fig 10).

Dry transfer materials are also popular for lettering and lining. Indeed, they have supplanted making lines, letters, and all kinds of shapes. Dry transfers come with adhesive on them. You just put the line (or whatever) in place, apply pressure, and lift off the backing. The line is on the paper perfectly. Such materials are available in a tremendous variety of line sizes and letters.

T square

This instrument is used for drawing lines parallel to the lower edge of the board. It consists of two parts—the head and the

Fig. 10. Technical fountain pen. Pens come with nibs of various sizes for lettering and drawing. Courtesy Koh-i-Noor.

161

blade. These two parts are fastened at an angle of 90° to each other, as shown in Fig. 11. This is the fixed-head type of square. The square may also be fitted with a movable head, as shown in Fig. 12, thereby permitting a line to be drawn at an inclined angle to the edge of the board. Fig. 13 shows the two types of squares in position on the board.

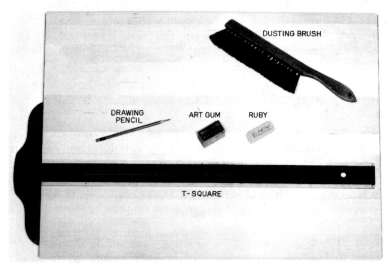

Fig. 11. Drawing board, T square, pencil, erasers, and dusting brush.

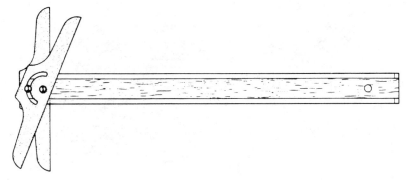

Fig. 12. A movable-head T square has a fixed head on one side and a movable head on the other; the movable head is pivoted so that it may be shifted to any angle with the blade.

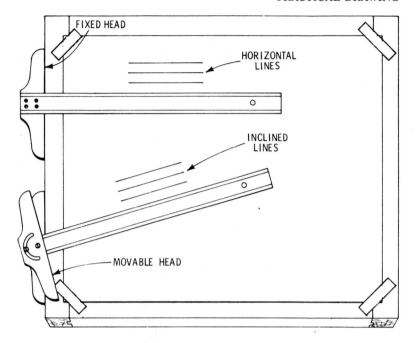

Fig. 13. *The fixed and movable-head T squares in position on the drawing board; horizontal lines are drawn with the fixed-head square, and inclined lines are drawn with the movable-head square.*

Triangles

For drawing other than horizontal lines, triangles are generally used.

Two triangles will ordinarily be required—the 45° triangle and 30° triangle—as shown in Fig. 14. Fig. 14A has two equal sides at right angles with the third side making an angle of 45° with the two legs; Fig. 14B also has two sides at right angles, but the third side makes a 30° angle with one leg and a 60° angle with the other leg. Fig. 15 illustrates the use of these triangles in conjunction with the T square.

Rules and Scales

Although triangular scales are found in every drafting room, most draftsmen prefer to work with flat scales. They are gener-

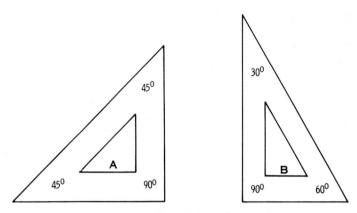

Fig. 14. The 45° and the 30° triangles.

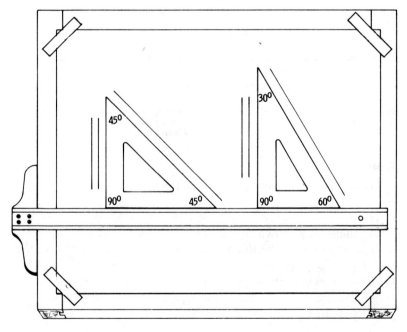

Fig. 15. The 45° and 30° triangles in position on the T square.

ally furnished in sets of three. When using the flat scales, the graduations are easier to see, and the proper graduations do not have to be selected every time the scale is picked up. The good scales are made of wood which is faced with plastic, or they are made entirely of solid plastic. Cheaper scales are made completely of wood, and they will not long withstand the hard use and constant cleaning which are common in modern and efficient drafting rooms.

When drawings are made to the same size as the object being drawn, that is, to full size, a common 1-foot rule is employed. However, when drawings are to be made larger or smaller than actual size, special scales are used. For architectural drawing, the various scales are divided into feet and inches with appropriate subdivisions. The most convenient forms are the usual flat or triangular scales shown in Fig. 16.

The triangular scale contains six different scales, as shown. The usual scales are:

3 inches=1 foot
1 1/2 inches=1 foot
1 inch=1 foot
3/4 inch=1 foot
3/8 inch=1 foot
1/4 inch=1 foot

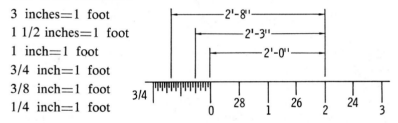

Other scales are available. The scales are usually designated by the length of the foot division, as for example, the 1½- or ¾-inch scale. On each scale, the first foot is divided into inches, and where the scale is large enough, it is divided into fractions of an inch.

Drawing Ink

India ink, rather than ordinary ink, is normally employed in drawing; it is made of lampblack pigments contained in solution. The ink is available in small bottles which have a quill or a small bulb dropper attached to the lid which is used to fill the pen.

Pencils

Drawings are generally made in pencil. Drawing pencils are made in various degrees of hardness, from *6B* (the softest) to *9H*

165

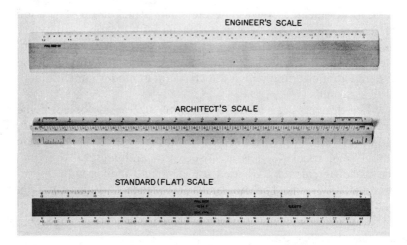

Fig. 16. Scales used by the draftsman.

(the hardest). The choice of hardness or softness depends on the type of drawing to be done and on the degree of precision desired. For ordinary work, such as when laying out house frames on a large scale, a *2H* or *3H* pencil is generally used. However, when drawing a roof-stress diagram, for example, for a scale of 1 inch = 2000 pounds, a pencil no softer than *H* should be used because a sharp point could not be maintained with a soft pencil, and precision could not be expected with a pencil having a blunt-like point.

Pencils are generally sharpened, with ⅜ to ½ inch of lead exposed, on a piece of sandpaper, as in Fig. 17, but some draftsmen prefer to sharpen them so the lead is wedge-shaped, as in Fig. 18. Many draftsmen prefer mechanical pencils, since leads of any desired hardness may be inserted instantly (Fig. 19). Sharpening of the leads is done on the sandpaper pad, and the leads may be used until they are quite short.

A mechanical lead pointer can also be used to sharpen the lead and in most cases is preferred by most draftsmen, Fig. 20. Once the lead is sharp the loose graphite should be wiped from the lead. The secret to good line quality is to keep a sharp point on the lead.

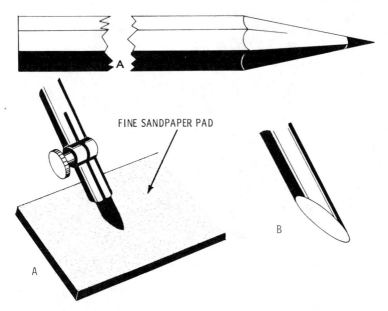

Fig. 17. Some draftsmen prefer to sharpen their drawing pencils to a conical point, as in A. The compass lead is normally sharpened as shown in B.

Fig. 18. The end and side views of a drawing pencil which has been sharpened with a wedge point.

Fig. 19. A typical mechanical pencil.

Erasers

Three kinds of erasers should be included in the basic drawing outfit:

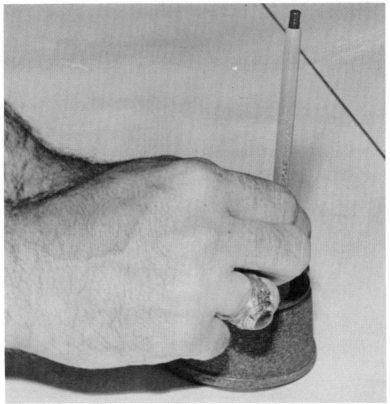

Fig. 20. A mechanical lead pointer which is used to sharpen the lead.

1. Pencil.
2. Ink.
3. Sponge (artgum).

For erasing any portion of a pencil line, a piece of prepared vulcanized rubber, small in size, and of rectangular shape, is best.

An ink eraser is made of a composition of rubber and ground glass, and it should be used sparingly on drawings because it roughens the paper and removes the gloss from its surface. Steel ink erasers (Fig. 21) are useful, although rarely used today, in

Fig. 21. A steel ink eraser.

removing defects, overrun lines, joint of lines if swollen, etc.; they have a fine point and can be used to advantage with a little practice; they are used with a scratching, not a cutting, motion, and they are available with replaceable razor-edge blades. If you do a great deal of pencil work, consider an electric eraser. There's a plug-in type and one that runs on batteries (Figs. 22 and 23).

Cleaning Powder

To keep the drawing clean while being worked on, cleaning powder is sprinkled lightly over the paper (Fig. 24). It readily absorbs graphite, dust and dirt. It is available in bag form or can be bought in small containers.

Electric eraser—Courtesy of Keuffel & Esser

Fig. 22. Electric eraser. Just plug it in and erase away.

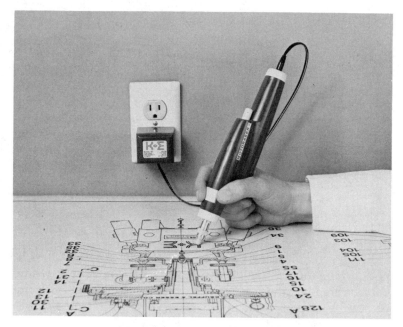

Battery operated eraser—Courtesy of Keuffel & Esser

Fig. 23. Battery-powered eraser being used with adapter.

Lettering Pens

Nearly all lettering is executed by a pen similar to a common writing pen but with a fine or wide point. The width of the point depends on the desired thickness of the letters. The pen must be kept clean at all times so that only clean-cut lines are obtained. Fig. 25 shows some usual styles of pens used for lettering.

Irregular Curves

For describing curves other than circles, special cut forms called irregular curves are used to guide the pen. These may be obtained in great variety. A set of two or three will frequently be found useful; several forms of these curves are shown in Fig. 26.

Protractor

This instrument is employed for laying off or measuring angles. Fig. 27 shows the ordinary form of protractor. Its outer

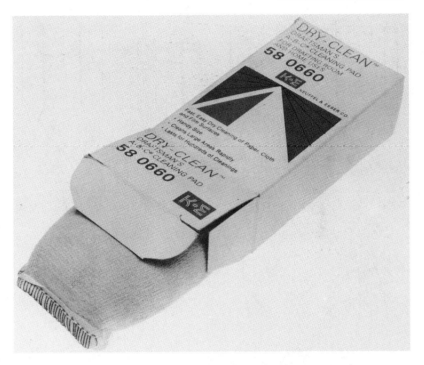

Fig. 24. *Cleaning powder used to keep drawing paper clean.*

edge, as shown in the illustration, is a semicircle with the center at 0; for convenience, it is divided into 180 equal parts, or degrees, from M to S, and in the reverse direction from L to F. Protractors are often made of transparent plastic to allow the drawing under it to be seen. A fine precision protractor is shown in Fig. 28.

HOW TO DRAW

In most drafting rooms the boards are covered with a removable and replaceable cover of some sort, either a heavy, hard and smooth manila paper or, preferably, a type of paper with a waterproof plastic glaze, which can be cleaned with a damp cloth. When dampened, or even under high air humidity, these plastic coverings are slightly inclined to expand and wrinkle until

171

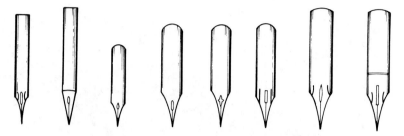

Fig. 25. Various shapes and sizes of lettering pens.

Fig. 26. Some typical irregular curves, which are quite useful when parabolic or elliptical curves are to be drawn.

dry; sometimes it may be necessary to loosen and restretch them, but on the whole they are satisfactory.

The drawing paper is stretched flat and smooth and is usually secured by means of small tabs of pressure-sensitive tape, as many as may be necessary. Use the T square to square the paper with the board. Most drawing is done directly on tracing paper of good quality which is normally purchased in rolls. Use pencils that are soft enough to make a good, legible black line. Prints may be made directly from the pencil drawing.

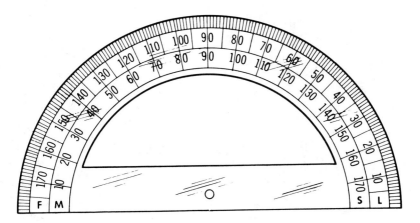

Fig. 27. A protractor is used to measure and lay out angles.

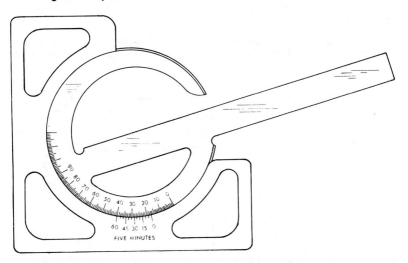

Fig. 28. A steel precision protractor. The blade is 8½ inches long, and graduations are read to degrees with a vernier reading to 5 minutes.

Straight Lines

To draw a straight line, use the T square or triangle, or both, depending on the direction of the line. Horizontal lines are drawn with the aid of the T square, as shown in Fig. 29; sometimes vertical lines are drawn by applying the head of the square to the lower, or horizontal, edge of the board.

173

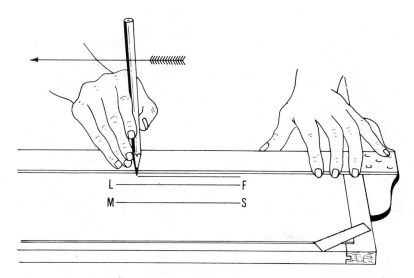

Fig. 29. Drawing parallel horizontal lines. The lines LF and MS are drawn by moving the pencil in the direction of the arrow, guided by the edge of the T square.

The usual method of drawing vertical lines is with the aid of both the T square and one of the triangles, as shown in Fig. 30. In this illustration, one of the legs of the triangle is used to guide the pencil. By using the hypotenuse of the 45° triangle, oblique parallel lines may be drawn, as in Fig. 31, and by using the hypotenuse of the 30° triangle, oblique lines may be drawn at 30° or 60°, as in Figs. 32 and 33.

By a combination of both triangles, as in Fig. 34, various other angles, such as 15°, 75°, 135°, may be obtained. Sometimes you may want to draw a line parallel to another line that is not inclined at any of the angles obtained with the triangles. This is done by placing the edge of one triangle parallel with the given line and sliding it on the other triangle, as in Fig. 35.

When drawing a line, it is important that the pencil be held correctly. Fig. 36 shows the wrong ways and the correct way to hold the pencil. It should not be inclined laterally, but in drawing a line (with either pencil or pen), it should be held with its axis in a plane perpendicular to the plane of the paper, slightly inclined

174

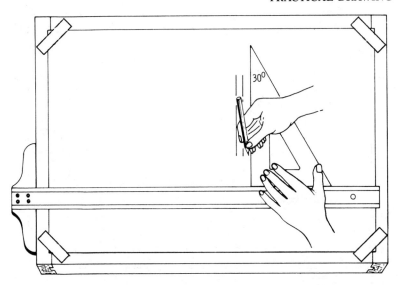

Fig. 30. Drawing parallel vertical lines with the T square and a right triangle. The triangle is held in contact with the T square and is shifted to any position where a vertical line is desired.

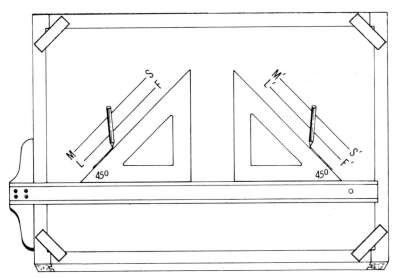

Fig. 31. Drawing parallel 45° oblique lines with a T square and a 45° right triangle.

175

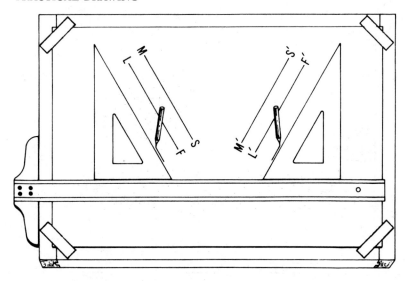

Fig. 32. Drawing parallel 60° oblique lines with a T square and a 30° right triangle.

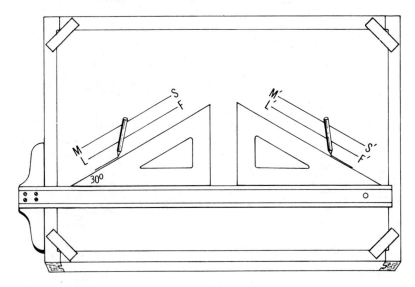

Fig. 33. Drawing parallel 30° oblique lines with a T square and a 30° right triangle.

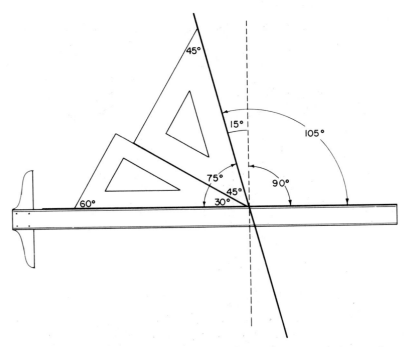

Fig. 34. The method of drawing angles other than 30°, 45°, or 60°.

in the direction in which it is being moved. If held as in Fig. 36A, the inclination is likely to vary, thereby resulting in a wavy line; if held as in Fig. 36B, a reference point R through which the line is to be drawn may not be visible or only partially visible. When held in a perpendicular plane, as in Fig. 36C, the line comes close to the lower edge, the reference point R can be plainly seen, and there is only a slight chance of drawing a wavy line. When drawing lines with a pencil which has been sharpened to a conical point, the pencil should be given a slight twisting motion while the line is being drawn; this procedure will tend to keep the point sharp. The line will also stay the same thickness.

Arcs and Circles

These are "described" with the compass. The compass and the proper positions for its use are shown in Fig. 37. Both points

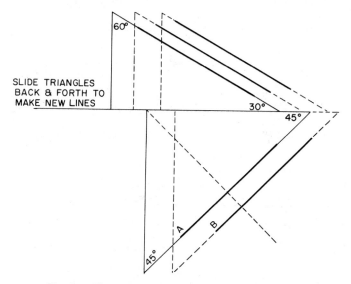

Fig. 35. The method of drawing slanting parallel
and perpendicular lines.

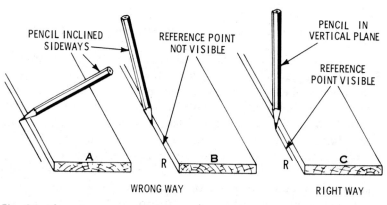

Fig. 36. The wrong ways and the right way of using the pencil to draw
lines.

should be approximately perpendicular to the paper, slightly inclined in the direction of movement. The starting position should
be such that the entire movement can be made in one continuous
sweep by grasping the handle at the pivot end by the thumb and

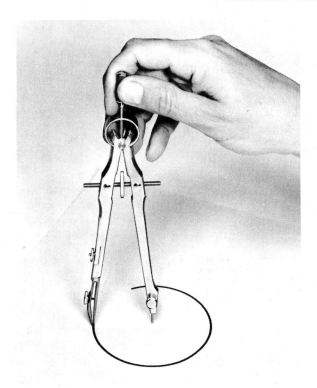

Fig. 37. The correct use of the compass. The compass is held by the handle only; the points are nearly perpendicular to the paper.

forefinger, thus obtaining a twisting motion by moving the thumb forward without stopping to shift the hold on the compass. Never hold the compass by the legs, even when the lengthening bar is used; to do so will tend to move the legs to a different radius, as shown in Fig. 38. Always have the center point in an upright position, otherwise indentation in the paper will be enlarged and untrue.

For extremely small circles, a smaller compass (called the bow compass) is used; it is more convenient and, having a screw adjustment, can be set with greater precision than the large compass. Particular attention is called to the result obtained by inclining the center point of a compass in describing circles, as

179

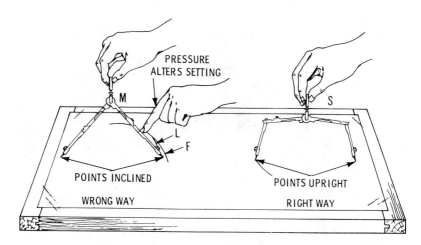

Fig. 38. The wrong way and the right way to use the compass when describing large circles. The points, especially the needle point, should be as nearly perpendicular to the paper as possible. Use only one hand to guide the compass, since the pressure of two hands may alter the setting, and part of the circle, as at L, will vary from the true path, F.

shown at S, Fig. 39. Since these centers must be used again if the drawing is inked, accurate work cannot be done if the center indentations are spoiled, as at S, by the wrong or careless use of the compass.

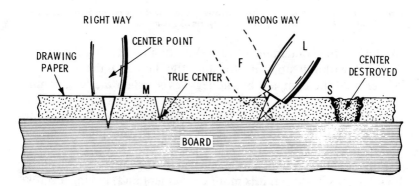

Fig. 39. The right way and the wrong way to position the center point of a compass. The center point of a compass should be provided with a shoulder, as shown, instead of being conical; this limits the depth of the indentation.

Spacing

Hair-spring dividers are used to accurately divide a given distance into several equal parts. If an exact length is to be laid off with the dividers, a large multiple of that length should first be laid off with the scale on a right-angle line and then exactly subdivided into the desired exact length by the dividers. This involves several trials. Set the dividers as close as possible to the desired length. Then test by spacing with the dividers along the line, as shown in Fig. 40. The setting of the dividers after each trial is adjusted by slightly turning the hair-spring adjustment screw until the correct length is obtained. For extremely fine divisions, the bow dividers are more conveniently used.

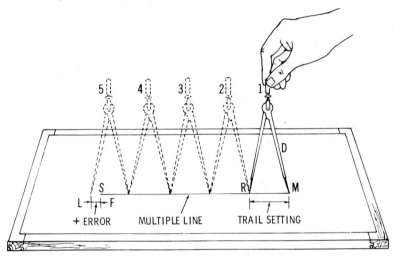

Fig. 40. Spacing with the dividers. To divide line MS into five equal parts, set the dividers "by eye" to ⅕ the distance, as MR. Space along the line by moving the dividers clockwise and counterclockwise to positions 2, 3, 4, and 5. If MR was taken too large, as shown by LF, adjust the setting, and respace the line until the correct results are finally obtained.

Hints on Penciling

The pencil drawing should resemble the ink drawing as closely as possible. A good draftsman leaves his work in such a state that any competent person can, without difficulty, ink in what he has drawn.

The pencil should always be *drawn*, not *pushed*. Lines are generally drawn from left to right and from the bottom to the top. Pencil lines should not be any longer than the proposed ink lines. By keeping a drawing in a neat, clean condition when penciling, the use of the rubber eraser on the finished inked drawing will be greatly diminished.

Inking

Very little inking is done in present-day drafting rooms because a pencil drawing usually prints satisfactorily. However, permanent or file drawings, or drawings intended for publication, may be inked. It should be pointed out that inked drawings make the clearest and, therefore, the best prints.

A drawing should be inked in only after the penciling is completed. Always begin at the top of the paper, first inking in all small circles and curves, then the larger circles and curves; next, ink in all horizontal lines, commencing again at the top of the drawing and working downward. Then ink in all vertical lines, starting on the left and moving toward the right; finally, ink in all oblique lines.

Irregular curves, small circles, and arcs are inked in first, because it is easier to draw a straight line up to a curve than it is to take a curve up to a straight line.

When inking in lines with a ruling pen, use it against the edge of the T square and triangles. The tool has two separate blades, or jaws, one of which is equipped with a spring to spread them apart. It is brought close to the other by an adjustable thumbscrew, or the blade is allowed to come away by turning the thumbscrew. In the better class of drawing pens, a hinge is wrought on one blade at the base, thus permitting the blade to open at a right angle so that it can be cleaned of any ink that may cake or adhere to it.

The drawing pen is applied by holding it perpendicular between the first and second fingers and thumb of the right hand, keeping the smooth blade close against the T square or triangle as required.

The ink is inserted between the jaws with a common writing pen or with the bulb dropper on the cork of the bottle of drafting ink, and any ink which remains outside must be cleaned off with a soft rag or piece of soft blotting paper. Similar directions must be followed when using the pen leg and point of compasses. The thicknesses of the lines are determined by the distance between the points of the blades; this distance is controlled by the regulating screw. By separating or bringing together the blades, a thick or thin line may be drawn, as desired. Arcs or circles are normally inked in by removing the pencil and inserting the pen end into the compass leg.

Using the technical pen is much less problematic. It is like using a regular pen. You just shake the pen to get an ink supply flowing, then use a straightedge or other template to make your mark. That's it. The width of the line is controlled by the nib size.

Drawing to Scale

Drawing to scale means that the drawing, when completed, bears a definite proportion to the full size of the particular part being drawn.

It must be understood that the scale on a drawing is not given for a shopman to take his dimensions from; such dimensions must all be taken from the dimension figures. The scale is only given for the draftsman's use, or for whoever may check the drawing, and also for the use of other draftsmen who may wish to make alterations or additions to the drawing at some future time.

Dimension Drawings

Every dimension necessary for the execution of the work indicated by the drawing should be clearly stated by figures on the drawing, so that no measurements need be taken in the shop by scale. All measurements should be given with reference to the base or starting point from which the work is laid out and also with reference to center lines.

There are two ways to dimension a drawing, the aligned system of dimensioning and the unidirectional system of dimensioning (Fig. 41). When using the aligned system, all dimensions are placed in line with the dimension line. If the unidirectional system is used, all dimensions are read from the bottom of the drawing.

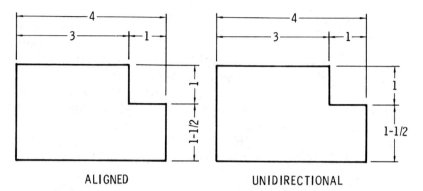

ALIGNED   UNIDIRECTIONAL

Fig. 41. The system of dimensioning.

There are certain types of lines used in dimensioning a drawing. The four basic lines are extension, dimension, center lines, and leaders (Fig. 42). Extension lines are extensions of the object lines. They start $1/16$ inch past the object and extend $1/8$ inch past the last dimension line. Dimension lines are placed between two extension lines and are terminated by arrowheads. In mechanical drawing, the dimension line is broken in the middle and the dimension is placed in the gap. In architectural drawing, the

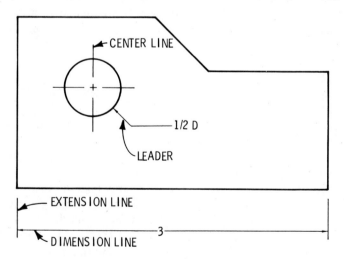

Fig. 42. Basic dimension lines.

dimension line is solid and the dimension is placed on top of the line.

Center lines are composed of long and short dashes and are used to locate the center of circles and cylindrical shaped objects. A leader is an inclined line that has a horizonal shoulder. The inclined line is terminated by an arrowhead and shows the location of a special feature.

All dimensions that a shopman may require should be put on a drawing, so that no calculations are required on his part. For instance, it is not enough to give the lengths of the different parts of the object, but the overall length, which is the sum of all these lengths, should be placed outside, in which case an arrow should be put in to indicate the proper position of the figures.

Lettering

When the information necessary to the reading of a drawing cannot be expressed by lines and scale dimensions, it must be indicated in the form of printed explanations, remarks, etc. Good lettering is not an easy task, and the totally inexperienced person should devote much time to practicing the art, working slowly. A great deal of time is required to make well-finished letters.

The character and size of the letters on all working drawings should be in harmony with the drawing on which they appear. It is desirable to have all lettering on a drawing made in the same style, differing only in size or finish of details. The lettering used on mechanical drawing is usually of the simplest character. The letters are composed of heavy and light strokes only; for headings, titles of large drawings, etc., comparatively large letters are used. However, the title should be conspicuous, but not too much so; subtitles should be made smaller than the main title. The "scale" and general remarks, which are usually placed in the margin of the drawing or near the title, should come next in size. All explanations and remarks on the view should not be larger than ⅛ inch. The vertical and inclined letters and figures shown in Fig. 43 are examples of the various sizes and styles often used.

After deciding on the size of the letters, lightly draw two parallel lines at a distance equal to the height of the letters. Good

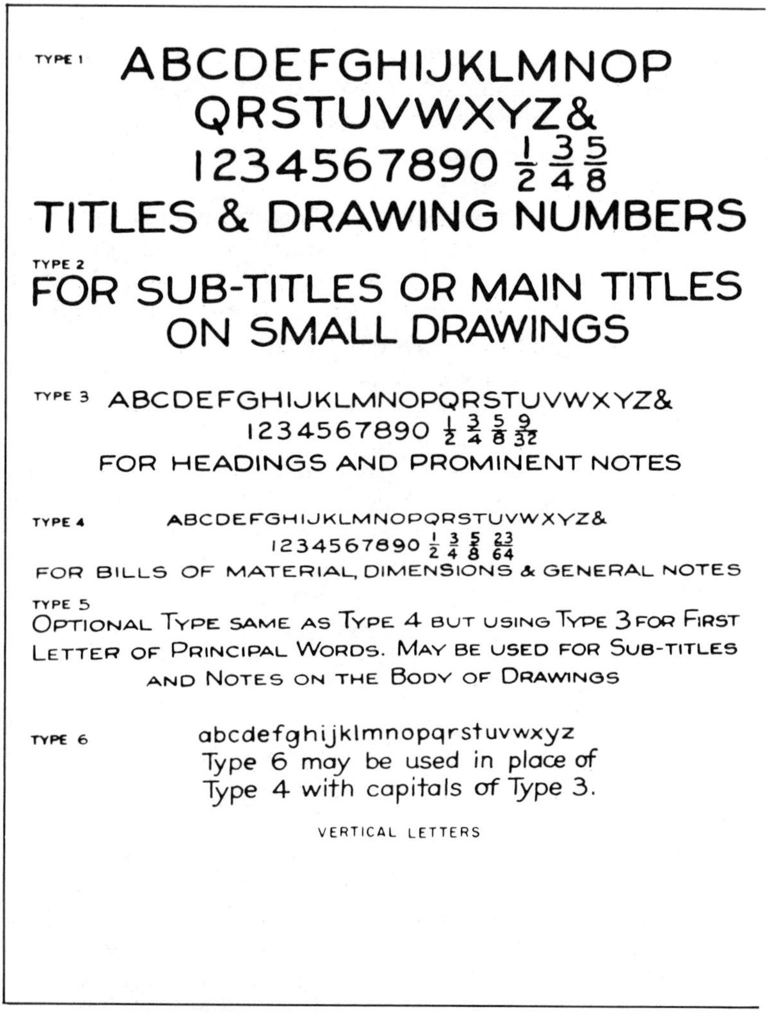

TYPE 1
ABCDEFGHIJKLMNOP
QRSTUVWXYZ&
1234567890 $\frac{1}{2}\frac{3}{4}\frac{5}{8}$
TITLES & DRAWING NUMBERS

TYPE 2
FOR SUB-TITLES OR MAIN TITLES
ON SMALL DRAWINGS

TYPE 3 ABCDEFGHIJKLMNOPQRSTUVWXYZ&
1234567890 $\frac{1}{2}\frac{3}{4}\frac{5}{8}\frac{9}{32}$
FOR HEADINGS AND PROMINENT NOTES

TYPE 4 ABCDEFGHIJKLMNOPQRSTUVWXYZ&
1234567890 $\frac{1}{2}\frac{3}{4}\frac{5}{8}\frac{23}{64}$
FOR BILLS OF MATERIAL, DIMENSIONS & GENERAL NOTES

TYPE 5
OPTIONAL TYPE SAME AS TYPE 4 BUT USING TYPE 3 FOR FIRST
LETTER OF PRINCIPAL WORDS. MAY BE USED FOR SUB-TITLES
AND NOTES ON THE BODY OF DRAWINGS

TYPE 6 abcdefghijklmnopqrstuvwxyz
Type 6 may be used in place of
Type 4 with capitals of Type 3.

VERTICAL LETTERS

Fig. 43. Vertical and slanted single-stroke Gothic

lettering requires considerable practice. Freehand lettering
should only be considered after the student is proficient in mechanical lettering; pencil-guide lines for letters and words should
be drawn. Letters should be placed so as not to interfere with

TYPE 1
ABCDEFGHIJKLMNOP
QRSTUVWXYZ&
1234567890 ½ ¾ ⅝ 7/16
TO BE USED FOR MAIN TITLES
& DRAWING NUMBERS

TYPE 2
ABCDEFGHIJKLMNOPQR
STUVWXYZ&
123456 7890 13/64 5/8 ½
TO BE USED FOR SUB-TITLES

TYPE 3
ABCDEFGHIJKLMNOPQRSTUVWXYZ&
1234567890 ½ ¾ ⅝ 7/16
FOR HEADINGS AND PROMINENT NOTES

TYPE 4
ABCDEFGHIJKLMNOPQRSTUVWXYZ&
1234567890 ½ ¼ 13/16 5/32 7/8
FOR BILLS OF MATERIAL, DIMENSIONS & GENERAL NOTES

TYPE 5
Optional Type same as Type 4 but using Type 3 for First
Letter of Principal Words. May be used for Sub-titles &
Notes on the Body of Drawings.

TYPE 6
abcdefghijklmnopqrstuvwxyz
Type 6 may be used in place of
Type 4 with capitals of Type 3

INCLINED LETTERS

characters are employed when lettering drawings.

the lines of the drawing and should clearly point out the part intended to be described. Any lettering on the drawing should be centered in the appropriate areas. It is a good practice to start with the middle letter of the inscription and work in both directions.

SUMMARY

A draftsman should use top quality instruments. There are many patterns and types of good drawing instruments currently available, and the would-be draftsman should purchase only the best and most suitable equipment for his particular needs. Drawing board, T square, triangles, pencils, compass, dividers, and technical pens are the main tools needed for general drafting work.

Drawing boards should be about 2 inches longer and 2 inches wider than the size of paper to be used. The edges of the board should be perfectly square to each other and smooth in order to provide a good working edge for the head of the T square to slide against.

The T square is used for drawing lines parallel to the lower edge of the board. It consists of two parts—the head and the blade, which are fastened at an angle of 90° to each other. A movable head or adjustable T square is also made, permitting a line to be drawn at an inclined angle to the edge of the board.

REVIEW QUESTIONS

1. What is the basic difference between a compass and a divider?
2. What is a T square and how is it used?
3. How is a protractor used in drawings?
4. What is a drafting machine?
5. Explain several advantages in purchasing good drafting instruments.

CHAPTER 5

How to Read Plans

There are various ways of representing objects in drawings, and a grasp of these different methods is essential if you are to read a drawing or blueprint well. The various methods of illustrating an object by a drawing are:

1. Perspective.
2. Oblique projection.
3. Isometric projection.
4. Orthographic projection.
5. Development of surfaces.
6. Sections.

Of these methods, the first three may be classed as "pictorial" in that they show the entire visible portion of the object in one view, whereas the fourth method requires several views to fully present the object and can be called "descriptive." It is this last method that is most generally used and requires a little study to understand.

A perspective drawing shows an object as it really appears to the eye, but it presents so many difficulties of construction that projection methods have been devised to overcome them. These projection methods will be considered before the perspective method.

OBLIQUE PROJECTION

In this system of drawing, the lines of an object are drawn parallel to three axes; one is horizontal, a second is vertical, and the third is inclined 45 degrees to the horizontal (Fig. 1). The horizontal axis lies in the plane of the paper, and the vertical and inclined axes lie in planes intended to appear to the eye as being at right angles to the plane of the paper. These axes lie in planes at right angles to each other and are known as the horizontal, vertical, and profile planes.

In cabinet projection, it should be remembered that:

1. All horizontal measurements parallel to the length of the object must be laid off parallel to the horizontal axis in their actual sizes.
2. All vertical measurements parallel to the height of the object must be drawn parallel to the vertical axis in their actual sizes.
3. It is not essential which side of the object is considered its length and which side is considered its thickness.
4. Place the principal face of the object parallel to the frontal plane of projection.
5. The receding line of the axes may be placed at any convenient angle, but a 45-degree angle is usually used.
6. In some cases the true length of the receding lines is reduced to one-half. This type of drawing is called cabinet projection (Fig. 2).

Steps in oblique drawing:

1. Draw the three axes OX, OY, and OZ (Fig. 3).

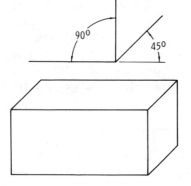

Fig. 1. **Oblique projection.**

Fig. 2. **Cabinet projection of a cube.**

2. Using the three axes, construct a box—use the correct dimensions (Fig. 4).
3. Block out any details and shapes (Fig. 5).
4. Darken all final lines (Fig. 6).

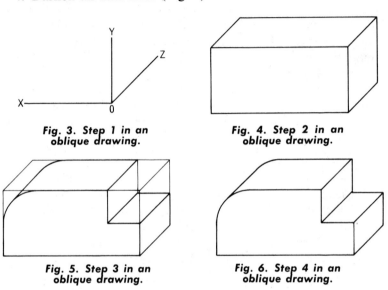

Fig. 3. Step 1 in an oblique drawing.

Fig. 4. Step 2 in an oblique drawing.

Fig. 5. Step 3 in an oblique drawing.

Fig. 6. Step 4 in an oblique drawing.

ISOMETRIC PROJECTION

By definition, the word "isometric" means equal distances, and, as applied here, an isometric projection is a system of drawing with measurements on an equal scale in every one of three sets of lines 120° apart and representing the three planes of dimension (Fig. 7). In other words, the axes are taken 120° apart,

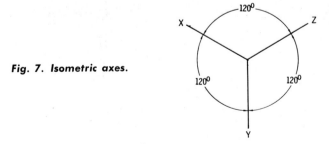

Fig. 7. Isometric axes.

and there is no profile shortening as in cabinet projection; all lines are drawn full length. Isometric projection also differs from cabinet projection in that none of the three planes lies in the plane of the paper.

If a line is parallel to one of the three axes, it is called an isometric line. However, if a line is not parallel to one of the three axes it is called a non-isometric line. A non-isometric line cannot be measured with a scale, but can be set off directly with the scale (Fig. 8).

Hidden lines are usually not used in isometric projection. They should be used only when a particular detail needs clarification. Center lines should also be used sparingly. They are used only to indicate symmetry, or they can be used for dimensioning.

1. Draw the three axes OX, OY, and OZ (Fig. 9). It is usually easier to lay out the angles for the bottom of the object. Using this technique, two 30-degree angles to the horizontal and one vertical line would be drawn.

2. Set off the dimensions of height, width, and depth (Fig. 10). These dimensions should be set off on one of the three axes.

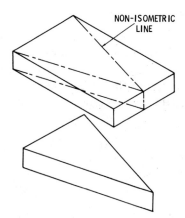

NON-ISOMETRIC LINE

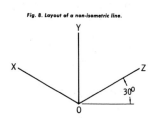

Fig. 8. Layout of a non-isometric line.

Fig. 8. Layout of a non-isometric line.

Fig. 9. Layout of the isometric axes.

3. Using the dimensions draw construction lines parallel to the axes (Fig. 11).
4. Block out any details and shapes (Fig. 12).
5. Darken all final lines (Fig. 13).

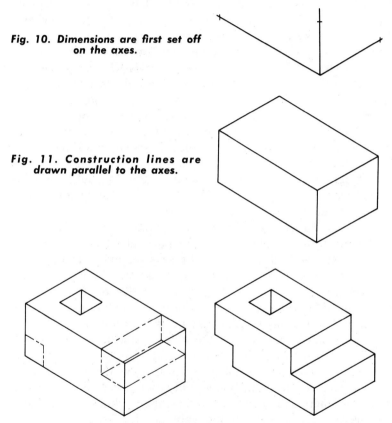

Fig. 10. Dimensions are first set off on the axes.

Fig. 11. Construction lines are drawn parallel to the axes.

Fig. 12. Details and shapes are blocked out.   **Fig. 13. Finished drawing.**

ORTHOGRAPHIC PROJECTION

Isometric drawing and cabinet projection are not very convenient methods to employ where it is necessary to dimension every part of the drawing for the purpose of reproducing it.

The most valuable use for pictorial drawings of any type—cabinet, isometric, or true perspective—is for comparison of two or more different designs, and to enable the draftsman or architect to show a design to best effect to a prospective client. Clients usually are not skilled in reading drawings. In such cases, architects often build extremely elaborate and expensive small-scale models, which are submitted to prospective owners. In any case, such pictorial drawings should not be sent to the shop or field. Foremen, superintendents, and other men in similar positions are used to reading the usual *working drawings* made by the orthographic projection method. The only requirements are that the drawings be legible and properly dimensioned.

In cabinet or isometric projections, three sides of the object are shown in one view, while in a drawing made in orthographic projection, only one side of the object is shown in a single view. To illustrate this, a clear pane of glass may be placed in front of the object intended to be represented. In Fig. 14 a cube is shown in a glass box. Now when the observer looks directly at the front of the object from a considerable distance, he will see only one side, in this case only the front side of the cube.

The rays of light falling on the cube are reflected into the eyes of the observer, and in this way he sees the cube. The pane of glass is placed so that the rays of light will pass from the object, through the glass in straight lines, to the eye of the observer. The front side of the object, by its outline, may be traced on the glass, and in this way a figure may be drawn on it (in this case, a square) which is the view of the object as seen from the front and is called the *front elevation*.

One view, however, is not sufficient to show the real form of a solid figure. In a single view, only two dimensions can be shown—length and height. Therefore, the thickness of an object will have to be shown by still another view, such as the top view, or *plan*.

Place the pane of glass in a horizontal position above the cube, as shown in Fig. 14; look at it from above, directly over the top face of the cube, and trace its outline on the pane. As a result, a square figure is drawn on the glass which corresponds to the appearance of the cube as seen from above. This square on the glass is the top view, or plan, of the cube. Fig. 14 shows

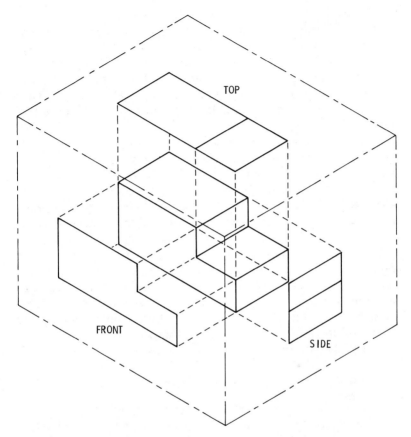

Fig. 14. *The various views of an object using the orthographic projection in which an imaginary pane of glass is placed in the different planes of projection.*

the manner in which a side view of the cube may be traced; the pane of glass is placed on the side of the cube, which rests on the table as before; the outline of the cube on the glass in this position is called its *side elevation*.

Usually, either two of the above mentioned views will suffice to show all dimensions and forms of the object, but to completely represent complicated objects, three or four views may be required. In complicated pieces of machinery, however, even more views may be required to adequately represent the proportions and forms of the different parts.

A drawing that represents the object as seen by an observer looking at it from the right side is called the *right-side elevation,* and a drawing showing the object as it appears to the observer looking at it from the left side is called the *left-side elevation.* In the case of a long object, a view at the end is called an *end view.* A view of the object as seen from the rear is called the *rear view* or *rear elevation,* and a view from the bottom is called the *bottom view.*

The different views of an object are always arranged on the drawing in a certain fixed and generally adopted manner. The front view is placed in the center; the right-side view is placed to the right of the front view, and the left-side is placed to the left; the top view is placed above the front view, and the bottom view is placed below it. The different views are placed directly opposite each other and are joined by dotted lines called *projection lines.*

With the aid of projection lines leading from one view to the other, measurements of one kind may be transmitted, or transferred, from one view to the other. For instance, the height of different parts of an object may be transmitted from the front view to either one of the side views. In a similar manner, the length of different parts of the object may be transmitted by the aid of projection lines to the bottom view and top view.

CENTER LINES

Objects that are symmetrical with respect to some axis drawn through their center are most easily drawn by first drawing this axis, or center line, and then drawing the object so that its center coincides with the center line. It is usual to make such lines broken by dots and dashes to distinguish them from the lines of the object.

Fig. 15A and B shows a rectangular built-up post drawn with center lines. Since the figure is symmetrical with respect to these lines, equal distances are conveniently spaced off from each side with the aid of dividers, and the drawing can be made quickly and with precision. To show the entire length of the post would require considerable space; it is therefore usual to "break it off," as at MS, by two ragged freehand lines, which indicate that part of its length is not shown.

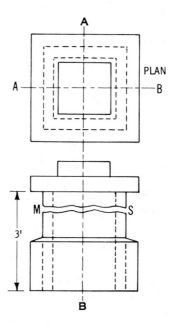

Fig. 15. *The orthographic projection drawings of a built-up post illustrate how to use center lines.*

Hidden Lines

Hidden lines are dashed lines used to describe details that cannot be seen (Fig. 16). These lines are just as important as visible lines. The dashes are about ⅛ inch in length and are separated by a $\frac{1}{32}$ inch gap. The dashes are not measured, but are carefully estimated.

DEVELOPMENT OF SURFACES

The principles of projection that have already been explained may readily be applied to the important problem of surface development. Whenever it is necessary to construct an object out of some thin material such as sheet metal, as in the case of elbows or tees for leader or stovepipe, the surface of the desired object is laid out on sheet metal, in one or in several pieces; these are called the *patterns* of the object. The pattern is first

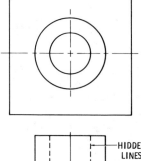

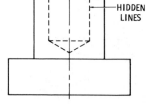

HIDDEN LINES

Fig. 16. Hidden lines are used to describe interior details.

laid out on the sheet metal and then cut out. When this is done, the separate pieces are ready to be fitted together to form the required object.

In all elbow work, the difficulty lies in obtaining the correct rise of the miter line. By the use of a protractor, this difficulty is overcome and the necessity of drawing a complete quadrant is avoided. The rise can be easily found when the throat and diameter of the pipe are known. Table 1 gives the rise of the miter line for elbows of various degrees and of various numbers of pieces.

The method by which the surface of an object is laid out on a plane is called the *development* of the object. A few exercises will sufficiently acquaint you with the methods used in problems of this nature.

Development of a Right Angle. A right-angle elbow is made by joining two pieces of pipe for the purpose of forming a right angle. It is really an intersection of two cylinders of equal diameters; the center lines of the two cylinders meet at one point, and since the joint is to be a right elbow, the center lines must be perpendicular to each other.

To develop the surfaces, divide the circumference of the cyl-

Table 1. Elbows

No. of pieces	Divide by	Degree of elbow	Rise of miter line
2	2	105	52½°
2	2	90	45°
2	2	70	35°
3	4	90	22½°
4	6	90	15°
6	10	90	9°

inder into any number of equal parts, and through the points of division draw lines parallel to the center line of the cylinder. On these parallel lines, mark the points which belong to the curve of intersection with another cylinder, or any other figure, and then roll out the surface of the cylinder into a flat plate. The rolled-out surface will be equal in length to the circumference of the cylinder. It will contain all the parallel lines which were drawn on the cylinder, with spaces between them just equal to the actual space between the parallel lines which were drawn on the surface of the cylinder. By marking the points of intersection on the parallel lines in the rolled surface, the development of the cylinder or its part is thereby obtained.

In Fig. 17, the circle showing the circumference of the pipe is divided into any number of equal parts by the divisions 1, 2, 3, etc. Lines are drawn through these divisions parallel to the center line of the vertical portion of the joint. The points on the parallel lines designate the curve of intersection. The development of the two branches of the right elbow is shown by the projection lines. The length of the development is equal to the circumference of the circle. To obtain this length, all spaces (1, 2, 3, 4, etc.) laid out on the circle in Fig. 17 are set off on a straight line; these spaces are marked by 1, 2, 3, etc. Perpendiculars 1I′, 2H′, 3G′, etc., on the elbow, are drawn through the points 1, 2, 3, etc., on the circle.

The required curve is traced through these points; the development 1I′I′1 is the pattern for the part of the right elbow shown in Fig. 17 as the circle. It will be noticed that the patterns do not

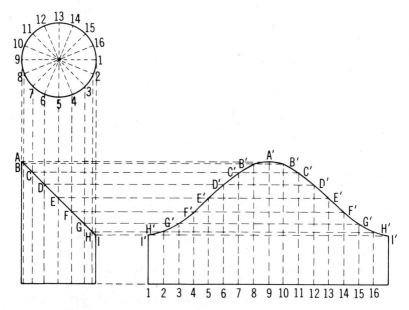

Fig. 17. The plan and elevation of a 90° pipe elbow illustrates the method of projecting dimensions for the development of a surface.

provide for the lap by which the two branches are held together. A lap of any desired width may be added to the pattern after it is constructed by drawing an additional curve parallel to the curve of the elbow pattern. The distance between the two curves is made equal to the width of the desired lap.

Sections

In many cases, an object cannot be adequately described with hidden lines. To help clarify the details, a section is made of a particular view. To make a sectioned view, an imaginary cutting plane is passed through the object and a portion of the object is removed, revealing the interior of the object (Fig. 18).

The cutting plane line is a dark dashed line terminated by arrowheads (Fig. 19). The arrowheads indicate the direction the observer is looking at the object. The area of the object that is touched by the cutting plane line should be cross-hatched. The cross-hatched lines (section lining) are usually drawn at a 45-degree angle and are drawn with a medium-grade pencil. The

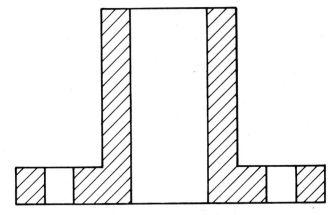

Fig. 18. A sectioned view.

Fig. 19. A cutting plane line.

cross-hatched lines are spaced by estimating the distance. The lines are usually spaced $1/16$ inch apart, but can vary from $1/32$ inch to $1/8$ inch. The distance between the lines depends on the size of the object.

There are five basic types of sectional views: full sections, half sections, broken sections, revolved sections and removed sections. A full section is drawn when the cutting plane line passes completely across the object and the front half of the object is removed (Fig. 20).

A half section is drawn when the cutting plane line passes only halfway through an object, Fig. 21. In a half section, one-quarter of the object is removed to show the interior details. In using this type of section both interior and exterior shapes and details can be shown. In most cases hidden lines are omitted from the half section unless they are needed for clarification.

A broken section is used to show only a small part of a particular object, Fig. 22. This type of section does not use a cutting plane line, but rather the location is indicated by a freehand break line.

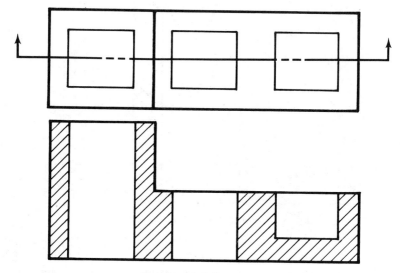

Fig. 20. A full section.

A revolved section is created when the cutting plane line passes through an object and the view is revolved to show the true shape of the object, Fig. 23. A revolved section is often used to describe the shape of spokes, arms, and cylindrical shaped objects.

A removed section is very similar to a revolved section, except the removed section is placed from its normal position to a more convenient location on the drawing, Fig. 24. It is not unusual to draw the removed detail to a larger scale. This is done to magnify any small detail that might need clarification.

PERSPECTIVE DRAWING

Perspective drawing is defined as the art of representing objects as they appear to the eye at a definite distance from the object. In orthographic (perpendicular) projection, the views represent the object as seen by the eye at an infinite distance. By the perspective method, then, the lines drawn from points on the object to the eye converge and intersect at the point of sight.

Before beginning the study of perspective projection, it is well

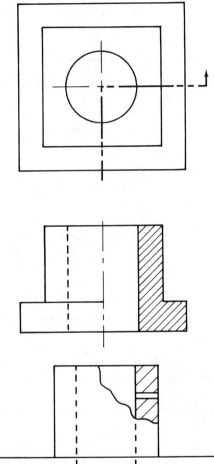

Fig. 21. A half section.

Fig. 22. A broken section.

to consider some of nature's phenomena of perspective. These phenomena become more apparent when we attempt to sketch from nature. We notice that the size of an object diminishes as the distance between the eye and the object increases.

If several objects of the same size are situated at different distances from the eye, the nearest one appears to be the largest and the others appear to be smaller, because they are farther and

203

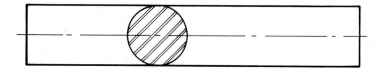

Fig. 23. A revolved section.

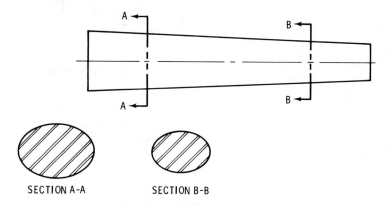

SECTION A-A   SECTION B-B

Fig. 24. A removed section.

farther away. At infinity, the distance between the lines becomes zero, and the lines appear to meet in a single point. This point is called the *vanishing point* of the lines, as shown in the two examples of Fig. 25.

By a closer investigation of a perspective drawing, it is found that:

1. The limit of vision is a horizontal line called the *horizon,* which is situated at the height of the eye.
2. Objects of equal size appear smaller with increasing distance.
3. Parallel lines converge into one point called the *vanishing point.* For horizontal lines, this point is situated at the height of the eye; that is, it lies in the horizon.
4. Vertical lines appear vertical.
5. The location of the observer's eye is called the *point of sight* and is located in the horizon.

A

B

Fig. 25. Perspective views with the vanishing point at the center of the drawing (A) and at the side of the drawing (B).

When an object in space is viewed, rays of light, called *visual rays*, are reflected from all points of its visible surface to the eye of the observer. If a transparent plane, Fig. 26, is placed between the object and the eye, the intersection of the visual rays will be a projection of the object on the plane. Such a projection is called the *perspective projection* of the object. The plane on

205

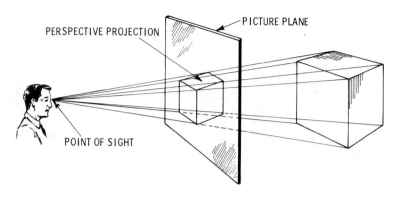

PERSPECTIVE PROJECTION

PICTURE PLANE

POINT OF SIGHT

Fig. 26. A picture plane illustrating the principles of perspective drawing.

which the projection is made is called the *picture plane*. The position of the observer's eye is the *point of sight*.

Perspective by Means of Plan and Elevation

This method of perspective can be put to practical use if we obtain a perspective projection in plan and elevation and then proceed by orthographic projection to obtain the perspective. Fig. 27 shows a prism in plan and elevation; its front face makes an angle with the picture plane. As a general rule, the object is placed behind the picture plane with one of its principal vertical lines lying in the picture plane. Point P is the point of sight (the observer's eye). Its distance A from the picture plane in the plan depends a great deal on the size of the object, and it is extremely important that the best viewpoint is obtained.

For example, if a house approximately 40 feet high is to be sketched, the point of sight should be taken at approximately 80 feet from the picture plane. A good rule to follow is to make this distance about twice that of the greatest dimension. When large objects are to be represented, the best results are obtained when the point is taken almost in front of the object. The distance of the horizon from the horizontal plane equals the height of the eye above ground and may be taken as approximately 5 feet 3 inches. For high objects, this distance may be increased; for low objects, decreased. In Fig. 27, it is shown slightly above the ob-

206

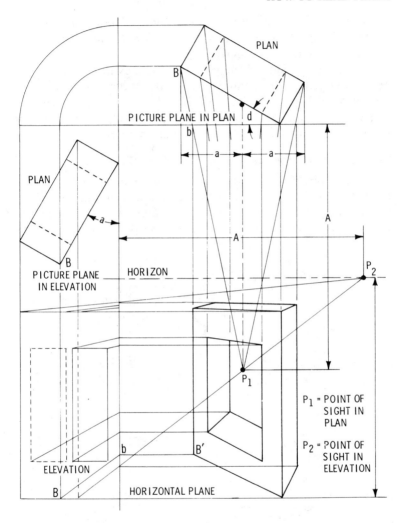

Fig. 27. *The perspective of a prism is drawn by means of the plan and elevation views.*

ject; P_1 is assumed on a vertical line halfway between two lines dropped from the extreme edges of the diagram. This is not necessary, but it usually ensures a more pleasing perspective projection.

207

To obtain the perspective of any point in the object, such as point B in Fig. 27, draw the visual ray in both the plan and elevation to P_1 and P_2, respectively. From the point of intersection b in the picture plane of the plan and the elevation, project perpendicularly, thereby obtaining point B_1 as the perspective picture of point B in the object. All the other points in the perspective are obtained in this way, and this method may be used wherever the plan and the elevation can be gotten.

Perspective by Means of Two Vanishing Points

An example of this method of perspective drawing is shown in Fig. 28, which illustrates a rectangular prism in plan and elevation resting on a horizontal plane. The first step in the construction of this drawing will be to redraw the plan, as with the first

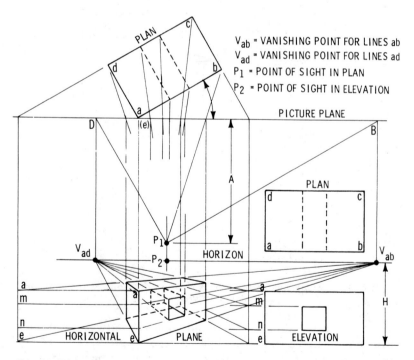

Fig. 28. The perspective of a rectangular prism by means of two vanishing points.

method, behind the picture plane in the plan, with the vertical line *ae* lying in the picture plane and positioned so that its long side makes an angle α (30°) with the picture plane. The point of sight P_2 is at a distance H above the floor and is located at the same height as the horizon.

Find the vanishing points for the different systems of lines in the object. There are three systems of lines in the prism; V*ab* and V*ad* are found by drawing lines P_1B and P_1D through P_1 parallel to *ab* and *ad* of the plan diagram and then dropping vertical lines from the intersection of these lines with the picture plane BD to the horizon, thereby producing the vanishing points V*ab* and V*ad*. The third system of lines embraces the vertical lines, which are actually drawn vertical and they are not converging toward one another.

The edge *ae* of the diagram lies in the picture plane and is called the *line of measures,* since it appears in its true size in the perspective view. From *a* and *e* in the perspective view, the lines will vanish at points V*ab* and V*ad*, respectively, thus establishing all the points desired by intersection with the vertical edges. In addition to this principal line of measures, other lines of measures may easily be established by extending any vertical plane in the object until it intersects the picture plane. This intersection, since it lies in the picture plane, will be shown in its true size, and all points in it will appear at their true height above the horizontal plane. If no line in the object lies in the picture plane, there will not be any principal line of measures, and some vertical plane in the prism must then be extended until it intersects the picture plane.

Instead of being some distance behind the picture plane, the prism might have been wholly or partly in front of the picture plane. In any case, find the intersection with the picture plane of some vertical face of the prism. This intersection will show the true vertical height of the prism.

Perspective by Means of One Vanishing Point

In this method, the plan is placed with one of its principal systems of horizontal lines parallel to the picture plane. This system, therefore, has no vanishing point, and since the vertical system has no vanishing point, only the third system of lines will

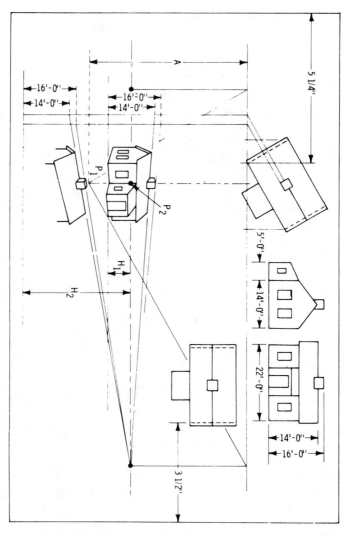

Fig. 29. The perspective of a house. The projections are given. The long side of the house makes an angle of 30° with the picture plane. The nearest vertical edge of the house is to lie in the picture plane. Two perspective views of the house will be obtained, since the house is viewed from two different points. Their common distance in plan A = 46'. The distances H₁ and H₂ of the point of sight above the horizontal are 6'6'' and 31'6'', respectively. The construction of both views is exactly the same.

have a vanishing point. In Fig. 30, the vertical face of the prism lies in the picture plane and is shown in its true size. Its edges are lines of measures. The construction of the perspective can be readily seen from the illustration. Another example of perspective by means of one vanishing point is shown in Fig. 31.

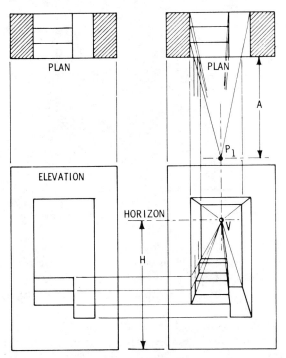

Fig. 30. The perspective view of a prism by means of one vanishing point.

SUMMARY

Various ways of representing object drawings are by perspective, cabinet projection, isometric projection, and orthographic projection. In cabinet projection drawings, the lines of an object are drawn parallel to three axes—one is horizontal, one is vertical, and the third appears to be inclined 45° to the horizontal. An isometric projection is a system of drawing with measurements on an equal scale in every one of three sets of lines 120° apart.

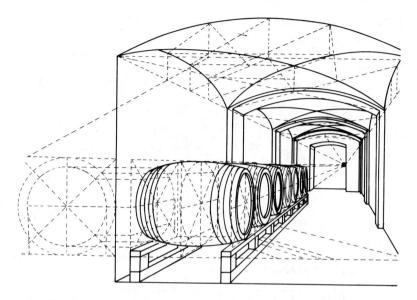

Fig. 31. The perspective of a row of barrels by means of one vanishing point.

In orthographic drawings, only one side is shown as compared to three sides of the object in cabinet or isometric projection. In orthographic drawings, it is not sufficient to show only one view. In some cases, many views must be shown in order to include important dimensions.

Perspective drawing is the art of illustrating objects as they appear to the eye at a definite distance from the object. In this type of drawing we notice that the size of an object diminishes as the distance between the eye and the object increases.

REVIEW QUESTIONS

1. What are the five methods of illustrating an object in drawings?
2. What is a conic section of a cone?
3. What are perspective drawings?
4. What is meant by the vanishing point in perspective drawings?
5. What is isometric projection?

CHAPTER 6

Architectural Drawing

It is always helpful for the neophyte in architectural drafting to have a background in building construction. Lacking this, he will find it difficult to avoid quite a few mistakes. It takes time before one becomes proficient enough to translate an architect's sketches, perhaps hastily done, into practical, workable drawings. We once saw an architect give a draftsman sketches on the back of an old envelope to "work out."

Almost invariably, the beginning architectural draftsman, who often has some good basic training and some real ability in simple drawing, will spend too much time on unimportant details. As a general rule, the draftsman should block out the plans and elevations before proceeding with the details. He should work out a definite system, blocking out the important parts—the overall dimensions—and then filling in the details. Sometimes the ¼-inch-scale working drawings are started at once and then altered as it is found necessary; a more usual preliminary is to make up sketches, perhaps freehand, with a ⅛-inch scale, which are then submitted to the client for approval. It is all right to copy other drawings, but this can result in difficulties for the beginning draftsman if he does not understand the underlying concepts.

Use a medium-soft pencil—*H, HB,* or *F.* These pencils require more frequent sharpening, but the lines are dense and black, erase more readily and print more clearly than the lines made with a hard pencil. Block in the outside walls first, then the partitions, doors, and windows. Most draftsmen prefer to work to the center lines of openings rather than to their edges.

Their positions may be influenced by the sizes of the furniture that will be used in the rooms or by the effect on the appearance of the outside. Almost without exception, Colonial-type homes have facades (faces or fronts) that are symmetrical about a center line. Even the chimneys are placed in the exact center of the roof, or two chimneys may be used, one in each gable. From the heating engineer's standpoint, inside chimneys are always preferable. Do not corbel a chimney out in the attic to make it loom large above the roof. It may be satisfying, architecturally speaking, but it is rather poor engineering because the enlarged top may prove to be an eternal nuisance from condensing creosote and water vapors in the smoke. Architecture, really, does not need to depend on fake details and the like for good appearance; when it deteriorates to that, it will no longer be an art.

You should consult a well-informed source, preferably an engineer, on questions concerning structural design. In general it is self-defeating to try to produce something that has not been done before. A certain amount of originality is desirable, but avoid very offbeat designs. They aren't necessarily good architecture, or even original architecture. In truth, very little architecture is original. Some "modern" architecture originated in the days of King Tut, and some of it looks like it. The type of architecture shown in Fig. 1 was developed thousands of years ago, but it is still in use in today's modern world. The Colonial types are nearly always pleasing, and will look good in almost any setting.

ARCHITECTURAL PRACTICE

It is, as it should be, the ambition of nearly every architectural draftsman to some day have his own architectural license and registration. Even though he is a graduate of an accepted architectural school, he must still pass an examination on the practical aspects of the profession, and a certain amount of practical experience is usually required. He must first learn his trade the same as a tradesman's apprentice before he can legally call himself an architect. He must also learn the duties of an architect, which go beyond making good drawings, though this is very important.

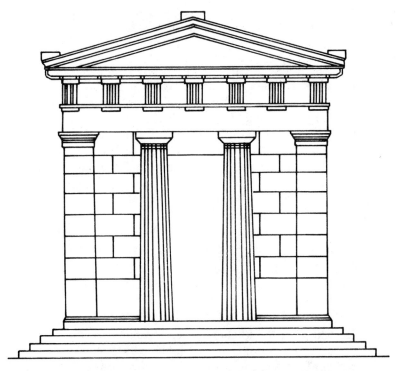

Fig. 1. The Temple of Diana Propylaea at Eleuses illustrates the characteristics of Greek architecture in its best and simplest form.

The first consultation the architect has with his client will usually result in the client setting forth what he wants or requires, such as the number of rooms, their sizes, the style of house he prefers, the kind of materials he wants to use, and probably that all-important factor—how much money he will need, or how much he has available. This first, or the first few, consultations may result in the architect making a dozen or more sketches. It is the architect's function to guide the client in such matters, for often, indeed usually, the client has no skill or aptitude for them. Later consultations may settle such things as lighting, heating, perhaps the quality and style of plumbing fixtures, and the make or quality of such appurtenances as air-conditioning, laundry, and dishwashing equipment. The architect usually makes sketches, probably freehands, for his client's approval. Among the many particulars that should be settled before the draftsman actually begins work:

1. The client may greatly prefer a house with a basement, but, perhaps for reasons of economy, he may be willing to accept a house on a concrete slab. The architect should be able to give him advice as to the advantages and disadvantages of the two systems along with the comparative cost of construction.

2. The client may have his mind set on a heating plant in the basement, but in the event that a house with no basement is agreed on, he should understand that the heating plant must be in a utility room.

3. He may insist that there be a well-equipped laundry in the basement. The client's wife may have some ideas on this subject.

4. He will probably insist that there be adequate closets for each bedroom. Again, the housewife may have some ideas as to exactly what "adequate" consists of.

5. He will want the kitchen to be convenient, with or without a garbage-disposal unit, probably with a dishwasher in a convenient location, possibly with room for a home freezer. The housewife again enters into the picture. Although "saving steps" is important to the housewife, sufficient room in the kitchen may be more important. Few housewives appreciate a kitchen that is too small—it greatly inhibits her style.

6. The client may wish a dining room, and not just "dining space" in one end of the living room, and he may think that a counter or bar and no partition between the kitchen and dining room is not sufficiently odor-resisting when cooking fish or corned beef and cabbage.

7. The client, or perhaps the architect himself, may have some ideas concerning privacy in the home. There may be some objections to "window walls" that are supposed to "bring the outdoors indoors," and a preference may be expressed for baseball-proof walls instead; perhaps the

housewife does not particularly like the idea of keeping large areas of glass clean and would be quite content to leave the "outdoors" outdoors if there is plenty of living space indoors.

8. Then there is the constant problem of sound resistance. Modern homes are often noisy, with air-conditioning, forced-heating, laundry, and dishwashing equipment, attic fans, kitchen fans, bathroom fans, radio and television, and many other noise-generating sources. It is the architect's duty and obligation to see that such noises are isolated insofar as is possible. Partitions should be noise-resistant, and plywood and pasteboard partitions definitely do not meet this requirement.

These are only a few of the problems of the modern home that the architect must understand; they are all with us and will probably be with us for many years to come. The client probably does not, possibly cannot, understand how to handle such problems. The architect can, and should. It is his function to guide his client's ideas or simple notions so that the home environment will be satisfactory as far as the client's means will permit. The architect will probably be blamed for any serious discrepancy, no matter if the client *did* insist on it. "He shouldn't have allowed me to do *that*," etc.

It is not only desirable, but absolutely necessary, that the good architectural draftsman be familiar with the dimensions of the equipment, furniture, and other appurtenances found in the home. While it is rarely necessary that they be accurately detailed, space must be allotted for each one of them, and space is expensive.

Almost all modern building is governed by codes of some sort. In all government-financed homes, the government's minimum standards are strictly enforced, and city codes are often much more restrictive. Electrical codes occasionally seem to be unreasonable, but the building designer must be governed by them. Plumbing is often, *too* often, seriously skimped when no one is watching. Many states have plumbing codes, but they do not have the force of law unless augmented and enforced by local authority. There is a National Plumbing Code and while it is

217

advisory, it is in line with good practice where there are no local codes. State and local boards of health may make it quite difficult for the designer of an inadequate plumbing system if the occasion arises.

For economy, kitchens and bathrooms should be placed back to back. A 3-inch copper soil pipe will fit into a partition of 2 × 4's whereas a 4-inch cast-iron soil pipe won't. In no case should two medicine cases be set back to back in the same partition. A conversation can easily be held through such an arrangement.

In perhaps most cases, the architect's duty is done when he prepares and delivers the drawings for a job. In some cases, he contracts to inspect the work at stated intervals, to assure that the work is satisfactorily done.

The draftsman should allow for the following thicknesses of walls in drawings:

1. Standard wood outside wall, ¾-inch wood or insulating board sheathing, 3½-inch studs, ½-inch sheetrock inside, 4¼ inches under the siding.
2. Inside partitions, 3½-inch studs, plaster ½ inch (both sides), 4½ inches.
3. Sound-resistant staggered-stud partitions, 3½-inch studs staggered 2 inches, gypsum lath and plaster (both sides) 7¼ inches.
4. Single-width brick veneer, ¾-inch sheathing, 3½-inch studs, ½-inch sheetrock, 9½ inches.
5. Concrete block, 8-inch plastered against the masonry, 8½ inches.
6. Concrete blocks, 8-inch, ¾-inch furring, ½-inch sheetrock, 9¼ inches.
7. Cavity masonry wall, 3¾-inch brick, 2½-inch air space, 4-inch concrete blocks, plaster on masonry, 10⅞ inches.
8. Chimneys—minimum wall thickness, 3¾-inch brick; liners, outside dimensions, 8½'' × 8½'', 8½'' × 13'', 8½'' × 18'', 13'' × 13''.
9. Ceiling heights—first floor, clear minimum, 7 feet 6 inches; basement, 6 feet 9 inches clear.
10. Stair wells—3 feet 2 inches × 9 feet, or clear head room 7 feet above nosing of treads, vertically.

AN EXAMPLE IN ARCHITECTURAL DRAWING

As an example in architectural practice, the series of illustrations presented in this section show the development of architectural drawings beginning with plans such as appear in newspapers and magazines from time to time. They give a prospective owner a good starting point, saving him much time and study, and they are appreciated by the draftsman who works up the final drawings.

Certain things, however, should be kept in mind. The magazine drawings were doubtlessly prepared by a registered architect. While the publishing of a design may imply that he has given approval that the design can be copied, it is best to get the written consent of the original designer, or at least to secure this consent from the publisher. A registered architect's plans are protected from being copied, and court decisions have ruled that minor changes, regardless of how many of them there are, do not release the copier from liability. Determine where you stand, legally, before copying designs of any sort. It may save you from a costly and embarrassing situation.

Let us assume that we start with the magazine plans shown in Figs. 2 and 3. These two plans were prepared by a capable and experienced architect who has given us a practical and logical arrangement of a house plan, with stairs, doors, windows, closets, etc.; he has also indicated a proper and reasonable size for the various rooms. Any proposed changes or additions that the owner may desire may be taken up with the architect or builder and may be easily whipped into form on his drawing board.

Conference with Builder

Let us now assume that the owner prefers to deal only with a carpenter or builder of his acquaintance, and asks him to prepare the drawings and give him an estimate on construction. We will also assume that while the builder understands his own business from start to finish, he does not pretend to be a good draftsman; he therefore calls us in for advice on the preparation of the drawings. Having decided on the main features of the plans and elevations, we will start with the first-floor plan of the

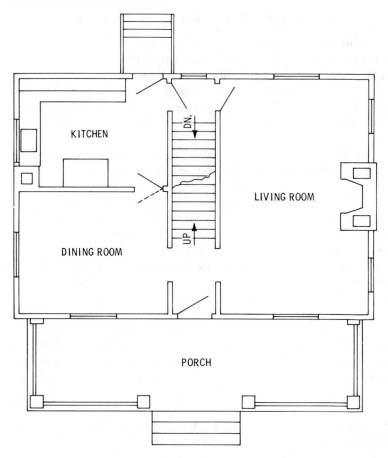

Fig. 2. First-floor plan from a magazine.

house, since that is always the controlling factor. Then, following the easy and usual method, we may trace the other plans (second floor and basement) over it.

Changes Agreed On

After a careful study of the first floor magazine plan, it is decided, first, to place the large chimney and fireplace inside the house against the stairs to conserve as much heat as possible, since considerable heat is necessarily lost from an outside wall.

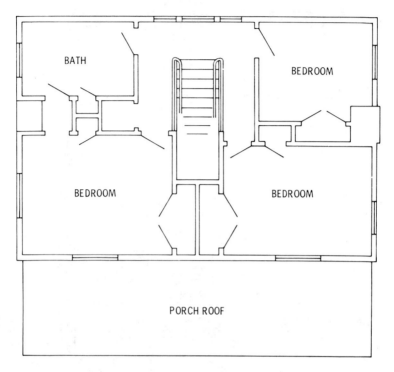

Fig. 3. Second-floor plan from a magazine.

Next, omit the kitchen chimney, since a gas range is to be used. Third, move the large porch to the end of the house, since it provides more privacy, and change the window to a door, as indicated in Fig. 4. Fourth, provide the paved entrance platform with a settee at the front entrance. Fifth, provide a coat closet at the front entrance. Sixth, enlarge the dining room, taking the space from the kitchen. Seventh, install a first-floor lavatory in the small new wing at the rear. These, along with other minor changes, such as turning the back steps, adding two small closets near the fireplace, and substituting round for square porch columns, create a much more convenient and valuable first-floor plan. The principal second-floor changes are made to save cost and involve a lowering of the front eaves line and decreasing the size of the front rooms.

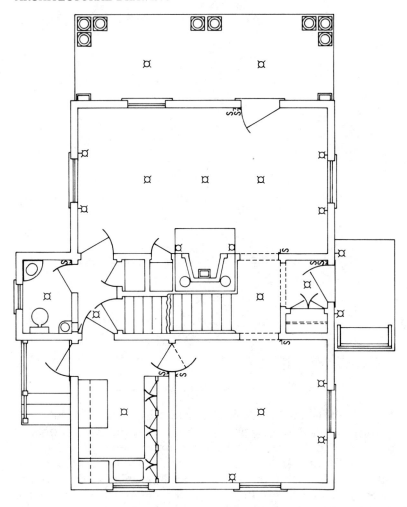

Fig. 4. The modified first-floor plan.

Drawing

Draw in light lines with an *H* or an *F* pencil the outside walls and inside partitions without regard to openings (doors and windows), stairs, chimney, fireplace, closets, stoops, porches, or any other of the many details to be shown later. The main center lines may now be drawn in lightly. This, then, completes the first stage of the work. For sheetrock construction, outer walls are to be drawn 6½ inches thick if plaster and lath are used, room partitions, 4½ inches thick, and closet partitions, 3 inches thick. They would be thicker if plaster and lath were depicted. Fig. 4 shows the modified first-floor plan after the changes have been agreed on, and Fig. 5 illustrates the completed drawing of the

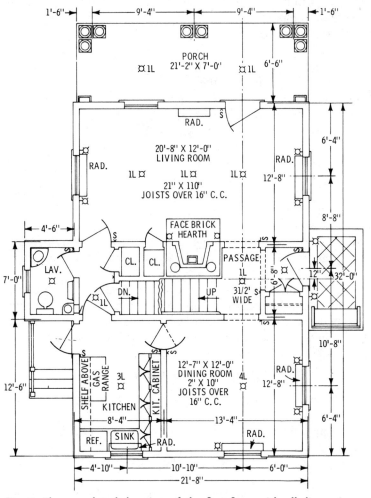

Fig. 5. The completed drawing of the first floor with all dimensions and specifications in detail.

first floor, with all the specifications and dimensions given in full detail.

SUMMARY

In architectural practice, the architect usually makes several sketches, probably freehand, for his client's approval. Among the many particulars which should be settled before the draftsman actually begins work are: will there be a basement, which determines the location of the heating plant; how many closets in each bedroom; will there be kitchen conveniences, like a garbage-disposer unit, dishwasher, and room for a home freezer.

These are only a few of the problems of the home that the architect must understand. The client probably does not know how to understand and handle such problems. The architect should know how to handle these problems and guide his client so that the home environment will be more than satisfactory when the work is completed.

It is absolutely necessary that a good architectural draftsman be familiar with the dimensions of the equipment, furniture, and other appurtenances found in the home. Electrical codes occasionally seem to be unreasonable, but the building designer must be governed by them. Plumbing is often seriously skimped unless local authorities have some kind of a ruling enforcing certain regulations.

Many times the future owner prefers to deal only with a carpenter or builder, and asks him to prepare the drawings and give him an estimate on construction. The builder therefore calls the architect in for advice on the preparation of the drawing.

REVIEW QUESTIONS

1. What must an architect know from his client before drawing up plans for a house?
2. Is it generally a good idea to change floor plans after construction has started?
3. Is the kind of material used in the construction important to the architect?
4. Is wall thickness, plumbing, and electrical wiring considered when drawing up plans?

CHAPTER 7

Specifications

By definition, a specification is a specific and complete statement detailing the nature and construction of the item to which it relates; as applied to the building trades, specifications describe briefly, yet exactly, each item in a list of the materials required to complete a contract for building an entire project.

Great care should be used when writing specifications to avoid misunderstandings and disputes. Each item entering into the construction should be defined and described with precision so that there can be no chance of misunderstanding or double interpretation. The language should be simple and brief. For the guidance of architects in writing specifications, the American Institute of Architects has prepared a number of sample documents, and these should be carefully studied and consulted by the architect when writing specifications for building and construction of any size project.

Specifications should refer to the contract form of which they are to become a part. This saves repetition of statements with regard to liability of contractor, owner, etc. The following is an example of specifications as ordinarily prepared by an architect.

Specifications
for
a frame dwelling

to be built for Mr._____of_____
in the county of_____and state of_____
on lot number_____on the_____side of _____

street in the city or borough of_____, county of
_____, state of _____. These
specifications relate to a set of attached drawings consisting of:

1. Plan of foundation and basement.
2. Plan of first floor.
3. Plan of second floor.
4. Plan of roof.
5. Four elevations.

(eight sheets in all)

Detailed working drawings to be furnished as required, all of which are a part herewith, and are to be considered as such with any contract that may be made.

Height of Ceilings—The following dimensions for these heights are:

Basement to be ....7 feet 2 inches clear of finish
First story to be ....8 feet 6 inches between timbers.
Second story to be ....7 feet 6 inches between timbers.

Interpretation of Drawings—For arrangement of floors, general finish, and measurements, reference must be made to the drawings. However, should any difference appear between the scale measurements and the figures, or between the wording of the specifications and the lettering on the drawings, the specification shall in all cases take precedence. If any error that is not explained either by reference to the drawings or specifications becomes apparent, the contractor shall refer them to the architect for correction before proceeding with the work.

Conditions—The contractor must see that all the work on the said building is performed in a thorough, workmanlike, and substantial manner by competent workmen and must also furnish all materials (the best of their respective kinds), labor, implements, transportation, etc., if not otherwise specified.

All painted parts of the exterior must have a prime coat of paint as fast as it is ready. The succeeding coats must not be applied within 3 days of the former, and then not in wet or freezing weather or other conditions specified by the paint manufacturer.

The contractor must protect all work while the building is in his hands, remove all superfluous materials or rubbish, and not obstruct the grounds around the foundation for grading and filling in as soon as the building is up. Figures are to take precedence over scale measurements.

Mason's Work—Excavate to the length, breadth, and depth required for the foundations, as shown on the architect's drawings. The top soil is to be removed and placed in a separate pile from the other excavated materials—25 feet away from the excavation where directed. Also, excavate for a septic tank and overflow 75 feet from the foundation, as will be directed, containing 28 cubic yards to be built of concrete, with baffles, drains, etc., all of which is set out in a special plan for same. The septic tank may be included in the plumbing subcontract. The main tank must be waterproof, although the overflow need not be. The tank shall be connected to the house at a point below the lowest fixture and below the frost line with a uniform declination of not less than 12 to 20 inches and will have no running U trap. The drain is to be made of 6-inch socket-jointed Transite tile laid in tight cement joints from a point 4 feet outside the foundation.

Foundation—Foundations and footings, as shown on the plans, are to be made of poured concrete with 8-inch walls and 16-inch footings.

Chimneys—Build two chimneys, as shown, of the same size and shape. Use an approved hard-red-pressed brick for all exposed parts of the outside chimney and for topping out. The fireplaces in the parlor, dining room, and bedroom are to be faced with the same brick (smooth inside the fireplaces), with 8 inches on the sides and 24 inches at the top. Buff the joints, and straighten the arches on 3½″ × 3½″ angle irons, unexposed. Use fire brick for the backs; lay the bricks in an approved refractory mortar (no fire clay). Spring trimmer arches for the hearths are to be laid with the same selected brick. All flues are to have tile linings, approved chimney pots, and clean outs.

Mortar—All mortar for brick work is to be grade specified by building code regulations

Installing Drywall—All walls, partitions, and ceilings, and all studded and furred places in all stories, are to be covered with ½-inch-thick Sheetrock, which will have joints covered with tape and joint compound. Two coats of compound will be used where wallpaper is used, three coats where paint is to be used. Panels used shall be 4 feet by 8 feet and will be installed horizontally on walls, across the framing members on ceilings. The panels are to be secured with 1⅜-inch blued ring shank nails and pieces staggered. Inside corners of the paneling shall be covered with inside corner molding, with nails placed 7 inches apart. Outside corners shall also be covered with metal molding. All joints will be smooth to the touch.

Tiling—The floors of bathrooms will be tiled with 3″ × 3″ octagonal and 1-inch-square vitrified tiling, colors to be selected. The side walls will be tiled 4 feet high of plain white glazed 2½″ × 4″ molded base and nosing, with a narrow tinted stripe at the top of the sanitary base and under the nosing. The floors will be properly prepared by the carpenter by setting the rough floor ½ inch below the top of the floor beams. All tiling will be set in adhesive recommended by the manufacturer, and the floors will be finished flush with the wood finish floors.

Other Floors—There will be a concrete floor in the furnace room, in the shop, and in the area from the west end turning east to the cross wall, as shown in the plans. All floors will be 3⅝ inches minimum, with 6″ × 6″ × No. 11 reinforcing mesh. The kitchen hearth will be built in the same manner.

Coping—There will be 4-inch caps of blue stone on all piers showing them, edged on four sides, 3 inches larger than the piers. Cope area walls, which are to be 8 inches, with 2″ × 10″ blue stone where circular, fitted to radius. *No* patching of stone will be permitted.

Timber—All timber will be thoroughly seasoned, No. 1 common pine, square, straight, and free from any imperfection that will impair its durability or strength. *No* individual piece is to have a moisture content of more than 19%; the architect will check this.

Framing—The framing will be as indicated on the drawings. Headers over openings will be the sizes indicated in detail. *No* header with a checked moisture content of over 15% will be acceptable. Frame so that sheathing will be flush with the foundation wall. All moldings are to be miter-spliced and mitered at angles. *No* butt ends will be showing in the finish.

Timber sizes will be as follows:

Sills .... 2″ × 8″
Girders .... 10″ standard I beams (25.4 pounds)
Corners .... 4″ × 6″ backed with 2″ × 4″
           or built up
Main plate .... 4″ × 4″ (2″ × 4″ doubled)
Rafter plate .... 4″ × 4″ (2″ × 4″ doubled)
Studding (general) .. 2″ × 4″
Closet studding ..... 2″ × 3″
Main rafters .... 2″ × 6″
Dormer rafters ..... 2″ × 4″
Ridge boards .... 1¼″ × 8″
First floor joists .... 2″ × 10″
Second floor joists .. 2″ × 8″
Second story
   ceiling beams .... 2″ × 6″

Spacing and Bridging—Place all studding, floor, and ceiling joists on 16-inch centers. In every span of flooring exceeding 10 feet, there will be a row of 1″ × 2″ bridging or 2″ × 3″ doubled nailed at each end. Rafters will be placed on 24-inch centers.

Partitions—All partitions are to be set plumb, well braced, and nailed; studs at all angles and openings are to be doubled, and extra block is to be set at door openings for base nailing. All partitions that are not supported below are to be firmly trussed and braced. Ceilings to all closets will be furred down to within 12 inches of the door head except in closets over 2 feet deep. Trued ⅞-inch grounds at top of base and around all openings.

Table 1. Relative Hardness of Woods

Shell Bark Hickory	100	Yellow Oak	60
Pignut	96	White Elm	58
White Oak	77	Hard Maple	56
Dog Wood	75	Red Cedar	56
Scrub Oak	73	Wild Cherry	55
White Hazel	72	Yellow Pine	54
Apple Tree	70	Chestnut	52
Red Oak	69	Yellow Poplar	51
White Beech	65	Butternut	43
Black Walnut	65	White Birch	43
Black Birch	62	White Pine	30

Lumber—All outside finish lumber will be clear white pine unless otherwise specified. All exterior finish lumber is to be free from large or loose knots and will also be clear and thoroughly dry.

Sheathing and Sheathing Paper—Cover all the exterior walls with ¾-inch plywood sheathing nailed to each stud with 8d nails. With joints cut on studs or backed for end nailing, cover with 15-pound tarred felt, well lapped and extending under all trim and around all corners to make a complete and tight job.

Exterior Finish—Windows, door casings, cornices, corner boards, water table, brackets, band courses, etc., are to be made to the detail furnished in the drawings. The stock moldings that are to be used are numbered on the drawings. The first story is to be covered with the best grade cedar lap bevel siding, laid at 4½ inches to the weather. The second story and gables are to be covered with 18-inch hand-split and resawn shakes, laid at 8½ inches to the weather. Use hot-dipped galvanized nails, whose length will be approved by the architect. Window casings will be laid 2½ inches to the weather, and the front door frames and casement windows will be according to detail shown in the plan.

Shingling—Cover all roofs with 8″ × 16″ Pennsylvania blue slate, laid 7 inches to the weather. All hips and other parts that require it are to be made secure against leaks by the proper use of slaters' cement and proper flashings. An ornamental galvanized-iron ridge crest will be placed on the main ridge; see details on drawings for this crest.

Flashing—Flash around chimneys, over all doors and windows, heads exposed to the weather, and where roofs join walls with 16-ounce sheet copper. Do the same in all valleys and wherever required to secure a tight job. Each side of the valleys is to have a water check turned up 1 inch in the metal.

Flooring—First and second stories are to have double floors, with a subfloor of $1'' \times 6''$ tongue and groove sheathing laid diagonally. The first- and second-story finish flooring is to be oak tongue and groove strip flooring, which is to be thoroughly seasoned and blind nailed over building paper. There will be no joints in the main hall and only one joint in the run of boards in other rooms of the first floor. The second-story floors are to be cleaned and sandpapered to a smooth finish for the painter. Oak thresholds are to be set to all outside doorways, and hard rubber-tip door stops are to be located behind all doors that open against a wall.

Window Frames—These are to be made of seasoned white pine.

Sash—All sash and frames are to be made by the Johnson Corporation and are to be of kiln-dried, vinyl sheathed white pine; the numbers are given on the drawings.

Screens—All windows that open are to be fitted with bronze- or copper-wire window screens.

Glazing—All sash and outside doors, where indicated, are to be glazed with Johnson insulated windows or their equivalent. All hall doors are to be glazed with French plate; the plate in the Dutch door will be beveled. The basement sash is to be glazed with a single strength glass.

Blinds—All windows, where indicated, are to be provided with an approved type of blind that will be 1⅛ inches thick and made of the best grade of seasoned white pine; all blinds will move freely after painting. The blinds are to be hung on approved cast-iron blind hangers.

Door Frames—All inside door frames in finished parts of the house, first and second stories, are to be made of white pine $^{25}/_{32}$ inch thick, set plumb and true, and blocked in four places on each side. Outside door frames are to be rabbeted for doors. All frames are to be flush with the plaster finish.

Doors—Unless otherwise specified, all inside doors are to be made of slab-type birch veneer with hollow cores and will be 1⅜ inches thick. Outside doors are to be 1¾ inches thick and will be made of solid-core, slab-type birch veneer. The front doors are to be of the design shown in the drawings. Hang all doors throughout with loose-joint ball-tip butts of sufficient size to throw them clear of the architraves. Doors are to have three 3½″ × 3½″ butts on 1⅜-inch doors and three 4″ × 4″ butts on 1¾-inch doors. A hardware schedule will be furnished. Hang both double-swing butlery doors on double-acting brass spring hinges. Furnish all nails, except those used for inside work, galvanized and all other hardware that will be necessary for the completion of the work in the proper manner.

Interior Trim—For the basement, the interior trim is to be selected cypress or redwood. For the first and second floors, the trim is to be unselected birch. There will be a 4-foot 6-inch paneled wainscoting in the dining room, first floor hall, and up stairway; this panel will be made of ¼-inch birch plywood, with trim as shown in the details. There will be a 5-inch cabinet plate shelf in the dining room, the bottom member of which will be a picture molding; this shelf will match the door head trim.

Stairs—The main staircase is to be made of unselected birch. The stringers and treads are to be 1⅛ inches thick, as shown in details. The risers are to be ¾ inch thick. The risers and treads are to be housed into the wall stringer and return-nosed over the outside string. The rails are to be 3″ × 3″ molded, with ramps as shown in the details. Balusters will be 1⅝ inches, taper turned, three to a thread, and proportionately more for increased widths. Newels and column newels are to be as shown in the details. The run on the first flight is to be 10¼ inches from face to face of the rise with 12-inch treads; the second flight and basement stairs are to be 9¾ inches of run with 11½-inch treads. For the basement stairs, cut 2″ × 12‴′s for the stringers and 2″ × 10″ yellow pine for the treads.

232

Mantels—There will be two mantels where indicated on the drawings. The contractor will figure them to cost $2000 each complete, including linings and face and hearth tile. This amount will be allowed the owner to use at his, her, or their option in the selection of same. The entire cost is to be figured in the contract price, including the setting of the mantels by the contractor.

Pantry Cabinets—There will be a cabinet, where indicated, with three glass doors, above the draining board; this cabinet will be 10 inches deep inside and will contain three shelves. The wall cabinets are to be constructed as shown in the details.

Closet Shelving—The trim on the inside of the cabinets is to be plain. There is to be an average of 10 feet of 12-inch shelving to a closet, with 6-inch clothes strips and 1 dozen clothes hooks, japanned. The kitchen closet and the closet under the kitchen stairs are to have suitable shelving and sufficient pot hooks and other fixtures. There will be 25 feet of shelving in the shop closet. There will also be 1 dozen clothes hooks under the basement front stairs.

Plumbing—All necessary materials for completing the plumbing installation, as hereafter set forth, in a correct and sanitary manner are to be included in the general contract. The state plumbing code shall be strictly followed.

Electric Wiring—No. 12 Romex sheathed cable is to be installed under and subject to the requirements and regulations of the *National Electrical Code* and all state, county, and municipal codes. The locations for all electrical outlets will be shown in the drawings.

Water Pipes—Water is to be brought from the street main into the house through ¾-inch copper tubing, or plastic if preferred. Copper water tubing is to be used on all straight-line work. Place a hose-bib cock on the main at a point against the house for hose purposes, both front and rear, with a stop and waste cock in the basement. Complete all necessary digging for the laying of sewer and water pipes to the house; no trenches are to be less than 36 inches below the grade at any point. The pipes are to enter the house in the basement at a suitable point for intersection with the inside piping system. The dirt is to be well rammed over the pipe in the trenches as it is refilled. The house sewer is to be installed by the plumber and it will consist of a perfect 4-inch glazed socket-jointed tile pipe to a point exactly 4 feet outside the foundation wall; the soil pipe is to be 4-inch cast iron. All water pipes must have a gradual fall from the fixtures which they supply, and they must open at their lowest point for drainage purposes. All the cast-iron waste pipe will be furnished with the necessary fittings. Furnish and install one 60-gallon gas-fired water heater of an approved type and manufacture; this water heater is to be supplied with water through a ¾-inch copper tube. Place a shutoff cock on the supply pipe. Take hot water from the water heater to and over the kitchen sink and to all other fixtures, except toilets, with ½-inch copper tubing. The supply to the toilets will be through ⅜-inch copper tubing. Cold water to all fixtures will be through separate pipe lines. There must be no depressions in any pipe, and hot water must be kept rising from the boiler head.

Kitchen Sink—Furnish and install a cast-iron enameled kitchen sink, with a garbage disposer of (*specify make and model*). Furnish and install an automatic dishwasher (*specify make and model*) where indicated in drawings.

Wash Trays—Provide and install where indicated on drawings, one two-part stone tub on galvanized iron legs. Supply the tub with hot and cold water through ½-inch copper tube and brass faucets, one for cold water, threaded 1½ inches waste, with traps, plugs, and chains complete. The waste drain is to be connected with the soil pipe through a 2-inch copper pipe.

Bathroom Fixtures—All bathroom fixtures are to be (*specify name of manufacturer*) make, as listed in their catalog. The basement bathroom water closet will be (*name and model*); lavoratory, (*name and model*); bathtub, 5-feet 6-inch (*name and model*). The other toilets are to be (*name and model*). The two second-story baths are to be (*name and model*), 18″ × 27″. Before any wall finishing is done, all supply pipes must be proven perfectly tight by a satisfactory test, and they must be left perfect at the completion of the test.

Painting—The entire exterior woodwork, except shingles, is to be painted with three coats of (*manufacturer's name*) best grade of ready-mixed paints, thinned as necessary and as specified by the manufacturer. The color of paint will be plain white, except for the shutters and shakes, which will be green and will be given two coats of (*manufacturer's name*) shake and shingle finish. The second-story floors will be sanded smooth and given three coats of (*manufacturer's name*) polyurethane varnish. The first-story floors are to be left bare for wall-to-wall carpeting or vinyl tiling. All interior birch trim is to be finished natural, with one coat of white shellac and two coats of (*manufacturer's name*) of flat varnish. The type and color of the interior wall paint for all interior walls will be specified by the owner.

Condition of Bids—The owner reserves the right to accept or reject any or all bids.

SUMMARY

A specification is a statement containing a detailed description or enumeration of particulars, as of the terms of a contract, and details of construction usually not shown in an architectural drawing. Great care should be used when writing specifications to avoid misunderstandings and disputes. Each item entering into the construction should be defined and described with such precision that there can be no chance of misunderstanding or double interpretation.

Framing will be indicated on the drawings. Specifications as to type of timber used, such as No. 1 common yellow pine, square, straight, and free from any imperfections that will impair its longevity, will be indicated. Headers over window and door openings will be indicated as for size and installation procedure.

Interior trim, including stair casing, will be shown. Moldings used throughout the house will indicate miter angles and type of lumber used. Ceiling height, as well as plastered or dry-wall construction, will be specified. Most plastered walls will be specified as to type of finish coat, which in most cases is at the option of the owner, and will also specify that exposed corners be protected with metal corner beads.

All necessary materials for completing the plumbing installation, as set forth in the specifications, shall meet all state and local regulations. All electrical wiring will be listed and must meet the requirements and regulation of the *National Electric Code* or state or local codes.

REVIEW QUESTIONS

1. Why should great care be used when writing specifications?
2. What information should be included in the specifications on framing a house?
3. What code should be followed when plumbing a house?
4. Can specification on a dwelling be changed or altered? If so, how?
5. What code should be followed when electric wiring is installed?

CHAPTER 8

Barn Construction

In practically all parts of agricultural United States, horses no longer furnish the power necessary to produce farm crops, and except in very isolated cases, horse barns and stables are but rarely found on farms; therefore, no horse barns are being built. However, there is still a need for dairy barns, and for structures that, depending on the area, must stand up to quite a lot of stress from weather. In the northern dairy region—Michigan, Wisconsin, Minnesota, and North Dakota—valuable dairy herds must be housed in substantial buildings that will keep the animals comfortable and healthy.

Farther south, in Ohio, parts of Michigan, Kansas, and Nebraska, there are less stringent demands, but there must be barns where animals can thrive.

At one time, barn design stressed the interior storage of hay and feed, but this emphasis has been dropped because feed and hay are now stored outside the barn proper, reserving the structure for the animals.

There are three basic kinds of barn design: the gambrel, the Gothic, and the pole. The first two refer to roof style, while the third reflects the type of foundation used. Although the gambrel and Gothic are still being built in some instances, the overwhelming favorite of today's farm builder is the pole-type construction where the barn rests on poles sunk in concrete-filled holes in the ground. As we shall see later in the chapter, this type of barn is easy and fast to build and economical, yet it can stand up to weather stresses and the like well.

FALSE ECONOMY AND STORM DAMAGE

In recent years, great emphasis has been placed on economy in construction. While economy is of vital importance, in some cases this has been carried to the point where strength and safety have suffered. If a building is to endure and give satisfactory service, something more than bare minimum construction is required.

The maintenance on jerry-built farm buildings is high, and insurance on them has become expensive. Windstorm damage of a farm building involves not only the cost of the building but also the damage or loss of the contents. The hazard to human life is usually not great, since only a few persons are in barns and outbuildings during windstorms, but a profitable herd of dairy cattle may be almost entirely destroyed. Insurance, no matter how complete the coverage, never includes compensation for the inconvenience caused by the loss, or the loss of income entailed. Indeed, the animals usually cost more than the barn.

While it is possible that no wood-framed barn building can be designed to withstand the full force of a tornado, some buildings are damaged much less than others. Examination of the wreckage, and of buildings that partially withstood the fury of the storms, emphasized the following:

1. Foundations were heavy. Poured concrete was better than concrete blocks. In any case, the buildings were firmly anchored to the foundations. Anchorage of the studs to the sills was equally vitally important.
2. The frames were adequately braced. Many owners emphatically disapprove of inside bracing, which restricts headroom or interferes with the desired use of the inside space, but the fact remains that good bracing is necessary if any significant degree of storm-resistance is to be built into the structure. In some cases the builder can reduce the objection by careful planning of the placement of the bracing.
3. Decay and termite damage seriously weaken otherwise good framework. All such damage is repairable, but if it is neglected too long, repairs become so expensive as to be impractical.

BARN DESIGNS

The builder is advised to confer with specialists on the subject when designing barns. Engineers in the Agricultural Engineering Departments of the various state universities should be consulted. Working drawings of approved construction are available from the Midwest Plan Service at all midwestern land-grant universities, or they are obtainable from the headquarters of the MPS at Iowa State University, Ames, Iowa. The cost of these services is usually free or nominal, and no builder can afford to ignore these sources of dependable information.

Naturally, the arrangement of the interiors of such buildings will be planned for efficiency, and labor-saving equipment of all kinds will be employed as fast as its use is recognized as economical. Since the methods of operating dairies are changing, the plans of barns now in use will certainly become obsolete in the future, and in most cases, well-built barns can be remodeled to accommodate more efficient equipment.

The large hay-mows necessary in years past are no longer required. Hay is now almost always chopped, or baled in the field, and much less storage space is required than when loose forage was used. It is much easier handled mechanically in this form, either in overhead or ground-level storage. In stall barns with mow storage, the high gambrel and Gothic roofs may now be made much lower and therefore less wind-vulnerable than formerly. This is academic in most areas of the country, however, because, as mentioned, the overwhelming favorite in barn design is the pole type.

When designing structures to resist winds, no separate provisions can be made for windward and leeward sides, since winds may come from any direction. Nails and spikes are efficient fastenings, within their obvious limitations, but in highly stressed joints some type of stronger fastenings may be desirable. For fastening planks (such as ties or rafters) to round poles, Table 1 may be informative. The figures given are based on the results of actual testing. Such companies as Teco also make special framing fasteners.

What follows is a close look at the construction of the three main types of barns.

Table 1.   Strength of Various Fastenings

These fastenings are inserted through pre-bored holes in 1 5/8 inch lumber into the round sides of pressure-creosoted southern yellow pine poles, with 4 7/8 inch to 7 7/8 inch diameters.

	Test load at .01 in. slip (pounds)	Recommended design loading (pounds)
5—40d plain common nails	2550	940
5—60d plain common nails	3660	1450
5—40d helically-threaded nails	2510	1210
5—60d helically-threaded nails	2180	1050
15—40d plain common nails	6310	2610
15—40d helically-threaded nails	5960	3080
2—2-1/2-inch split-ring connectors	6330	2990
3—5/8-inch bolts	7320	2720
2—1-inch bolts	6950	3120

Design loads contain a reduction factor of 4 1/2 applied to the average ultimate loadings.

(Abridged from a paper given by John N. Walker and Harold V. Walton at a meeting of American Society of Agricultural Engineers, Ithaca, New York, June, 1959. Testing done under direction of H. V. Walton at Pennsylvania State University, 1958.)

GAMBREL ROOF

The gambrel roof was especially adaptable to mow-type barns where large storage space was needed for hay. Loose hay is bulky, a ton occupying about 450 cubic feet. In barns designed for loose hay feeding the roofs were often very high, with vertical side walls in the mow of 4 to 8 feet.

The modern dairy barn is also frequently gambrel roofed, but the lower or stable story is now generally lower than in the older barns—only about 8 feet clear. The modern mow has no vertical side walls, the rafters setting on a plate at the mow floor line. This makes the modern building much lower than the ones built years ago, and consequently the modern building is less vulnerable to storms.

Very little loose hay is stored in barns, as mentioned. Baled loosely, a ton of hay will occupy 200 cubic feet, and baled tightly, from 150 to 170 cubic feet. Chopped hay, blown loosely into the mow, will occupy approximately 170 cubic feet per ton, and put through the hammer-mill, it may occupy only 100 to 130 cubic feet per ton. Today's barn, with hay storage overhead, requires only a third to a half as much dry forage space as formerly to feed the same number of animals for the same length of time.

It is not the intention here to discuss the interiors and mechanical equipment of such barns. Such arrangements may soon become passé, and mechanical equipment is constantly being developed and improved. The builder must be familiar with the equipment that will be used, for often special provision must be made for this. The following power-operated equipment is found in many dairy barns:

1. Ventilating fans.
2. Mechanical gutter cleaner.
3. Mechanical manure conveyor, or stacker.
4. Silo unloaders.
5. Feed conveyors.
6. Mechanical hay driers.
7. Milking equipment.
8. Milk cooling and handling equipment.

PLANS AND PERSPECTIVES, GAMBREL-ROOFED BARNS

Fig. 1 is a plan of a dairy barn, 36'0'' × 86'0'', with stalls for 20 cows. It may readily be lengthened, preferably in 4'0'' multi-

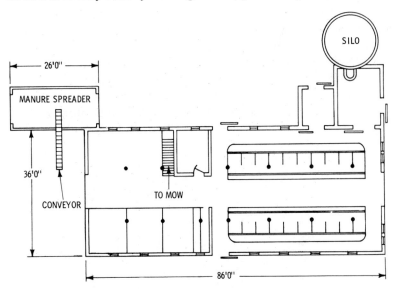

Fig. 1. A plan of a dairy barn for 20 cows.

ples, but the 36'0'' width is standard for stall barns with the cows facing outward and a drive through the center. The left-hand end of this plan is presumably loose pens for dry cows, heifers, and calves, but by housing them elsewhere the number of stalls may be increased to about 32. The milk-house may be attached to the barn at any convenient location.

Fig. 2 shows the perspective of a barn of this description with a gambrel roof. Fig. 3 is a cross-section showing the type of framing when trussed rafters are used.

GOTHIC ROOF

Fig. 4 shows a barn with the same 36'0'' width as in Fig. 2, but with a Gothic roof and bent laminated rafters. Fig. 5 shows the general roof framing. Factory-built arches of this description are obtainable from prefabricating firms, through your lumber dealer, or they may be built up on the site. With the quality of materials and workmanship required, it is doubtful that a builder inexperienced in arch fabrication can compete with factory-fabricated ones. Fig. 5 is an illustration showing the general appearance of this roof framing. The storage capacity of both the mows shown in Figs. 3 and 5 may be estimated at about 1 ton of loose-baled hay per lineal foot.

Gothic roofs of this type are popular, and their appearance is exceptionally good. In most tests, however, either in the laboratory wind tunnel or under actual storm exposure, they do not usually show the wind resistance of well-built braced-rafter gambrel roofs or pole-construction barns. In fact, properly built

Fig. 2. A gambrel-roof dairy barn. The oldest dairy barn design.

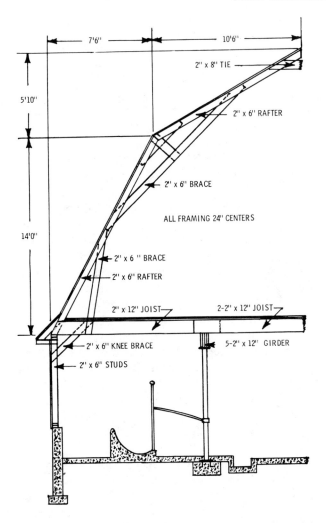

7'6"   10'6"

2" x 8" TIE

5'10"

2" x 6" RAFTER

2" x 6" BRACE

ALL FRAMING 24" CENTERS

14'0"

2" x 6 " BRACE

2" x 6" RAFTER

2" x 12" JOIST   2-2" x 12" JOIST

2" x 6" KNEE BRACE   5-2" x 12" GIRDER

2" x 6" STUDS

Fig. 3. The trussed-rafter gambrel barn roof.

roofs of the other types have in many cases shown really re-
markable wind resistance, even though the sheathing and roof
coverings have been ripped off during windstorms.

Fig. 4. A dairy barn with a low Gothic-type roof. An extremely good appearing structure, and extremely practical.

FOUNDATIONS

Solid foundations for barns are preferably of poured concrete, because of its stabilizing weight and the facility with which the framing may be tied to the foundations. Above grade, the walls may be of hollow masonry, but the anchor bolts should extend down through the masonry and be embedded in the concrete. In a foundation of the type shown in Fig. 6, the wall below grade is 9 or 10 inches thick, above grade it may be 8 inches. It is desirable that the foundation extend down below the frost line. Where there is some ground cover, frost over most of the midwest rarely penetrates deeper than 36 inches. In northern Michigan where there is no ground cover (as in feed lots and roadways), there are records of frost penetrations to 54 inches, while in parts of Minnesota and North Dakota, 60 to 72 inches have been recorded. It is doubtful, however, if there is any serious danger of frost damage to foundations 48 inches deep, even in these areas.

Fig. 6 shows one of the most effective methods for tying the studs to the sills. A 30-inch strap of 18-gauge *galvanized* steel is passed under the sill, bent up on both sides, and nailed to the edges of each stud. There is usually no difficulty encountered in placing these ties, even after the frame is erected. If the nuts on the anchor bolts are loosened the sill may be wedged up and the ties slipped under. Such ties are symmetrical on both sides of the studs, and are economically sheared in any sheet-metal shop. Nails *can* be driven through 18-gauge metal, but with some difficulty. Some care must be taken when setting the anchor bolts so that they do not interfere with the straps. At the

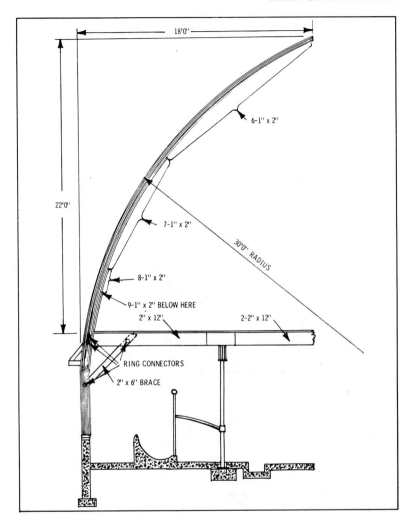

18'0''

22'0'

6-1'' x 2''

7-1'' x 2''

30'0'' RADIUS

8-1'' x 2''

9-1'' x 2'' BELOW HERE

2'' x 12''

2-2'' x 12''

RING CONNECTORS

2'' x 6'' BRACE

Fig. 5. *The Gothic-roof bent laminated dairy barn frame. Such arches are obtained from commercial fabrications.*

top, a similar metal strip about 20 inches long should be used to tie the rafters to the studs. Incidentally, the junction of the rafters with the plate is one of the most critical of all the joints in the frame.

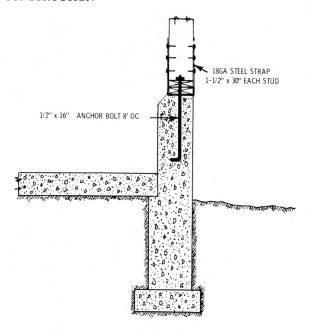

18GA STEEL STRAP
1-1/2" x 30" EACH STUD

1/2" x 16" ANCHOR BOLT 8' OC

Fig. 6. *A poured concrete foundation for a dairy barn, showing an excellent method for tying sills to the foundation. Through the cyclone belt, some designers prefer to place the anchor bolts 5 feet on center instead of the standard 8 feet.*

LOOSE-TYPE BARNS FOR DAIRY HERDS

Throughout Ohio, Indiana, lower Michigan, Kansas, and Nebraska, where winters are relatively mild and snowfall not usually heavy, most dairy farmers prefer loose-type shelters for the animals. This enables the animals to move about freely, with access to a mechanical feeding "bunk" and to a feeding-fence along a ground-level hay storage barn, and to a common water supply instead of the individual drinking cups that are necessary in the stall barn. Many more animals can be handled in this way (where climate permits) and a great deal less labor is required.

A layout for such a building is shown in Fig. 7. As the layout shows, there are facilities for 100 head of milk cows and up to 80 dry cows and heifers. Up to at least 150 milk cows could be

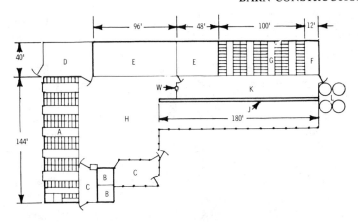

Fig. 7. A layout of a modern dairy barn using the pole-type building. A. loose-stall barn for 100 cows; B. milking rooms; C. holding pens for milk cows; D. manure storage, paved; E. ground-level hay barns, with feeding fences; F. bedding storage; G. loose-stall barn for heifers and dry cows; H. paved lot, for producing cows; J. mechanical feeding bunk; K. paved lot, for heifers and dry cows; L. silos; W. water supply.

handled if the dry cows and heifers are sheltered in other buildings.

The layout shown will certainly not be satisfactory for all dairy farmers. Orientation is important, for the open sides of the buildings should face away from prevailing winter winds, and a maximum amount of sunlight is desirable. The holding pens are preferably roofed, and in all cases should be sheltered from the wind. The areas around drinking water, feed bunks, and self-feeding areas, should be paved. Some states *require* 75 to 100 square feet of paving per cow. Cleaning of such areas is easier done with a tractor equipped with a scraper blade, and suitable gates or exits should be provided for this purpose.

POLE-TYPE BUILDINGS

The most popular barn design, the pole-type, requires no foundation. The buildings are mounted on round pole vertical members that are set in the ground and adequately anchored to resist uplift. For most buildings of appreciable size, the poles are set in round holes about 5 feet deep. Projecting nails or lag screws are placed in the pole 6 or 8 inches from the bottom, or holes are bored through which tight-fitting pieces of rod are driven to project a couple of inches on each side. After the poles are placed and positioned in the holes provided, about 12 inches of concrete is poured around the bottom ends and the holes filled with earth.

Satisfactory joining of rafters and other framing members to the round poles may be made by properly using any standard connecting device, including plain bolts, split-ring connectors, toothed-ring connectors and plain-shank common nails.

The idea of the pole-type building is not new. This type of construction was well known at least 75 years ago, but it was generally used only on inexpensive and temporary buildings. The modern pole building can hardly be placed in this category. The poles used are now pressure-treated with a preservative such as Penta or a water-borne type preservative and have a long life even under most adverse conditions. Modern timber fastenings are far superior to anything that our forefathers had available.

Where rafters or trusses connect to the poles, it is preferable that the poles be flattened at the contacting surfaces. Cast-iron spike-grids with one side curved to conform to the round side of the pole have been satisfactorily used; however, simple bolts are also often used.

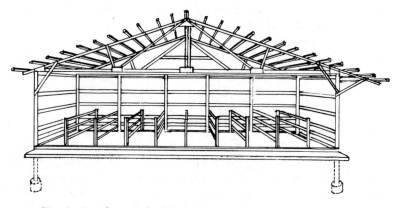

Fig. 8. A pole-type building showing loose stall construction.

The builder and the prospective owner may be interested in the survey made by investigators at the University of Missouri regarding relative depreciations on farm buildings. Their findings were as follows:

1. Pole-frame hay and feeding barns, no foundations, 4.04% per annum.
2. Conventional-framed hay and feeding barns, stone or concrete foundations, 2.20% per annum.
3. Dairy barns, conventional framing, concrete floors and foundations, 2.55%. These figures, of course, do not include losses from obsolescence, fires, or acts of God. The pole-frame building is by far the most economical to build, and although maintenance will be much higher than on the conventional building, this may be largely or entirely offset by the lower first cost of the pole building.

Fig. 8 is a perspective cross-section view (indicated at A and G in Fig. 7) of the loose-stall barn, an enlarged detail of the framing being shown in Fig. 9. These illustrations show a trussed, self-supporting roof with 2 × 6 knee braces. Working drawings for other types of trusses are available from many sources.

Fig. 10 is a cross-section of the hay-storage barns (E) with "feeding fence," indicated in Fig. 7. The widths of such buildings may be from 24 to 48 feet, and of any desirable length. The roof shown is not trussed, but the roof rafters (or beams) are heavily braced. Mechanical pilers are often used in such hay barns, and so the side walls may be from 14 to 20 feet. Where pilers are used, bales piled 200 feet high are common. Trussed roofs are often used in buildings of this kind, eliminating the inside poles.

SUMMARY

The builder is advised to consult a specialist on the subject when designing a barn. Today, great emphasis is being placed on economy in construction. While economy is truly of vital importance, the trend in many cases has been carried to the point

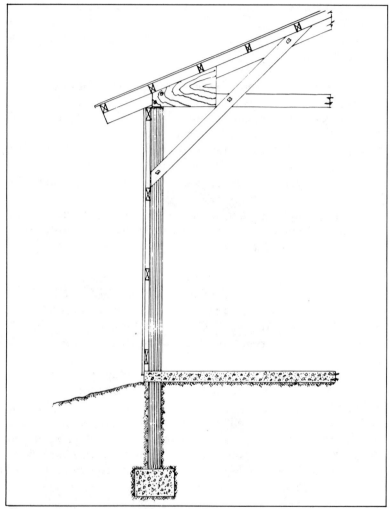

Fig. 9. Enlarged detail of a pole and truss connection.

where strength and safety have suffered. If a building is to endure and give satisfactory service, something more than bare minimum construction is demanded. In the northern states where the dairy industry is large, substantial and tight buildings must be built to house dairy herds and protect them from winter temperature and heavy snowfall.

250

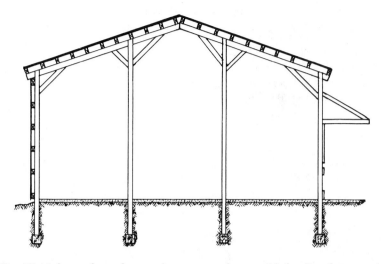

Fig. 10. A bent of a pole-type hay storage barn, with feeding fence and canopy at the right. Roofs of these buildings may be trussed, eliminating the interior poles. Bents may be set 12 to 16 feet on centers.

The arrangement of the interior of such buildings must be planned for efficiency and for labor-saving equipment. The large haymows necessary in years past are no longer required because hay is chopped or baled in the field, and much less space, if any, is required inside the barn.

The gambrel roof is adaptable to mow-type barns where large storage space is needed for hay. With this type of roof, the barn can still be designed to give the lower look because of the lower side walls. Gothic-roofed barns do not show the wind resistance of braced-rafter gambrel roofs.

The material used for barn stalls and solid foundations should be poured concrete, because of its stabilized weight and the facility with which the framing may be tied to the foundations. Another advantage to concrete stalls is their ease in cleaning.

A pole-type building, the most popular barn style, requires no foundation. The buildings are framed on round poles set in the ground and adequately anchored to resist uplift. The idea for pole-type buildings is not new, as this type of construction was well known at least 75 years ago.

REVIEW QUESTIONS

1. What is the difference in design between Gothic- and gambrel-roofed barns?
2. Which of the two roofs is more wind resistant?
3. What is a pole-type building?
4. Why are stalls and foundations constructed of concrete in dairy barns?

CHAPTER 9

Small House Construction

Ideally, every home should be designed by a talented and experienced architect to achieve the best possible design, but this is impossible, for not everyone can afford the architect's services. In many cases the home designing will be done, actually, by the owner himself, advised and assisted by the builder.

If you are a prospective homeowner, you need not feel abandoned. It is the function of the architect, and the function of the good builder, to lead and direct the client, to adopt his ideas when they are good, and to discourage ideas when they are impractical. The tastes and needs of two clients will not be the same, and so long as the client pays the bills, he has a right to his own ideas.

Whoever designs it, a home design has a number of fundamental considerations.

The house may be built of wood, masonry, concrete or metal, in one of the many styles called modern, or it may be of traditional architectural style such as Georgian, Cape Cod Colonial, Greek Revival, Southern Colonial, or it may be a so-called ranch type. Any of these houses are adaptable to modern living requirements, but in no case will the house be any better than the summation of its materials and workmanship, and above all, its *livability,* or actual utility. In any case, neatness, orderliness, and harmony should be the aim of the designer. A conglomeration of too many materials on the exterior, or too many frills or too much ornamentation is a common trap that the inexperienced designer falls into. It is not within the scope of this work to discuss the subtleties of harmony, line, scale, balance, color, and texture. The tasteful use of these properties is the function of the skilled architect, although many builders and others do very well here.

It is the primary responsibility of the builder to erect a *good* house. No matter where he sees it, the builder must know a good building when he sees it, and, of equal importance, the building must have a pleasing appearance.

You may have a choice of a single-story or a two-story house. It is possible almost to double the floor space in some one-story houses by finishing the attic and basement. Ordinarily, the same space built in a two-story house will cost less than when it is built in one story. The one-story house will have more roof, more basement or foundation walls, extra plumbing and heating, and more wiring.

There is debate over the merits of the house with a basement versus the house without a basement. It should be noted that most of the arguments against basements seem to come from developers and prefabricators. A basement will add something to the cost of a house and likewise to the selling price, which are sometimes its one and only sales appeal. A house without a basement allows the use of the very economical *slab on the ground floors,* which is currently being superseded by the somewhat more expensive but more desirable joisted construction, and the difference between the costs of a crawl space and a basement is not too great. Our advice is to accede to the wishes of the prospective owner and cooperate with him. If he has previously lived in a house with a basement heating plant, laundry, and children's playroom, he will probably want them again. Most builders agree such a basement is usually worth its cost, except where excavation is difficult, as in bedrock, or where the natural water table is too close to the surface preventing drainage. Exceptions may be elderly persons who find it difficult to climb stairs or young people building their first house who find it necessary to economize drastically.

THE TWO-STORY NEW ENGLAND COLONIAL HOUSE

Some two hundred houses of the Colonial style of architecture, many of them built in the late 1600's, are still standing in the New England states.

Many of the original houses were much larger than the one shown in Figs. 1 and 2, built to accommodate the larger families, but certain architectural details were common in all of them. One feature found in most of the original houses was moderate to steep roof slopes, often the one-third pitch shown in the illustration. This was necessary to allow the use of wood shingles or shakes, about the only roof covering then generally available. Narrow eaves, with little or no projection at the gables, had the lap siding cut against wide corner boards. The siding was *always* narrow; corner boards were *always* used. The wide lap siding we sometimes call colonial, with so-called mitered corners, was not found in the New England Colonial home. Plank frames were used for the windows, and there were no casings or very narrow casings outside. Entrances, however, were usually elaborate, sometimes with finely scrolled and carved pediments. Good, authentic replicas of many of these entrances are obtained today. In the later and more pretentious houses built in this era, side lights were often used at the entrances, and sometimes the doors were double. The relatively wide pilasters at the sides were

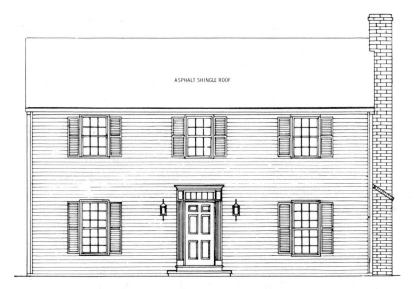

ASPHALT SHINGLE ROOF

Fig. 1. Front elevation of a Colonial-type home.

255

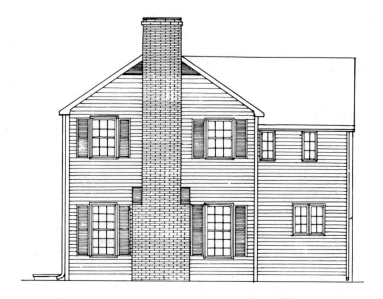

Fig. 2. Right side elevation of a Colonial-type home.

usually fluted or molded. A type of door that originated in England was paneled, three high, two wide, with a small, nearly square, pair of panels at the top. The rails in the upper part of the door form the Christian cross.

The front of the house was symmetrical about the central entrance. Although there were some exceptions to this design, symmetry was the rule. Invariably, second-story windows were placed directly over lower story openings. Small covered entrances were uncommon, porches and verandas virtually unknown. The central entrance hall was universal, with the stairway to the upper floor. In the earlier and smaller Colonial houses the stairway was often steep and tortuous, often with tricky winders, but in the later and better homes the stairs were often beautiful, tastefully designed and elaborately carved, with superb craftsmanship. Needless to say, such stairs cannot be duplicated today.

While the basic design was rectangular, many of the Colonial homes had attached ells or sheds. With a roof continuous down over a one-story shed at the rear, this house becomes the well-known *salt-box,* with a claim to fame all its own. All types of Colonial homes use windows of small glass or lights, often rectangular, sometimes diamond-shaped. In the early days the muntins were often made of lead; later wood muntins were used. Large sheets of glass were almost unknown, and very expensive.

A predominant feature in the Colonial house is the *privacy* afforded, the privacy that is lacking, and so often deplored, in many modern designs. There are no unnecessarily large areas of glass to give one the eerie feeling of being spied upon at night. While the angle at the rear is an ideal location for a private patio (if the head of the house persists in having cookouts), there is a convenient escape route to the living room where one can eat his hamburger in air-conditioned comfort if he happens to be allergic to mosquitoes or if he doesn't especially care for the onslaught of ants! The large living room allows mother to entertain the local church bazaar committee undistracted by the older daughter who is entertaining her boy friend in the dining room across the hall, while the small fry with their noise are isolated back in the family room. As for father, he has escaped to his lair in the basement where he is indulging in his favorite drink and reading a magazine, or doing just about anything he wishes, and will be undisturbed by the many activities of the rest of the family.

Aside from the fact that this house is excellent in architecture, it need not be an expensive house (relative to other houses) to build, and the plan shown in Figs. 3 and 4 shows the advantages of the two-story house for families of five or more. The downstairs bathroom is convenient, and the two complete bathrooms upstairs help prevent congestion. A complete basement is suggested for convenience to heating and plumbing, plus storage space. Included in the original plans is an adjacent garage with a covered breezeway connecting it with the outside door of the family room.

A HOUSE OF MODERN ARCHITECTURE

Architects who have pride in their originality often prefer an unusual custom design, as shown in Fig. 5. This does not mean that a house of unusual appearance such as this one, no matter

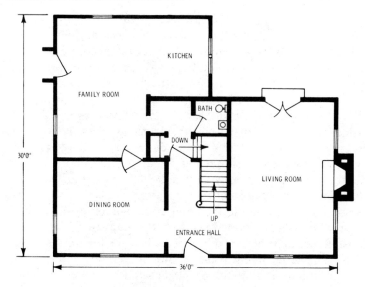

Fig. 3. First-floor plan of a Colonial-type home.

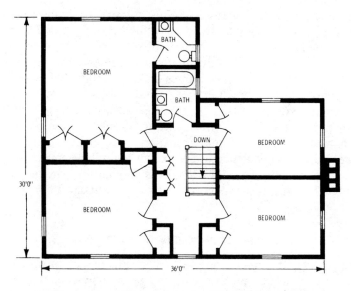

Fig. 4. Second floor plan of a Colonial-type home.

how good the appearance, can be placed on the odd lot in a
street of Colonial houses and have a pleasing effect. Houses
such as this one need a proper setting, preferably a rugged and
individual setting. It is able to do its own advertising in about
any environment, but when it is automatically compared with
houses of more conventional designs it may be discordant, and
discord in architecture, as in music, is never agreeable.

The design is bold, and reflects the lively imagination of its
designer, with an unusually pleasant result. Usually modern
practice makes use of large areas of glass, but these areas are
effectively shaded by the wide overhangs, which make them
much more acceptable than the large unprotected areas of glass
in many modern designs.

The outstanding feature of this house is the roof. Although
decidedly unusual, the pitches are regular, 45 degrees, and the
roof is composed of simple intersecting planes. The roof framing
is actually rather simple, for there are no *warped* planes. The
architect has used diagonal lines on the roof instead of the commonly used vertical and horizontal accents. The effect is strik-
ing, especially on a sloping site, but working drawings are available which adapt it to level sites as well.

Although imaginative and unusual, the plan is in right-angled
shapes for ease and economy of construction. The roof is
formed of intersecting planes, with steep pitches. The roof
treatment is important, as it dominates the entire view.

In the plans, Figs. 6 and 7, designations of rooms, and dimen-

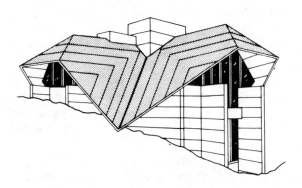

Fig. 5. A house of modern architecture.

259

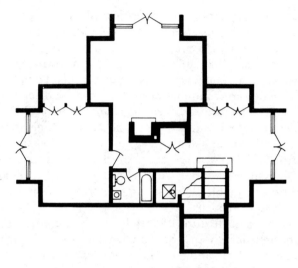

Fig. 6. *The lower-floor level of the modern house. If the entrance is at this level, the room with the fireplace will certainly be used as the living room.*

sions, are intentionally omitted. Naturally, the uses of the rooms will depend upon the contour of the ground. The large room with the fireplace will undoubtedly be used for a living room, depending upon whether the entrance is at the second-story level as it may be if the house is built on a sloping site, or at the first floor level, as it may be if the ground is level. The plan is flexible enough to allow considerable leeway in deciding upon the exact room arrangements, and their subsequent uses.

Specifications

In general, the walls are 12-inch lightweight concrete blocks, their cavities filled with insulation, with head joints cut smooth, and horizontal joints struck. The roof shown in Fig. 8 is sheathed with plywood. With a roof so steep, many types of roof coverings may be used, but probably one of the modern types of mopped down roof covers would be most acceptable, with a granule-coated roll roofing as a cap sheet. The horizontal and diagonal roof lines are obtained by the use of battens.

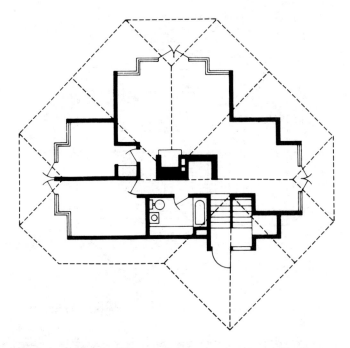

Fig. 7. The upper-floor level. If the entrance is at this level, the room with the fireplace will certainly be used as the living room.

THE A-FRAME HOUSE

The A-frame structure is the simplest, most primitive, of all types. In years past, the A-frame was not popular, probably because the use of the interior space was restricted by the steeply sloping walls. In A-frame designs, it is necessary in nearly every case to use vertical knee-walls along the sides. Upper stories, if any, are very much reduced in area due to the roof line. In Fig. 9, the architect has ingeniously extended the upper floor joists and introduced a dormer to obviate this difficulty.

The A-frame has more inherent rigidity than any other type of structure, primarily because of its shape. The triangle is the only polygonal frame whose rigidity is not dependent upon either bracing or rigid joints. The analysis of the A-frame is simple, and any desirable strength is obtainable. In contrast with the

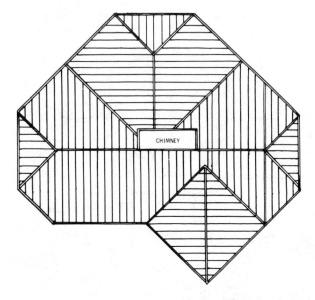

Fig. 8. The roof framing plan of the modern house.

Fig. 9. A typical A-frame cottage.

semicircular roof, or Quonset-hut type, which also is a true arch, much depends upon its shape for strength and rigidity, and the use of the interior space is restricted by sloping side walls. If the A-frame is properly handled by a good designer, an excellent structure can be the result. Because of its inherent strength and rigidity, the A-frame can be used along the seashore and in the mountains where high winds are prevalent and where snow accumulations may be many feet deep. The A-frame is popular for use as a summer home in the mountains; it may be inaccessible and abandoned or left unattended during winter, but its pleasing and unusual appearance makes it popular almost everywhere. Some fine examples of church architecture are A-frame types.

The A-frame is essentially a three-hinged arch, and must be analyzed as such. In common with all arches, it produces a considerable *outward* reaction at the bearings. It may be necessary to design the foundations to resist this outward thrust, but in the example illustrated the floor joists are designed to resist these horizontal components of the reactions by means of straight tension. The frames in this example are actually triangular, and there is no horizontal reaction. Only simple foundations, designed to resist vertical loadings, are required.

One difficulty with A-frame designs in most parts of the United States is the difficulty of obtaining suitable long timbers for the legs. This is largely overcome by using glued-laminated timbers, which are equally acceptable.

An outstanding feature of the example given is the circular staircase, rising from almost the center of the house, opposite to the entrance. Because of the sloping sides, it may be quite difficult to get a conventional stair into an A-frame without taking up too much valuable room. The circular stair elminates this difficulty. The *drum* is 7 ft. 5½ in. in diameter, and the stair design given in this cottage is rather plain, built of stock materials, and not beyond the ability of most good workmen. Needless to say, a great deal of money may be spent on millwork for a circular stair if this is preferred.

The design given is good in appearance, and very practical. While it may be most desirable as a second home, it may readily be equipped for year around living.

THE CONTEMPORARY HOUSE

This house is called contemporary architecture, for it embodies most of the features desired in homes of the present era. Among these features we may enumerate the following:

- This house is a split-level, not a new idea, but always popular.
- It allows adequate windows in the lower level rooms, and the stairway down is short.
- The living room is moderately large, and with the connected dining area it is ample for the needs of most moderately large families.
- The bedrooms are all of practical, usable size. The spare room in the basement is a useful stand-by.
- The access door to the two-car garage is convenient.
- The family room and the party room in the basement remove some of the inevitable activities of a large family from the living room.
- A concrete patio at the rear is convenient for the usual outdoor living activities of the modern family.

Fig. 10. A split-level house.

264

Construction Details

Glass has been used with discretion. Although the glazed areas are moderately large, they are not unreasonably so, at the expense of privacy and to the detriment of heating and air-conditioning.

Architecturally, this house is susceptible to many variations of materials. In the house illustrated in Fig. 10, uncoursed native stone has been tastefully used, with vertical siding on the overhanging upper story.

The roof has sufficient pitch to fill its primary function which is to shed water, but it also gives a lower *spread out* look to the house.

It is possible with the proper use of a steel beam to enlarge the party or family room. This could be done by removing the wall between party room and spare room, to make one big room in an "L" shape. Floor plans of the house are shown in Fig. 11.

SUMMARY

Many of the two-story New England houses built in the 1600's are still standing today. Features found in most original houses were steep roof slopes, wood shingles, narrow eaves, and wide corner boards. The siding was always narrow when used in conjunction with the wide corner boards. Entrances, however, were usually elaborate, sometimes with finely scrolled and cornered pediments.

The A-frame house is the simplest and most primitive of all types. Until recent years the A-frame was not popular because the use of the interior space was limited by the steeply sloping walls. It is necessary, in nearly every case, to use vertical knee-walls along the sides. If the structure has a second floor, the area is reduced due to roof line. If the A-frame is properly handled by a good designer, some outstanding examples can be constructed. The A-frame is very popular as a summer home in the mountains or at the seashore, and gives rigid strength in areas where high winds are prevalent.

The contemporary house could be considered a modern home of the present era. Among the many styles in contemporary

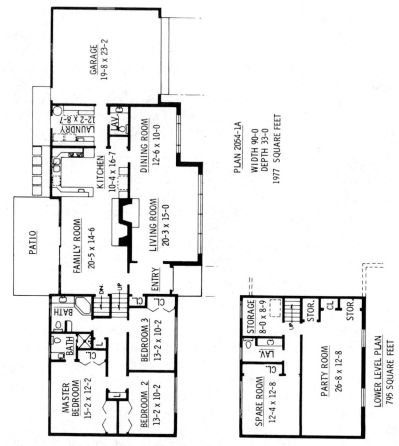

Fig. 11. Floor plans for the contemporary house.

homes is the split-level, popularly called the tri-level. There are advantages to this type of house; the same space built in a split-level house will cost less than when it is built in a one-story.

REVIEW QUESTIONS

1. What type of house was constructed in the 1600's?
2. What are some advantages in the A-frame construction?
3. What is a split-level house?
4. What are some advantages in the split-level house?
5. Give a few advantages and disadvantages of a basement.

CHAPTER 10

Motels

Motel building is a somewhat specialized branch of construction. Some motels are more hotels than motels; there are a great many of these, especially in the warmer winter-resort sections of the country. They often have every comfort and recreational facility known. The rates for these accommodations are high. The greater number of motels, however, are relatively modest, with probably not more than 20 rooms, and may or may not include a simple coffee bar or small restaurant, and/or a gasoline station.

The owners of these smaller motels come from about every walk of life. They are often an elderly couple, retired or semiretired, who have risked a major portion of their available capital in the venture, hoping for a good return on their investment without too much manual labor. It is these people who need the help and advice of a good builder to make their limited budget give them the best possible design for the type of people who will actually use the motel. The builder should know the typical clientele.

First is the tourist trade. These travelers usually stay only one night and are on their way early in the morning. They usually consist of small groups of three or four people who like informal service and free access to their parked automobiles. They are usually traveling for pure pleasure, and usually take such trips but once a year, during the summer vacation season. They need large rooms, and often their traveling budget is limited and they do not care to pay for dispensable frills or useless service. This class of clientele will most likely select a modest, clean, well-kept motel where the rental is less than it would be at larger complexes.

Second are the commercial travelers. These include salesmen and other business representatives who travel the same territory several times a year and may be repeaters. They are usually singles and may make a good motel the base of their operations in a nearby city, preferring it to the more formal and less convenient city hotel. They may stay several nights, and the business they bring the motel owner is almost a steady income summer and winter. Many of them have good expense accounts, and they prefer to stay where good food and liquor are served. They usually require individual telephone service and are willing to pay for it. Many prefer a central lounge, though many motels do not have this accommodation, and they like to be very close to their cars for ready access to sample cases, etc. Good-sized, usable desks in the rooms are a necessity for these guests to write up reports and orders.

Third are the sportsmen. They frequent the areas devoted to seasonal sports—skiing, fishing, boating, etc. The motels in the regions where winter sports are popular find that lounges with good solid furniture and efficient fireplaces, even in the living units, are attractive. Good food, of course, is necessary for this type of motel.

A fourth type of clientele is often worth considering when planning a motel. This consists of persons who are attending regional conferences or meetings. To attract this type of guest, the motel must include a sizeable meeting hall. Few of the smaller motels have accommodations of this kind and, considering the investment and the possibility that it will be used but seldom, it may not be profitable. At best, such a layout may be a considerable gamble to include when planning a motel.

In nearly all cases, services and accommodations at a motel should be flexible enough to attract all kinds of clientele that the owner will be called upon to serve. People from all walks of life and economic strata, it should be remembered, will pay for the motel that is most complete, comfortable, and convenient.

For the prospective motel operator who does not wish to serve food, proximity to a good restaurant is important. It may be (and this often happens) that the prospective owner has had some restaurant or food service experience. He may wish to emphasize the food service first and expand the motel business around this base.

It is presumable that the factors enumerated will have been evaluated in the mind of the prospective owner before he consults with a builder. From this point on, the well-informed builder can give the owner valuable advice, especially regarding the different types of construction, their costs, and many other factors that may directly affect the owner's investment. After all, it is the primary function of a motel, as with all commercial enterprises, to return a reasonable profit on the investment. It cannot, of course, exist otherwise.

PRELIMINARY CONSIDERATIONS

The builder should be familiar with local building ordinances, zoning restrictions, and state laws which govern such installations. The builder (or the owner) should have the property surveyed to avoid trouble later because of possible encroachment upon the property. By all means, make sure that an adequate water supply is available. This can be an exceedingly costly oversight. Equally as important is to determine what provision can be made for sewage disposal, since a simple septic tank system will usually not meet the requirement of local ordinances. Consult with your local Health Officer or with your State Board of Health.

A readily accessible location, and within one or two miles of town along a well-traveled highway, is preferable. The nature of the highway to town is important; if it is lined with interesting stores and restaurants, a motel will be more apt to prosper. If the proposed site is bare, grade it before starting actual construction. If it is wooded, or if it is landscaped in any way, go easy with the bulldozer.

CONSTRUCTION DESIGNS

First consideration for the motel units is that they should be as quiet as it is possible; *location* is important. There should be no railroad switching yards or noisy factories nearby, and the proximity of busy airports is undesirable. Keep the installation as far back from a busy highway as possible. In most cases, walls and partitions must be effectively sound-resisting. Concrete block walls are good (and inexpensive), but not particularly handsome. Double-studded walls are nearly always satisfactory, even as partitions between units. It should be noted that *acoustic treatment* that uses fiber tiles or boards *isn't* soundproofing. Such treatment may lower the noise level in the room where it originates some 5 decibels or so, but it is *not,* nor was it ever intended to be, effective in resisting *transmitted* noise.

Regular window glass is a very poor sound barrier; heavy plate glass is slightly better. Attempts to control noises from the outside are accomplished by using *double sash* (such as windows with storm sashes) which develops a thin air-cavity of 6 to 8 inches between glass.

In air-conditioned motels, storm sashes are sometimes left in place the year round, but then ventilation may become a problem.

HEATING THE MOTEL

It is best that the builder confer with a heating specialist when planning heating facilities for the motel. For the larger motels, a central heating plant seems to be the most practical answer. If proper provision is made when they are installed, such plants are readily expandable if at any time the owner decides to add more rental units. Natural gas, where it is available, is probably the most trouble-free fuel. Oil firing is extremely practical, but usually more expensive. Either gas or oil-fired plants can be made almost entirely automatic. Stoker-fired coal is usually the most economical fuel, if any fuel today can be called economical.

Throughout the midwest and northern parts of the country, winter is the slack season for the motel business (except where there is an attraction such as skiing, ice-boating, or some other winter sport). It may not be an economical proposition to keep all available units heated when there is a probability that they will not be occupied, but they must be kept above freezing temperature to protect the plumbing. If there is any probability of late guests, it is best to keep the baths well heated. The first refuge of the tired and belated guest is the bathroom, and a cold bathroom is not friendly.

For the smaller courts, individual room heaters are most satisfactory. With this kind of heating there is no difficulty about expanding the heating plant if it is ever found desirable to add rental units. Natural gas is the most satisfactory fuel, with oil a second choice. Where natural gas is not available, bottled or LP gas is extremely satisfactory. Where the units are not kept continuously warm, a quick warm-up may be desirable, and this means heaters with some reserve capacity. Radiant heat that utilizes a ceiling or floor does not have a *reserve* capacity for quick warmups. Steam heat is satisfactory, but it cannot be regulated to any desired temperature. Hot water heating is extremely flexible, but radiator temperatures are relatively low, which means larger radiator surfaces, and warmup time will be much longer than with steam. *All direct-fired heaters must be vented to the outside.* Common sense demands it, and it is specified by codes, ordinances, and state laws. Under no conditions are unvented gas heaters allowable, although they are occasionally used, especially in the south. *Gas-burning fireplaces must have chimneys.* Simple sheet-metal vent ducts are not safe for fireplaces, for a tenant may build a fire in such a fireplace with any fuel that is handy.

Leave the actual design of the heating system to a heating specialist; he understands all the problems involved. Some special construction details may be necessary to accommodate certain heating installations, and it will be necessary for the builder to determine what they may be by a conference with the heating plant designer.

WHAT IS DEMANDED IN A MOTEL

The crowded, cramped, small overnight cabin is a thing of the past. Even with low prices, that kind of accommodation rarely attracts the traveler. Today's automobile tourist demands a reasonable-sized sleeping room ($14'0'' \times 16'0''$ is common) and bath. A room of this size can accommodate an extra bed should the travelers wish it, and the patronage is not restricted to singles and doubles. Many women detest a shower bath; many men prefer it. We can't settle this controversy; so perhaps the answer is that the motel operator should have both types available.

Many operators think a long, full-length mirror in each unit is a good investment. In any case, the bath should have a convenient shaving mirror, with lights on both sides and an electric outlet for a razor. A medicine cabinet is not necessary, but plan an ample ledge or shelf under or near the mirror where toilet articles, razors, and toothbrushes will be in plain sight. Then they will not be forgotten. Some operators prefer that clothes closets be open-faced (no doors) for the same reason. Some prefer that window ledges slope sharply so that they cannot serve as a repository for personal belongings which would be left on the window sill, hidden by the curtains, when the owner leaves.

There are many possible furniture arrangements. This feature is almost entirely at the discretion of the owner. It is a wise preliminary precaution for the builder to furnish the owner with a large-scale plan of the proposed units (with pieces of pasteboard, proper scale, representing the various pieces of furniture proposed) so that he can arrange and rearrange until a satisfactory arrangement is decided upon. There can be no great flexibility in furniture arrangement. The necessity for keeping exits and bathroom doors clear and windows unobstructed prevents any great change in the furniture positions.

The units are preferably (and most economically) built in pairs, with bathrooms back to back. No great diversity of arrangement of fixtures is possible in bathrooms, but the six layouts shown in Fig. 1 have all been used satisfactorily in motels. In Example B, the ever popular lavatory mounted in a countertop with cabinets below is shown. While the cabinets will not be especially useful to the overnight guest, they will be for those who stay longer.

The arrangement of the motel units on the plot is entirely at the discretion of the owner. It may be dictated by the shape or contour of the plot, or by the proximity of streets. Figs. 2, 3 and 4 are given to illustrate a most convenient and satisfactory arrangement. The units are set diagonally with the drive to facilitate entrance to and exit from the individual car ports. Any

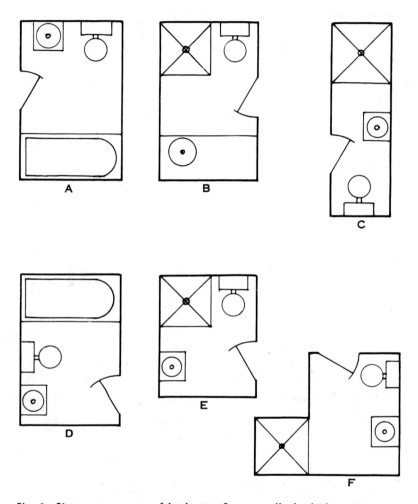

Fig. 1. Six arrangements of bathroom fixtures, all of which are in common use in motels today.

number (preferably an even number) of such units may be connected. The attached individual car port has been found to be one of the greatest drawing factors in motel operation. All automobile travelers prefer to have their cars as convenient as possible, and this arrangement is the last word in such convenience, especially appreciated during winter or stormy summer weather.

273

Fig. 2. An excellent motel room layout, with bathrooms back to back. The units are set diagonally with the drive, making access to the car ports extremely easy. An even number of units may be connected.

AIR-CONDITIONING THE MOTEL

Air-conditioning is imperative in the south and over most of the central U.S. Individual room units may be used, and for the small operation they are generally preferred. For larger motels, a central system may be preferred. It is very wise to install a system with excess capacity in case additional rentals are added later. Heavy heat insulation in walls and ceilings will reduce the load on air-conditioning equipment, whatever the climate. In most cases, a ½-ton through-the-wall unit will be found adequate for each rental.

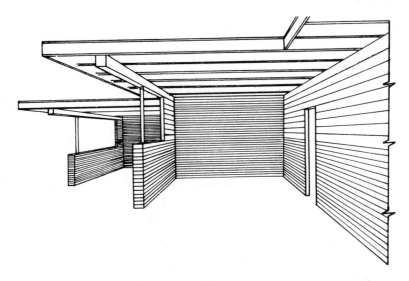

*Fig. 3. A view along the driveway side of the motel units with the plan
shown in Fig. 2. This design has a flat, or nearly flat roof.*

SOUND INSULATION

Motel patrons will insist upon (and have a right to expect) a
quiet night's rest for their money. This means good noise insulation from both the adjoining units and from the outside. The mechanics of soundproofing are not too well understood, and we
are giving the accompanying Table 1 to allow comparison of various types of sound-resisting walls. Regular insulation is important, but heat insulation and sound insulation should not be confused, nor should sound *resistance* and sound *absorption* be
confused. Actually, heat insulation is generally very poor sound
insulation, for sound-energy passes through porous materials of
all kinds. Packing the cavity between staggered-stud double
walls with loose heat insulation is certainly not worth the expense if the object is to increase its sound resistance. On the
other hand, the R-factor heat-transmission resistance of the wall
will be greatly improved, an important consideration in terms of
fuel savings.

The builder will do well to remember that there are two invar-

275

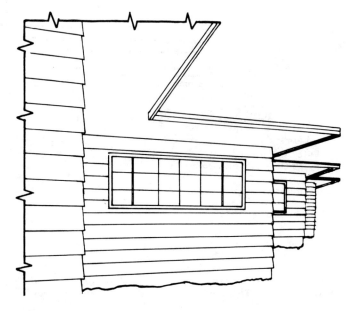

Fig. 4. A view along the rear side of the motel units with the plan shown in Fig. 2. The illustration is shown with wood siding, but the exterior may be masonry, or any other approved type of construction.

iably effective methods of controlling sound transmission through barriers. The first method is by adding weight. Sound is transmitted *by* walls, not *through* walls, if they are not porous or perforated. The wall is set into vibration by the energy in the sound waves, and the vibrations are re-transmitted as sound on the other side. Heavy walls are not readily set into vibration by the very low-energy sound impulses. The amount of energy *absorbed* by the wall surface is not significant. Second, double walls that are completely disconnected from the two sides are effective sound barriers, because the air between the two sides is very elastic and does not transfer the vibrations from one wall to the other. You cannot improve on this air space by filling the cavity between the two walls with insulation. Insulating materials are usually very light in weight, and have very little sound-proofing ability, as mentioned earlier.

Avoid the construction illustrated in Fig. 5. It is a common

Table 1.   Sound Proofing Guide

Sound Transmission Resistance of Various Walls and Ceilings, in decibels

8" brick, 5/8" sanded gypsum plaster both sides	50 dB.
4" brick, 5/8" sanded gypsum plaster both sides	48 dB.
Staggered 2" x 4" studs, 16" OC, 2" offset, fiberboard lath and 1/2" sanded gypsum plaster both sides	54 dB.
Staggered 2" x 3" studs, 16" OC, perforated gypsum lath and 1/2" sanded gypsum plaster both sides	49 dB.
2" x 4" studs 16" OC, wood lath and sanded gypsum plaster both sides, 7/8" grounds	41 dB.
2" x 4" studs 16" OC, 1/2" gypsum board, both sides, joints filled and taped	35 dB.
2" x 4" studs 16" OC, gypsum lath and 1/2" sanded plaster both sides	41 dB.
2" x 4" studs 16" OC, spring-mounted gypsum lath and 1/2" sanded gypsum plaster both sides	52 dB.
Double ceiling framing, roof joists 2" x 4", 3/4" sheathing, ceiling joists 2" x 4" staggered, 1/2" fiberboard lath and 1/2" sanded gypsum plaster	53dB.
2" x 8" floor joists, double floor above, 1/2" gypsum board ceiling hung on resilient springs below	52 dB.

(Courtesy U. S. Bureau of Standards)

8" cinder block wall, plain	33.3 dB.
8" sand-gravel concrete block wall, plain	51.8 dB.

These block walls may be improved approximately 9 dB by coating with 2 coats of cement base paint, and up to 18 dB with sanded gypsum plaster both sides. *Don't use light weight or acoustic plaster if maximum sound transmission resistance is desired. It is added weight that you want, and sanded plaster is heaviest.*

(Courtesy Portland Cement Association)

Drywall has less resistance to sound than plaster, but plaster (which is used only in perhaps 10% of new construction) is much more expensive. Doubling up on the drywall would aid sound transmission resistance.

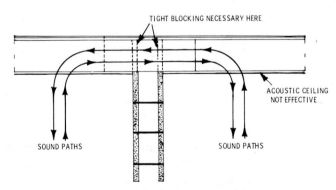

TIGHT BLOCKING NECESSARY HERE

ACOUSTIC CEILING NOT EFFECTIVE

SOUND PATHS   SOUND PATHS

Fig. 5. *A common source of sound transmission trouble in motels. Sound waves pass through acoustic tile ceilings, and will have an unobstructed path into the adjoining room. An attic above the ceiling (with tight blocking as shown) is very good in preventing noise transmission.*

source of trouble in motels. Run the sound-resisting partition tight up against the roof sheathing and build the ceilings *between* the walls, not *over* them. Acoustic tile ceilings are almost entirely ineffective in cases such as the one illustrated. If you wish to use acoustic ceilings, back them up with lath and sanded plaster, or with ½- or ⅝-inch drywall. Good wall-to-wall carpeting and padding will stop impact noises (which are usually footsteps) from passing through to the floor below where they originate. The carpeting and padding absorb sound nearly as effectively as acoustic tiles or boards.

When ceiling finishes are applied directly to the under side of roof joists (as is common in flat-roofed motel construction), resistance to outside noises is often very unsatisfactory. It is usually best to use *two* sets of joists; one set carrying the roof above and one set carrying the ceiling below. To economize, the joists may be staggered, but there should be no mechanical connection whatever between the two framing systems, such as nails, cleats, or wires.

BATHROOM REQUIREMENTS

Space requirements in bathrooms for public accommodations (such as motels) is governed by Board of Health regulations in most states. The builder should make himself familiar with all the legal requirements in his district.

The usual bathtub length is 60 inches, but 54-inch and 66-inch lengths are available, with widths usually 28 to 30 inches. The square corner bathtubs are 42″ × 48″, and are usually more expensive than the standard.

The standard shower stall is 36″ × 36″, but 32″ × 32″ sizes are available and usually are quite satisfactory. Tub and shower combinations are also available, which in most cases is more practical. Space can be saved if bath and shower are desired, plus it gives the overnight guest a preference. Needless to say, an installation such as this should have tile on the walls, to eliminate the hard job of cleaning. The tile will also waterproof the area involved, eliminating the need for frequent repair and painting of the walls.

For flush toilets, the usual space requirements are from side to side, not less than 2 feet 8 inches; from front to back, not less than 4 feet 6 inches.

Lavatories are available in many different sizes. Clearance in front of them should never be less than 18 inches, and always more if possible.

Bathroom ventilation is almost always controlled by statutes. Common requirements are that the bath shall have an outside window for ventilation, with an openable area not less than 5% of the area of the floor. Where outside windows are not compulsory, an inside bathroom shall have forced ventilation supplying not less than 1.5 cubic feet of air per minute per square foot of floor. To assure that it will be used, some authorities require that the ventilating fan be controlled by a switch which closes when the door is closed. Occupants generally do not like this provision, as it makes a bathroom drafty.

Sewage disposal, when no sanitary sewers are available, is generally strictly controlled by State Health Authorities. If it must be by means of septic tanks and seepage-fields, consult with them. The proximity of the disposal tile lines and disposal field to water supplies is rigorously specified, and limitations are strictly enforced.

SUMMARY

The right location, the right area, and the right accommodations are a must to a profitable motel business. A motel must also be designed to supply the general needs of the people who will actually use the court.

There are travelers who usually stay only one night and are on their way early in the morning. These groups usually consist of three or four people who like informal service and free access to their parked automobiles. They are usually traveling for pleasure, and usually take the trip once a year during the summer vacation season. These people will select a modest, clean, well-kept motel where the rental is less than in an elaborate unit.

Other clientele using the facilities of a motel are commercial travelers, such as salesman and businessmen. These men travel the same territory several times a year and may be repeaters. They are usually singles who may make a good motel the base of their operations. They may stay several nights, and are generally liberal spenders looking for good food and well-furnished lounges or meeting rooms.

An important consideration in motel construction is sound-proofing. Keep the installation as far back from a busy highway as possible. In most cases, walls and partitions must be effectively sound-resisting. Concrete block walls are good, but not particularly beautiful. Double-studded walls are nearly always satisfactory.

REVIEW QUESTIONS

1. What are the primary considerations when building a motel?
2. What are the advantages and disadvantages of locating a motel a few miles from a city?
3. What is the best way to soundproof motel rooms without spending too much money?
4. Is it always necessary to operate a restaurant with your motel?
5. Should a motel be air conditioned? If so, how?

CHAPTER 11

Home Workshop Layout

The placement of stationary power tools for their most efficient use is based on several basic principles, each playing an important role not only in the matter of tool selection but in the final cost and all-around satisfaction as well. It is, of course, necessary in a shop to have adequate electrical wiring and a sufficient number of power and light outlets in addition to proper ventilation.

MINIMUM-SIZE LAYOUT

In a projected workshop having a limited available area of, for example, 8 × 10 feet, it is obviously impossible to plan for a complete set of single-purpose power tools without unduly restricting the necessary working space. When conditions permit, the use of one compact multipurpose power tool should be considered for any limited workshop area. The comparison in layouts and tool arrangement for an 8 × 10-foot workshop is given, with various single-purpose power tools (Fig. 1) and one multipurpose tool (Fig. 2).

When checking the layouts, it should be noted that although both arrangements are possible, a considerable saving in floor space is obtained when using the multipurpose tool. When placed as shown, that is, near the center of the floor, the multipurpose tool enables the operator to work on long boards or large panels without ramming the work against the wall during the operation. Prior to the purchase of any power tool, therefore, a careful analysis of the necessary workshop space should

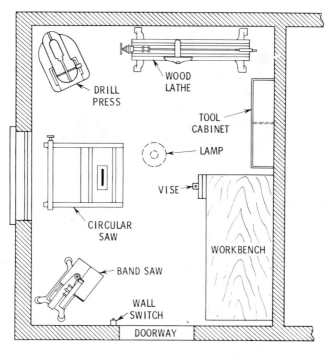

Fig. 1. A typical 8' × 10' basement workshop layout with four single-purpose power tools. Since other arrangements are possible, the location of the various power tools as well as the number of tools required should be carefully considered in each instance.

be considered. This again will depend on the type of work contemplated, the amount of space required for hardware and lumber storage, etc.

If a moderate amount of workshop space, for example, 13 × 18 to 13 × 20 feet, is available, and single-purpose power tool units are required, the individual machines may be placed for most efficient use as illustrated in Fig. 3. Note that the circular saw and jointer are placed near the center of the workshop for free movement when working with long boards and large panels.

The jigsaw is also placed in the fairway, but off center to avoid interference with nearby machines. The remainder of the power tools, namely the lathe and the drill press, may be grouped against the wall, since in most operations, the work

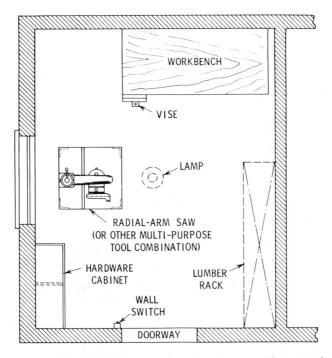

Fig. 2. A typical 8′ × 10′ basement workshop layout with one multipurpose power tool. Multipurpose power tools are frequently employed where the floor area and production requirements are limited.

done with these tools does not generally project beyond these machines. In addition, ample workbench and counter space is provided along the walls for convenience and efficiency. Here the various hand tools, portable power tools, and lumber may be arranged to suit individual preferences.

MAXIMUM-SIZE LAYOUT

In locations where there is ample basement space available, and where a full complement of single-purpose power tools is needed, the various machines may be located as shown in Fig. 4. An arrangement of this type requires a minimum floor area of 13 × 30 feet or more.

283

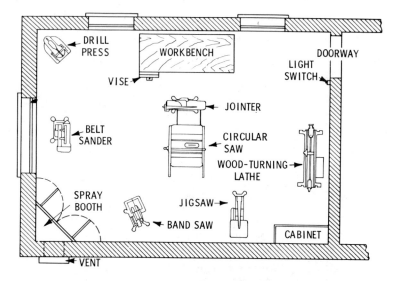

Fig. 3. A typical 13' × 18' basement workshop layout with seven basic single-purpose power tools.

With no premium on space, the problem actually resolves itself into how best to locate the various power units for greatest convenience and efficiency without unnecessary cramping of the working area. One area that may be set off from the rest is the finishing bench and its surroundings. In the spray-booth enclosure, articles may be left to dry after painting without fear of dust or smearing. See your insurance man before building a spray booth. Spray booths are a fire hazard and may result in increased insurance rates if they are not properly constructed and vented.

It should also be observed that with ample space, advantage should be taken of outside doorways for the delivery and storage of lumber and supplies. By placing lumber storage near the door, it is possible to add supplies without interfering with the shop itself. In locations where an irregular floor area exists, a satisfactory power-tool workshop layout may be obtained only if proper attention is paid to every known detail.

Sometimes it may be advantageous to lay out the available workshop area on a suitable sheet of paper to a certain scale,

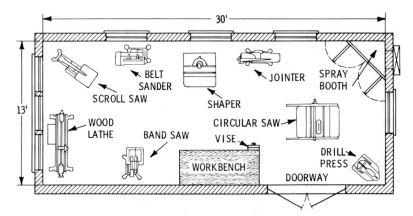

Fig. 4. A typical 13' × 30' above-ground workshop layout with eight single-purpose power tools. A shop of this size (containing almost 400 square feet) will readily lend itself to the production of medium to large work. When erecting a shop outside the house proper, the floor area required should be calculated to provide the most efficient service. For example, the ideal all-around shop area for production work may be built in the form of an "L" rather than in the form of a rectangle or a square. Doors and windows must be properly dimensioned for free unobstructed movement of work and materials as well as for lighting requirements.

such as 1:6, or 2 inches equals 1 foot of the actual floor dimensions. Using the same scale, make up a cardboard pattern for each of the machines to be installed, being careful to note and record the *maximum horizontal floor area* covered by each.

By placing these machine patterns on the scaled floor plan, each in its contemplated position, and by moving them about until the most advantageous location of each power tool is found, a good deal of miscalculation and future trouble may be avoided. When this method is used, the available space between each machine, as well as any other dimension, may easily be found by simple measurement to scale.

MISCELLANEOUS WORKSHOP LAYOUT

In case of insufficient basement space, workshops are sometimes erected in the furnace room, as noted in Fig. 5. Here the various power tools are placed along the walls, with the workbench and circular saw against the far wall opposite the entrance

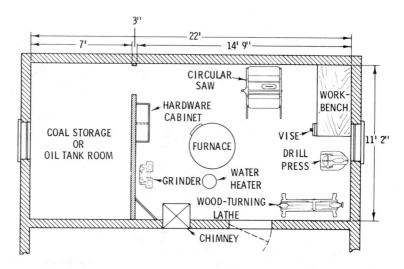

Fig. 5. A typical basement workshop with power tools placed in the furnace room of a divided basement. Since the suitable basement space is, in many instances, occupied by laundry equipment, storage, etc., some consideration should be given to utilizing the furnace space for only a few of the most needed power tools.

door. When contemplating a workshop installation in the furnace side of the basement, it is important to fully establish the space requirements prior to the purchase of various power tools, since in a great many instances a multipurpose tool would perhaps be more suitable. The placement of each tool should be carefully considered in order that a logical layout can be fully realized.

A typical workshop layout in a converted two-car garage is illustrated in Fig. 6. To obtain a suitable working area, however, it is suggested that a partition wall be erected to isolate the workshop from the car space proper. In cold climates, a suitable gas or oil heater may be used to provide the necessary heat requirements. Since the average workshop activity, however, demands a good deal of body movement, a temperature of approximately 60 to 65 degrees F. is usually sufficient, although individual requirements will dictate this factor.

It will, of course, be necessary to change the existing electric wiring system; that is, an additional motor circuit of adequate capacity must be installed, and under no conditions should the

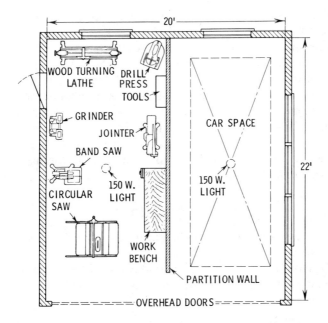

Fig. 6. A typical workshop housed in a divided two-car garage. By erecting a suitable wallboard partition to enclose the workshop area, an almost ideal space can be obtained. One advantage of having the workshop housed in this manner is the prevention of noise and vibrations from reaching the living area of the home, since the garage is usually located outside the house proper. In locations where the available shop area is insufficient for the proper placement of the necessary single-purpose power tools, some consideration should be given to the use of one or more multipurpose tools.

motor or motors be installed, and under no conditions should the motor or motors be allowed to operate from the lighting circuits. This rule should always be observed irrespective of the workshop location.

SUMMARY

When checking out a workshop area, considerable saving in floor space is obtained when using multipurpose tools. If power tools are near the center of the floor, long boards and large panels can be handled without ramming the work against the wall during operation. Prior to the purchase of any power tool, a careful analysis of the necessary workshop space should be considered.

If floor space is no problem, a survey should be made of outside doorways and window area. Advantage should be taken of doorways for the delivery and storage of lumber and supplies. Also, many times projects are made and assembled in the workshop but cannot be removed because doorways are too small.

It will, of course, be necessary to change the existing electric wiring system. An additional motor circuit of adequate capacity must be installed, and under no condition should the light level be below minimum standards.

REVIEW QUESTIONS

1. Should the floor space available influence the type of power tools to purchase? If so, why?
2. Why should electric circuits be added in the workshop?
3. Should doorways and window area be examined? If so, why?

Index

INDEX

E

Elastic limit, timber, 124
Erasers, 167
Example of architectural drawing, 219
Extension bar, compass, 159

F

Factor of safety, timber, 124
False economy, barn construction, 238
Finding divisors of numbers, 11
Force, timber, 124
Foundation, barn, 244
Fractions, 13
Functions of numbers, 88-90

G

Gambrel-roofed barn, 240
Geometrical problems, 45
Geometry, 40
  angles, 40
  lines, 40
  plane figures, 40
  solids, 41
Gothic-roofed barn, 242
Gradienter, 115

H

Hair-spring dividers, 159
Heating a motel, 270
Hidden lines, 197
Home workshop layout, 281-288
  maximum size, 283
  minimum size, 281
  miscellaneous, 285
Horizontal shears, 131
How to draw, 171
How to read plans, 189-212

I

Ink, drawing, 165
Inking, 182
Instruments, drawing, 153, 156
  compass, 157
  extension bar, 159
  hair-spring dividers, 159
  rules and scales, 163
  triangle, 163
  T square, 161
Irregular curves, 170
Isometric projection, 191

L

Lateral deflection of beams, 148
Lettering, 185
  pen, 170
Leveling rod, 97
Level, surveying, 91
  bubble, 94
  lines, 94
Linear measure, 30
Line measurement, 65
Lines, geometry, 40
Liquid measure, 33
Load of timber, 124
Loose-type barn, 246

M

Mathematics for carpenters and
  builders, 9-90
Maximum-size layout, workshop, 283
Measurement of
  lines, 65
  solids, 76
  surfaces, 67
Measures, 29
  board or lumber, 33
  circular, 36
  cubic, 32
  linear, 30
  liquid, 33
  of weight, 34
  square, 31
  time, 35
Member of structure, 124
Mensuration, 64
Methods of leveling, 98
Metric system, 36-40
Minimum-size layout, workshop, 281
Modern house, 257
Modulus of elasticity, timber, 124, 138
Motels, 267-280
  air-conditioning, 274
  bathroom requirements, 278
  construction design, 269
  demands of, 271
  heating, 270
  preliminary consideration, 269
  sound insulation, 275
Multiplication of
  common fractions, 15
  decimals, 21
  fractions by cancellation, 16

INDEX

**Over a Century of Excellence
for the Professional
and
Vocational Trades and the Crafts**

**Order now from your local bookstore
or use the convenient order form at
the back of this book.**

AUDEL

These fully illustrated, up-to-date guides and manuals mean a better job done for mechanics, engineers, electricians, plumbers, carpenters, and all skilled workers.

Contents

Electrical

House Wiring sixth edition
Roland E. Palmquist
5½ x 8¼ Hardcover 256 pp. 150 illus.
ISBN: 0-672-23404-1 $13.95

Rules and regulations of the current National Electrical Code® for residential wiring, fully explained and illustrated: • basis for load calculations • calculations for dwellings • services • nonmetallic-sheathed cable • underground feeder and branch-circuit cable • metal-clad cable • circuits required for dwellings • boxes and fittings • receptacle spacing • mobile homes • wiring for electric house heating.

Practical Electricity fourth edition
Robert G. Middleton; revised by L. Donald Meyers
5½ x 8¼ Hardcover 504 pp. 335 illus.
ISBN: 0-672-23375-4 $14.95

Complete, concise handbook on the principles of electricity and their practical application: • magnetism and electricity • conductors and insulators • circuits • electromagnetic induction • alternating current • electric lighting and lighting calculations • basic house wiring • electric heating • generating stations and substations.

II

Guide to the 1984 Electrical Code®
Roland E. Palmquist
5½ × 8¼ Hardcover 664 pp. 225 illus.
ISBN: 0-672-23398-3 $19.95

Authoritative guide to the National Electrical Code® for all electricians, contractors, inspectors, and home-owners: • terms and regulations for wiring design and protection • wiring methods and materials • equipment for general use • special occupancies • special equipment and conditions • and communication systems. Guide to the 1987 NEC® will be available in mid-1987.

Mathematics for Electricians and Electronics Technicians
Rex Miller
5½ x 8¼ Hardcover 312 pp. 115 illus.
ISBN: 0-8161-1700-4 $14.95

Mathematical concepts, formulas, and problem solving in electricity and electronics: • resistors and resistance • circuits • meters • alternating current and inductance • alternating current and capacitance • impedance and phase angles • resonance in circuits • special-purpose circuits. Includes mathematical problems and solutions.

Fractional Horsepower Electric Motors
Rex Miller and Mark Richard Miller
5½ x 8¼ Hardcover 436 pp. 285 illus.
ISBN: 0-672-23410-6 $15.95

Fully illustrated guide to small-to-moderate-size electric motors in home appliances and industrial equipment: • terminology • repair tools and supplies • small DC and universal motors • split-phase, capacitor-start, shaded pole, and special motors • commutators and brushes • shafts and bearings • switches and relays • armatures • stators • modification and replacement of motors.

Electric Motors
Edwin P. Anderson; revised by Rex Miller
5½ x 8¼ Hardcover 656 pp. 405 illus.
ISBN: 0-672-23376-2 $14.95

Complete guide to installation, maintenance, and repair of all types of electric motors: • AC generators • synchronous motors • squirrel-cage motors • wound rotor motors • DC motors • fractional-horsepower motors • magnetic contractors • motor testing and maintenance • motor calculations • meters • wiring diagrams • armature windings • DC armature rewinding procedure • and stator and coil winding.

Home Appliance Servicing fourth edition
Edwin P. Anderson; revised by Rex Miller
5½ x 8¼ Hardcover 640 pp. 345 illus.
ISBN: 0-672-23379-7 $15.95

Step-by-step illustrated instruction on all types of household appliances: • irons • toasters • roasters and broilers • electric coffee makers • space heaters • water heaters • electric ranges and microwave ovens • mixers and blenders • fans and blowers • vacuum cleaners and floor polishers • washers and dryers • dishwashers and garbage disposals • refrigerators • air conditioners and dehumidifiers.

Television Service Manual

fifth edition
Robert G. Middleton; revised by Joseph G. Barrile
5½ x 8¼   Hardcover   512 pp.   395 illus.
ISBN: 0-672-23395-9 $15.95

Practical up-to-date guide to all aspects of television transmission and reception, for both black and white and color receivers: • step-by-step maintenance and repair • broadcasting • transmission • receivers • antennas and transmission lines • interference • RF tuners • the video channel • circuits • power supplies • alignment • test equipment.

Electrical Course for Apprentices and Journeymen

second edition
Roland E. Palmquist
5½ x 8¼   Hardcover   478 pp.   290 illus.
ISBN:0-672-23393-2 $14.95

Practical course on operational theory and applications for training and re-training in school or on the job: • electricity and matter • units and definitions • electrical symbols • magnets and magnetic fields • capacitors • resistance • electromagnetism • instruments and measurements • alternating currents • DC generators • circuits • transformers • motors • grounding and ground testing.

Questions and Answers for Electricians Examinations eighth edition

Roland E. Palmquist
5½ x 8¼   Hardcover   320 pp.   110 illus.
ISBN: 0-672-23399-1 $12.95

Based on the current National Electrical Code®, a review of exams for apprentice, journeyman, and master, with explanations of principles underlying each test subject: • Ohm's Law and other formulas • power and power factors • lighting • branch circuits and feeders • transformer principles and connections • wiring • batteries and rectification • voltage generation • motors • ground and ground testing.

Machine Shop and Mechanical Trades

Machinists Library

fourth edition   3 vols
Rex Miller
5½ x 8¼   Hardcover   1,352 pp.   1,120 illus.
ISBN: 0-672-23380-0 $38.95

Indispensable three-volume reference for machinists, tool and die makers, machine operators, metal workers, and those with home workshops.

Volume I, Basic Machine Shop
5½ x 8¼   Hardcover   392 pp.   375 illus.
ISBN: 0-672-23381-9 $14.95

• Blueprint reading • benchwork • layout and measurement • sheet-metal hand tools and machines • cutting tools • drills • reamers • taps • threading dies • milling machine cutters, arbors, collets, and adapters.

Volume II, Machine Shop
5½ x 8¼   Hardcover 528 pp. 445 illus
ISBN: 0-672-23382-7 $14.95

• Power saws • machine tool operations • drilling machines • boring • lathes • automatic screw machine • milling • metal spinning.

Volume III, Toolmakers Handy Book
5½ x 8¼   Hardcover   432 pp.   300 illus.
ISBN: 0-672-23383-5 $14.95

• Layout work • jigs and fixtures • gears and gear cutting • dies and diemaking • toolmaking operations • heat-treating furnaces • induction heating • furnace brazing • cold-treating process.

Mathematics for Mechanical Technicians and Technologists

John D. Bies
5½ x 8¼   Hardcover   392 pp.   190 illus.
ISBN: 0-02-510620-1 $17.95

Practical sourcebook of concepts, formulas, and problem solving in industrial and mechanical technology: • basic and complex mechanics • strength of materials • fluidics • cams and gears • machine elements • machining operations • management controls • economics in machining • facility and human resources management.

Millwrights and Mechanics Guide

third edition
Carl A. Nelson
5½ x 8¼   Hardcover   1,040 pp.   880 illus.
ISBN: 0-672-23373-8 $22.95

Most comprehensive and authoritative guide available for millwrights and mechanics at all levels of work or supervision: • drawing and sketching • machinery and equipment installation • principles of mechanical power transmission • V-belt drives • flat belts • gears • chain drives • couplings • bearings • structural steel • screw threads • mechanical fasteners • pipe fittings and valves • carpentry • sheet-metal work • blacksmithing • rigging • electricity • welding • pumps • portable power tools • mensuration and mechanical calculations.

Welders Guide third edition

James E. Brumbaugh
5½ x 8 ¼   Hardcover   960 pp.   615 illus.
ISBN: 0-672-23374-6 $23.95

Practical, concise manual on theory, operation, and maintenance of all welding machines: • gas welding equipment, supplies, and process • arc welding equipment, supplies, and process • TIG and MIG welding • submerged-arc and other shielded-arc welding processes • resistance, thermit, and stud welding • solders and soldering • brazing and braze welding • welding plastics • safety and health measures • symbols and definitions • testing and inspecting welds. Terminology and definitions as standardized by American Welding Society.

Welder/Fitters Guide

John P. Stewart
8½ x 11   Paperback   160 pp.   195 illus.
ISBN: 0-672-23325-8 $7.95

Step-by-step instruction for welder/fitters during training or on the job: • basic assembly tools and aids • improving blueprint reading skills • marking and alignment techniques • using basic tools • simple work practices • guide to fabricating weldments • avoiding mistakes • exercises in blueprint reading • clamping devices • introduction to using hydraulic jacks • safety in weld fabrication plants • common welding shop terms.

Sheet Metal Work

John D. Bies
5½ x 8¼   Hardcover 456 pp.   215 illus.
ISBN: 0-8161-1706-3 $17.95

On-the-job sheet metal guide for manufacturing, construction, and home workshops: • mathematics for sheet metal work • principles of drafting • concepts of sheet metal drawing • sheet metal standards, specifications, and materials • safety practices • layout • shear cutting • holes • bending and folding • forming operations • notching and clipping • metal spinning • mechanical fastening • soldering and brazing • welding • surface preparation and finishes • production processes.

Power Plant Engineers Guide

third edition
Frank D. Graham; revised by Charlie Buffington
5½ x 8¼   Hardcover   960 pp.   530 illus.
ISBN: 0-672-23329-0 $16.95

All-inclusive question-and-answer guide to steam and diesel-power engines: • fuels • heat • combustion • types of boilers • shell or fire-tube boiler construction • strength of boiler materials • boiler calculations • boiler fixtures, fittings, and attachments • boiler feed pumps • condensers • cooling ponds and cooling towers • boiler installation, startup, operation, maintenance and repair • oil, gas, and waste-fuel burners • steam turbines • air compressors • plant safety.

Mechanical Trades Pocket Manual

second edition
Carl A. Nelson
4 × 6   Paperback   364 pp.   255 illus.
ISBN: 0-672-23378-9 $10.95

Comprehensive handbook of essentials, pocket-sized to fit in the tool box: • mechanical and isometric drawing • machinery installation and assembly • belts • drives • gears • couplings • screw threads • mechanical fasteners • packing and seals • bearings • portable power tools • welding • rigging • piping • automatic sprinkler systems • carpentry • stair layout • electricity • shop geometry and trigonometry.

Plumbing

Plumbers and Pipe Fitters Library

third edition   3 vols
Charles N. McConnell; revised by Tom Philbin
5½x8¼   Hardcover   952 pp.   560 illus.
ISBN: 0-672-23384-3 $34.95

Comprehensive three-volume set with up-to-date information for master plumbers, journeymen, apprentices, engineers, and those in building trades.

Volume 1, Materials, Tools, Roughing-In
5½ x 8¼   Hardcover   304 pp.   240 illus.
ISBN: 0-672-23385-1 $12.95

• Materials • tools • pipe fitting • pipe joints • blueprints • fixtures • valves and faucets.

Volume 2, Welding, Heating, Air Conditioning
5½ x 8¼   Hardcover   384 pp.   220 illus.
ISBN: 0-672-23386-x $13.95

• Brazing and welding • planning a heating system • steam heating systems • hot water heating systems • boiler fittings • fuel-oil tank installation • gas piping • air conditioning.

Volume 3, Water Supply, Drainage, Calculations
5½ x 8¼   Hardcover   264 pp.   100 illus.
ISBN: 0-672-23387-8 $12.95

• Drainage and venting • sewage disposal • soldering • lead work • mathematics and physics for plumbers and pipe fitters.

Home Plumbing Handbook

third edition
Charles N. McConnell
8½ x 11   Paperback   200 pp.   100 illus.
ISBN: 0-672-23413-0 $10.95

Clear, concise, up-to-date fully illustrated guide to home plumbing installation and repair: • repairing and replacing faucets • repairing toilet tanks • repairing a trip-lever bath drain • dealing with stopped-up drains • working with copper tubing • measuring and cutting pipe • PVC and CPVC pipe and fittings • installing a garbage disposals • replacing dishwashers • repairing and replacing water heaters • installing or resetting toilets • caulking around plumbing fixtures and tile • water conditioning • working with cast-iron soil pipe • septic tanks and disposal fields • private water systems.

The Plumbers Handbook

seventh edition
Joseph P. Almond, Sr.
4 × 6   Paperback   352 pp.   170 illus.
ISBN: 0-672-23419-x $10.95

Comprehensive, handy guide for plumbers, pipe fitters, and apprentices that fits in the tool box or pocket: • plumbing tools • how to read blueprints • heating systems • water supply • fixtures, valves, and fittings • working drawings • roughing and repair • outside sewage lift station • pipes and pipelines • vents, drain lines, and septic systems • lead work • silver brazing and soft soldering • plumbing systems • abbreviations, definitions, symbols, and formulas.

Questions and Answers for Plumbers Examinations

second edition
Jules Oravetz
5½ x 8¼   Paperback   256 pp.   145 illus.
ISBN: 0-8161-1703-9 $9.95

Practical, fully illustrated study guide to licensing exams for apprentice, journeyman, or master plumber: • definitions, specifications, and regulations set by National Bureau of Standards and by various state codes

• basic plumbing installation • drawings and typical plumbing system layout • mathematics • materials and fittings • joints and connections • traps, cleanouts, and backwater valves • fixtures • drainage, vents, and vent piping • water supply and distribution • plastic pipe and fittings • steam and hot water heating.

HVAC

Air Conditioning: Home and Commercial

second edition
Edwin P. Anderson; revised by Rex Miller
5½ x 8¼   Hardcover   528 pp.   180 illus.
ISBN: 0-672-23397-5 $15.95

Complete guide to construction, installation, operation, maintenance, and repair of home, commercial, and industrial air conditioning systems, with troubleshooting charts: • heat leakage • ventilation requirements • room air conditioners • refrigerants • compressors • condensing equipment • evaporators • water-cooling systems • central air conditioning • automobile air conditioning • motors and motor control.

Heating, Ventilating and Air Conditioning Library

second edition   3 vols
James E. Brumbaugh
5½ x 8¼   Hardcover   1,840 pp.   1,275 illus.
ISBN: 0-672-23388-6 $42.95

Authoritative three-volume reference for those who install, operate, maintain, and repair HVAC equipment commercially, industrially, or at home. Each volume fully illustrated with photographs, drawings, tables and charts.

Volume I, Heating Fundamentals, Furnaces, Boilers, Boiler Conversions
5½ x 8¼   Hardcover   656 pp.   405 illus.
ISBN: 0-672-23389-4 $16.95

• Insulation principles • heating calculations • fuels • warm-air, hot water, steam, and electrical heating systems • gas-fired, oil-fired, coal-fired, and electric-fired furnaces • boilers and boiler fittings • boiler and furnace conversion.

Volume II, Oil, Gas and Coal Burners, Controls, Ducts, Piping, Valves
5½ x 8¼   Hardcover   592 pp.   455 illus.
ISBN: 0-672-23390-8 $15.95

• Coal firing methods • thermostats and humidistats • gas and oil controls and other automatic controls •

ducts and duct systems • pipes, pipe fittings, and piping details • valves and valve installation • steam and hot-water line controls.

Volume III, Radiant Heating, Water Heaters, Ventilation, Air Conditioning, Heat Pumps, Air Cleaners
5 1/2 x 8 1/4 Hardcover 592 pp. 415 illus.
ISBN: 0-672-23391-6 $14.95

• Radiators, convectors, and unit heaters • fireplaces, stoves, and chimneys • ventilation principles • fan selection and operation • air conditioning equipment • humidifiers and dehumidifiers • air cleaners and filters.

Oil Burners fourth edition
Edwin M. Field
5 1/2 x 8 1/4 Hardcover 360 pp. 170 illus.
ISBN: 0-672-23394-0 $15.95

Up-to-date sourcebook on the construction, installation, operation, testing, servicing, and repair of all types of oil burners, both industrial and domestic: • general electrical hookup and wiring diagrams of automatic control systems • ignition system • high-voltage transportation • operational sequence of limit controls, thermostats, and various relays • combustion chambers • drafts • chimneys • drive couplings • fans or blowers • burner nozzles • fuel pumps.

Refrigeration: Home and Commercial second edition
Edwin P. Anderson; revised by Rex Miller
5 1/2 x 8 1/4 Hardcover 768 pp. 285 illus.
ISBN: 0-672-23396-7 $17.95

Practical, comprehensive reference for technicians, plant engineers, and homeowners on the installation, operation, servicing, and repair of everything from single refrigeration units to commercial and industrial systems: • refrigerants • compressors • thermoelectric cooling • service equipment and tools • cabinet maintenance and repairs • compressor lubrication systems • brine systems • supermarket and grocery refrigeration • locker plants • fans and blowers • piping • heat leakage • refrigeration-load calculations.

Pneumatics and Hydraulics

Hydraulics for Off-the-Road Equipment second edition
Harry L. Stewart; revised by Tom Philbin
5 1/2 x 8 1/4 Hardcover 256 pp. 175 illus.
ISBN: 0-8161-1701-2 $13.95

Complete reference manual for those who own and operate heavy equipment and for engineers, designers, installation and maintenance technicians, and shop mechanics: • hydraulic pumps, accumulators, and motors • force components • hydraulic control components • filters and filtration, lines and fittings, and fluids • hydrostatic transmissions • maintenance • troubleshooting.

Pneumatics and Hydraulics fourth edition
Harry L. Stewart; revised by Tom Philbin
5 1/2 x 8 1/4 Hardcover 512 pp. 315 illus.
ISBN: 0-672-23412-2 $15.95

Practical guide to the principles and applications of fluid power for engineers, designers, process planners, tool men, shop foremen, and mechanics: • pressure, work and power • general features of machines • hydraulic and pneumatic symbols • pressure boosters • air compressors and accessories • hydraulic power devices • hydraulic fluids • piping • air filters, pressure regulators, and lubricators • flow and pressure controls • pneumatic motors and tools • rotary hydraulic motors and hydraulic transmissions • pneumatic circuits • hydraulic circuits • servo systems.

Pumps fourth edition
Harry L. Stewart; revised by Tom Philbin
5 1/2 x 8 1/4 Hardcover 508 pp. 360 illus.
ISBN: 0-672-23400-9 $15.95

Comprehensive guide for operators, engineers, maintenance workers, inspectors, superintendents, and mechanics on principles and day-to-day operations of pumps: • centrifugal, rotary, reciprocating, and special service pumps • hydraulic accumulators • power transmission • hydraulic power tools • hydraulic cylinders • control valves • hydraulic fluids • fluid lines and fittings.

Carpentry and Construction

Carpenters and Builders Library
fifth edition 4 vols
John E. Ball; revised by Tom Philbin
5 1/2 x 8 1/4 Hardcover 1,224 pp. 1,010 illus.
ISBN: 0-672-23369-x $39.95
Also available in a new boxed set at no extra cost:
ISBN: 0-02-506450-9 $39.95

These profusely illustrated volumes, available in a handsome boxed edition, have set the professional standard for carpenters, joiners, and woodworkers.

Volume 1, Tools, Steel Square, Joinery
5 1/2 x 8 1/4 Hardcover 384 pp. 345 illus.
ISBN: 0-672-23365-7 $10.95

• Woods • nails • screws • bolts • the workbench • tools • using the steel square • joints and joinery • cabinetmaking joints • wood patternmaking • and kitchen cabinet construction.

Volume 2, Builders Math, Plans, Specifications
5 1/2 x 8 1/4 Hardcover 304 pp. 205 illus.
ISBN: 0-672-23366-5 $10.95

• Surveying • strength of timbers • practical drawing • architectural drawing • barn construction • small house construction • and home workshop layout.

Volume 3, Layouts, Foundations, Framing
5 1/2 x 8 1/4 Hardcover 272 pp. 215 illus.
ISBN: 0-672-23367-3 $10.95

• Foundations • concrete forms • concrete block construction • framing, girders and sills • skylights • porches and patios • chimneys, fireplaces, and stoves • insulation • solar energy and paneling.

Volume 4, Millwork, Power Tools, Painting
5 1/2 x 8 1/4 Hardcover 344 pp. 245 illus.
ISBN: 0-672-23368-1 $10.95

• Roofing, miter work • doors • windows, sheathing and siding • stairs • flooring • table saws, band saws, and jigsaws • wood lathes • sanders and combination tools • portable power tools • painting.

Complete Building Construction
second edition
John Phelps; revised by Tom Philbin
5 1/2 x 8 1/4 Hardcover 744 pp. 645 illus.
ISBN: 0-672-23377-0 $19.95

Comprehensive guide to constructing a frame or brick building from the footings to the ridge: • laying out building and excavation lines • making concrete forms and pouring fittings and foundation • making concrete slabs, walks, and driveways • laying concrete block, brick, and tile • building chimneys and fireplaces • framing, siding, and roofing • insulating • finishing the inside • building stairs • installing windows • hanging doors.

Complete Roofing Handbook
James E. Brumbaugh
5¹⁄₂ x 8¹⁄₄   Hardcover   536 pp.   510 illus.
ISBN: 0-02-517850-4 $29.95

Authoritative text and highly detailed drawings and photographs,on all aspects of roofing: • types of roofs • roofing and reroofing • roof and attic insulation and ventilation • skylights and roof openings • dormer construction • roof flashing details • shingles • roll roofing • built-up roofing • roofing with wood shingles and shakes • slate and tile roofing • installing gutters and downspouts • listings of professional and trade associations and roofing manufacturers.

Complete Siding Handbook
James E. Brumbaugh
5¹⁄₂ x 8¹⁄₄   Hardcover   512 pp.   450 illus.
ISBN: 0-02-517880-6 $23.95

Companion to *Complete Roofing Handbook*, with step-by-step instructions and drawings on every aspect of siding: • sidewalls and siding • wall preparation • wood board siding • plywood panel and lap siding • hardboard panel and lap siding • wood shingle and shake siding • aluminum and steel siding • vinyl siding • exterior paints and stains • refinishing of siding, gutter and downspout systems • listings of professional and trade associations and siding manufacturers.

Masons and Builders Library
second edition   2 vols
Louis M. Dezettel; revised by Tom Philbin
5¹⁄₂ x 8¹⁄₄   Hardcover   688 pp.   500 illus.
ISBN: 0-672-23401-7 $23.95

Two-volume set on practical instruction in all aspects of materials and methods of bricklaying and masonry: • brick • mortar • tools • bonding • corners, openings, and arches • chimneys and fireplaces • structural clay tile and glass block • brick walks, floors, and terraces • repair and maintenance • plasterboard and plaster • stone and rock masonry • reading blueprints.

Volume 1, Concrete, Block, Tile, Terrazzo
5¹⁄₂ x 8¹⁄₄   Hardcover   304 pp.   190 illus.
ISBN: 0-672-23402-5 $13.95

Volume 2, Bricklaying, Plastering, Rock Masonry, Clay Tile
5¹⁄₂ × 8¹⁄₄   Hardcover   384 pp.   310 illus.
ISBN: 0-672-23403-3 $12.95

Woodworking

Woodworking and Cabinetmaking
F. Richard Boller
5¹⁄₂ x 8¹⁄₄   Hardcover   360 pp.   455 illus.
ISBN: 0-02-512800-0 $16.95

Compact one-volume guide to the essentials of all aspects of woodworking: • properties of softwoods, hardwoods, plywood, and composition wood • design, function, appearance, and structure • project planning • hand tools • machines • portable electric tools • construction • the home workshop • and the projects themselves – stereo cabinet, speaker cabinets, bookcase, desk, platform bed, kitchen cabinets, bathroom vanity.

Wood Furniture: Finishing, Refinishing, Repairing second edition
James E. Brumbaugh
5¹⁄₂ x 8¹⁄₄   Hardcover   352 pp.   185 illus.
ISBN: 0-672-23409-2 $12.95

Complete, fully illustrated guide to repairing furniture and to finishing and refinishing wood surfaces for professional woodworkers and do-it-yourselfers: • tools and supplies • types of wood • veneering • inlaying • repairing, restoring, and stripping • wood preparation • staining • shellac, varnish, lacquer, paint and enamel, and oil and wax finishes • antiquing • gilding and bronzing • decorating furniture.

Maintenance and Repair

Building Maintenance second edition
Jules Oravetz
5¹⁄₂ x 8¹⁄₄   Hardcover   384 pp.   210 illus.
ISBN: 0-672-23278-2 $9.95

Complete information on professional maintenance procedures used in office, educational, and commercial buildings: • painting and decorating • plumbing and pipe fitting

• concrete and masonry • carpentry • roofing • glazing and caulking • sheet metal • electricity • air conditioning and refrigeration • insect and rodent control • heating • maintenance management • custodial practices.

Gardening, Landscaping and Grounds Maintenance
third edition
Jules Oravetz
5¹⁄₂ x 8¹⁄₄   Hardcover   424 pp.   340 illus.
ISBN: 0-672-23417-3 $15.95

Practical information for those who maintain lawns, gardens, and industrial, municipal, and estate grounds: • flowers, vegetables, berries, and house plants • greenhouses • lawns • hedges and vines • flowering shrubs and trees • shade, fruit and nut trees • evergreens • bird sanctuaries • fences • insect and rodent control • weed and brush control • roads, walks, and pavements • drainage • maintenance equipment • golf course planning and maintenance.

Home Maintenance and Repair: Walls, Ceilings and Floors
Gary D. Branson
8¹⁄₂ x 11   Paperback   80 pp.   80 illus.
ISBN: 0-672-23281-2 $6.95

Do-it-yourselfer's step-by-step guide to interior remodeling with professional results: • general maintenance • wallboard installation and repair • wallboard taping • plaster repair • texture paints • wallpaper techniques • paneling • sound control • ceiling tile • bath tile • energy conservation.

Painting and Decorating
Rex Miller and Glenn E. Baker
5¹⁄₂ x 8¹⁄₄   Hardcover   464 pp.   325 illus.
ISBN: 0-672-23405-x $18.95

Practical guide for painters, decorators, and homeowners to the most up-to-date materials and techniques: • job planning • tools and equipment needed • finishing materials • surface preparation • applying paint and stains · decorating with coverings • repairs and maintenance • color and decorating principles.

Tree Care second edition
John M. Haller
8½ x 11 Paperback 224 pp. 305 illus.
ISBN: 0-02-062870-6 $9.95

New edition of a standard in the field, for growers, nursery owners, foresters, landscapers, and homeowners:
• planting • pruning • fertilizing
• bracing and cabling • wound repair
• grafting • spraying • disease and insect management • coping with environmental damage • removal
• structure and physiology • recreational use.

Upholstering
updated
James E. Brumbaugh
5½ x 8¼ Hardcover 400 pp. 380 illus.
ISBN: 0-672-23372-x $12.95

Essentials of upholstering for professional, apprentice, and hobbyist: • furniture styles • tools and equipment • stripping • frame construction and repairs • finishing and refinishing wood surfaces
• webbing • springs • burlap, stuffing, and muslin • pattern layout • cushions
• foam padding • covers • channels and tufts • padded seats and slip seats
• fabrics • plastics • furniture care.

Automotive and Engines

Diesel Engine Manual fourth edition
Perry O. Black; revised by William E. Scahill
5½ x 8¼ Hardcover 512 pp. 255 illus.
ISBN: 0-672-23371-1 $15.95

Detailed guide for mechanics, students, and others to all aspects of typical two- and four-cycle engines: • operating principles • fuel oil • diesel injection pumps • basic Mercedes diesels • diesel engine cylinders • lubrication • cooling systems • horsepower • engine-room procedures • diesel engine installation • automotive diesel engine
• marine diesel engine • diesel electrical power plant • diesel engine service.

Gas Engine Manual third edition
Edwin P. Anderson; revised by Charles G. Facklam
5½ x 8¼ Hardcover 424 pp. 225 illus.
ISBN: 0-8161-1707-1 $12.95

Indispensable sourcebook for those who operate, maintain, and repair gas engines of all types and sizes:
• fundamentals and classifications of engines • engine parts • pistons
• crankshafts • valves • lubrication, cooling, fuel, ignition, emission

control and electrical systems
• engine tune-up • servicing of pistons and piston rings, cylinder blocks, connecting rods and crankshafts, valves and valve gears, carburetors, and electrical systems.

Small Gasoline Engines
Rex Miller and Mark Richard Miller
5½ x 8¼ Hardcover 640 pp. 525 illus.
ISBN: 0-672-23414-9 $16.95

Practical information for those who repair, maintain, and overhaul two-and four-cycle engines – with emphasis on one-cylinder motors – including lawn mowers, edgers, grass sweepers, snowblowers, emergency electrical generators, outboard motors, and other equipment up to ten horsepower: • carburetors, emission controls, and ignition systems • starting systems • hand tools
• safety • power generation • engine operations • lubrication systems
• power drivers • preventive maintenance • step-by-step overhauling procedures • troubleshooting • testing and inspection • cylinder block servicing.

Truck Guide Library 3 vols
James E. Brumbaugh
5½ x 8¼ Hardcover 2,144 pp. 1,715 illus.
ISBN: 0-672-23392-4 $45.95

Three-volume comprehensive and profusely illustrated reference on truck operation and maintenance.

Volume 1, Engines
5½ x 8¼ Hardcover 416 pp. 290 illus.
ISBN: 0-672-23356-8 $16.95

• Basic components · engine operating principles • troubleshooting
• cylinder blocks • connecting rods, pistons, and rings • crankshafts, main bearings, and flywheels • camshafts and valve trains • engine valves.

Volume 2, Engine Auxiliary Systems
5½ x 8¼ Hardcover 704 pp. 520 illus.
ISBN: 0-672-23357-6 $16.95

• Battery and electrical systems
• spark plugs • ignition systems, charging and starting systems
• lubricating, cooling, and fuel systems • carburetors and governors
• diesel systems • exhaust and emission-control systems.

Volume 3, Transmissions, Steering, and Brakes
5½ x 8¼ Hardcover 1,024 pp. 905 illus.
ISBN: 0-672-23406-8 $16.95

• Clutches • manual, auxiliary, and automatic transmissions • frame and suspension systems • differentials and axles, manual and power steering
• front-end alignment • hydraulic, power, and air brakes • wheels and tires • trailers.

Drafting

Answers on Blueprint Reading
fourth edition
Roland E. Palmquist; revised by Thomas J. Morrisey
5½ x 8¼ Hardcover 320 pp. 275 illus.
ISBN: 0-8161-1704-7 $12.95

Complete question-and-answer instruction manual on blueprints of machines and tools, electrical systems, and architecture: • drafting scale • drafting instruments
• conventional lines and representations • pictorial drawings • geometry of drafting • orthographic and working drawings • surfaces • detail drawing • sketching • map and topographical drawings • graphic symbols • architectural drawings
• electrical blueprints • computer-aided design and drafting. Also included is an appendix of measurements • metric conversions
• screw threads and tap drill sizes
• number and letter sizes of drills with decimal equivalents
• double depth of threads • tapers and angles.

Hobbies

Complete Course in Stained Glass
Pepe Mendez
8½ x 11 Paperback 80 pp. 50 illus.
ISBN: 0-672-23287-1 $8.95

Guide to the tools, materials, and techniques of the art of stained glass, with ten fully illustrated lessons:
• how to cut glass • cartoon and pattern drawing • assembling and cementing • making lamps using various techniques • electrical components for completing lamps
• sources of materials • glossary of terminology and techniques of stained glasswork.

Macmillan Practical Arts Library
Books for and by the Craftsman

World Woods in Color
W.A. Lincoln
7 × 10   Hardcover   300 pages
300 photos
ISBN: 0-02-572350-2 $39.95

Large full-color photographs show the natural grain and features of nearly 300 woods: • commercial and botanical names • physical characteristics, mechanical properties, seasoning, working properties, durability, and uses • the height, diameter, bark, and places of distribution of each tree • indexing of botanical, trade, commercial, local, and family names • a full bibliography of publications on timber study and identification.

The Woodturner's Art: Fundamentals and Projects
Ron Roszkiewicz
8 × 10   Hardcover   256 pages   300 illus.
ISBN: 0-02-605250-4 $24.95

A master woodturner shows how to design and create increasingly difficult projects step-by-step in this book suitable for the beginner and the more advanced student: • spindle and faceplate turning • tools • techniques • classic turnings from various historical periods • more than 30 types of projects including boxes, furniture, vases, and candlesticks • making duplicates • projects using combinations of techniques and more than one kind of wood. Author has also written *The Woodturner's Companion.*

The Woodworker's Bible
Alf Martensson
8 × 10   Paperback   288 pages   900 illus.
ISBN: 0-02-011940-2 $12.95

For the craftsperson familiar with basic carpentry skills, a guide to creating professional-quality furniture, cabinetry, and objects d'art in the home workshop: • techniques and expert advice on fine craftsmanship whether tooled by hand or machine • joint-making • assembling to ensure fit • finishes. Author, who lives in London and runs a workshop called Woodstock, has also written *The Book of Furnituremaking.*

Cabinetmaking and Millwork
John L. Feirer
7⅛ × 9½   Hardcover   992 pages
2,350 illus. (32 pp. in color)
ISBN: 0-02-537350-1 $47.50

The classic on cabinetmaking that covers in detail all of the materials, tools, machines, and processes used in building cabinets and interiors, the production of furniture, and other work of the finish carpenter and millwright: • fixed installations such as paneling, built-ins, and cabinets • movable wood products such as furniture and fixtures • which woods to use, and why and how to use them in the interiors of homes and commercial buildings • metrics and plastics in furniture construction.

Cabinetmaking: The Professional Approach
Alan Peters
8½ × 11   Hardcover   208 pages   175 illus.
(8 pp. color)
ISBN: 0-02-596200-0 $29.95

A unique guide to all aspects of professional furniture making, from an English master craftsman: • the Cotswold School and the birth of the furniture movement • setting up a professional shop • equipment • finance and business efficiency • furniture design • working to commission • batch production, training, and techniques • plans for nine projects.

Carpentry and Building Construction
John L. Feirer and Gilbert R. Hutchings
7½ × 9½   hardcover   1,120 pages
2,000 photos (8 pp. in color)
ISBN: 0-02-537360-9 $50.00

A classic by Feirer on each detail of modern construction: • the various machines, tools, and equipment from which the builder can choose • laying of a foundation • building frames for each part of a building • details of interior and exterior work • painting and finishing • reading plans • chimneys and fireplaces • ventilation • assembling prefabricated houses.